ISBN 978-1-331-50306-4
PIBN 10198867

1 MONTH OF
FREE
READING

at

www.ForgottenBooks.com

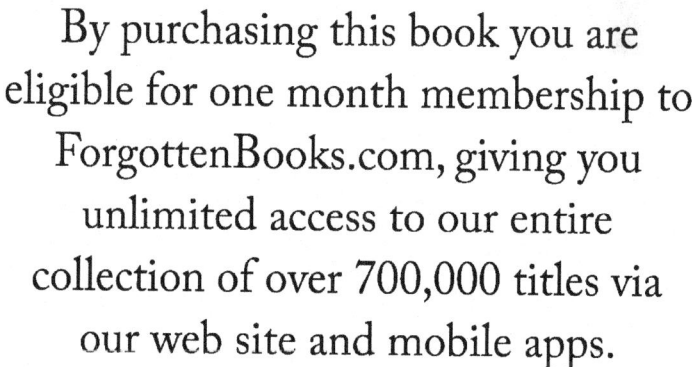

By purchasing this book you are eligible for one month membership to ForgottenBooks.com, giving you unlimited access to our entire collection of over 700,000 titles via our web site and mobile apps.

To claim your free month visit:
www.forgottenbooks.com/free198867

LIFE AND LETTERS OF
FATHER JOHN MORRIS, S.J.

QUARTERLY SERIES. VOLUME NINETY-FIVE.

ROEHAMPTON : PRINTED BY JAMES STANLEY.

THE LIFE AND LETTERS OF

ATHER JOHN MORRIS,

Of the Society of Jesus.

1826—1893.

BY

FATHER J. H. POLLEN, S.J.

LONDON: BURNS AND OATES LIMITED.

NEW YORK, CINCINNATI, CHICAGO: BENZIGER BROTHERS.

1896.

PREFACE.

THE following pages will, it is hoped, sufficiently explain themselves to Father Morris's friends, for whom they have been written. Yet a few words of preface may not be out of place to indicate the sources whence the Life has been drawn, and the use that has been made of them.

Though there do not exist for the life of Father Morris those sources, to which a biographer would most naturally turn, no diaries, no long series of familiar letters, and though his life was rather such as to lead him to make frequent fatal holocausts of such papers as he would otherwise have been glad to keep, yet the materials for his biography, especially for certain portions of it, are sufficiently abundant. He began to write reminiscences "of the many interesting persons and things" he had seen in life, and his brother, Mr. Henry Morris, has continued the record as far as he could. Finally, his correspondents have allowed me to inspect many hundreds of his letters, which they had considered worth preserving. Material then has not been wanting.

*a**

But it has not been all equally eligible. His reminiscences remain a mere fragment, for it seems that when he found he could hardly help writing an autobiography, he was not inclined to persevere. His brother's continuation covers indeed one most important episode, but a very short one The many letters I have seen, are written almost all simply for the purposes of business or literature, or in answer to questions about religious life and conduct, and though I gathered from them a number of extracts on the latter subjects, of which a selection will be found in the Life, the number of paragraphs about himself and his own doings will be comparatively few, and for some periods altogether wanting.

This notwithstanding, the business of the biographer has been rather to curtail than to expand. It is true that some of Father Morris's friends may be disappointed at finding much omitted, which was interesting in itself, and doubly so to them. But, had a larger scale been adopted, the generality of readers might have been misled by the very profusion of the materials offered, and might have imagined that an undue importance was being attached to Father Morris's life. Especially would this have been so if descriptions of his personal qualities, spiritual and intellectual, weak and strong, had been too minute. To have enlarged unduly here would have produced in turn the ill effects of panegyric and of hyper-criticism. By preference, the materials are set briefly before the reader. One of the chief claims to respect which men such as Father Morris possess, is that they desire to live in retirement and to be left in peace. This biography desires in its measure to imitate that love of reserve, and to have the credit of reticence as well as of candour.

It only remains for me to return thanks to His Eminence Cardinal Vaughan, to Henry Morris, Esq. and Mr. Malcolm Morris, to the Hon. Mrs. Scott Murray, to' Dr. Jessop, Mrs. de Lisle, the Rev. Mother Superioress of the Bar Convent, York, the Rev. Mother Prioress at Haywards Heath, Miss Laura Jackson, and others, who have lent letters, and helped me in various ways.

P.S.—Since writing the above, in the autumn of last year, I have been fully occupied abroad with other work, and another has undertaken for me the task of seeing this volume through the press. For the thoroughness and care with which he has done his work I cannot be sufficiently grateful. I should add that the chapter concerning Cardinal Manning was in print before the appearance of Mr. Purcell's biography. My best thanks are due to the Cardinal's executors for their kind permission to publish the letters I have there used.

J. H. P.

246, Via di Ripetta, Rome.
April 9, 1896.

CONTENTS.

CONTENTS.

CHAPTER I.

FATHER JOHN MORRIS, who is the subject of this
biography, was a man of great mental activity, of a
strong personal character, and of a keen and lively
disposition, and these qualities combined to develope
his mind at an early age. His thoughts soon turned
to religious questions, and enlightened and aided by
grace, led him to embrace the Catholic faith when only
twenty years of age. Within the Church he was, after
his theological studies, at once promoted to different
active charges in Rome itself, and in the dioceses
of Northampton and Westminster, bringing him into
immediate relations with Cardinals Wiseman and
Manning. His devotion to the Church and the very
keen interest he had taken in historical and ecclesiastical researches connected with the period of the
" Reformation " in England, led him to become a foremost champion of the cause of the English Martyrs.
As a member of the Society of Jesus, Father Morris,
after doing good work in the offices of Professor of
Church History and Canon Law, of Rector of the
College in Malta, and of Master of Novices at Manresa,
was devoted during the last ten years of his life to that
literary work and to that fruit of his skill in the spiritual

B

direction of souls with which his name will be most permanently associated.

He was born, on July 4th, 1826, at Ootacamund, a sanatorium on the Nilgiri Hills, in the Madras Presidency. He was the eldest son of John Carnac Morris, F.R.S., a member of the Madras Civil Service, author of some works on the Telugu language, and for some time editor of the *Madras Journal of Literature and Science.* His mother, Rosanna Curtis, daughter of Peter and Mary Cherry, was born on the 4th of August, 1803, and married in February, 1823. She outlived her son by several months, dying in 1894 at the ripe age of ninety-one. Father Morris's grand-parents on the father's side were John Morris, born August 16, 1765, who died July 27, 1840, and Sarah Mackay, born March 27, 1773, who was married December 15, 1791, and died October 1, 1831. He himself was the eldest of a large family of fifteen children, ten of whom were sons, and five were daughters. Of this number two died in infancy, and a second boy was carried off by illness, when eleven years old.

In the year 1888, while recovering from the effects of a rather serious illness, Father Morris wrote a few reminiscences of his boyhood, and from these we take, amongst other details, the following account of his father's sufferings at the hands of his doctors, as being thoroughly characteristic both of the man and of the medical empiricism of those days. " My father had lost the use of his legs by a fever in India, and he came to England on furlough to spend all his substance on physicians. This he did, no doubt, but he was nothing the better for it. A sanguine man, if ever there was one, when the physicians failed, he turned to the quacks. Mohammed, of the baths at Brighton, tried his hand on him; and the awful quack, St. John Long. This last horror had been tried for his life for

JOHN MORRIS IN 1831

To face p 3

having caused the death of a young lady, and on his acquittal a Duchess drove him in her carriage round Hyde Park. In later years he was experimented upon once more, and after my ordination I recollect going to see him in Mansfield Street, when he had had the *tendon Achilles* cut in both heels. It was a curious operation that only cost a single drop of blood, thanks to the skill with which it was performed. The tendon, when cut through, flew apart with a noise like a pistol shot. The idea was that as the tendon reformed, it might be made longer by the foot being set in a frame with a graduated scale, and the angle being altered a very little every day. The operation did him no good, but rather harm, for he walked with still greater difficulty after it; but no disappointment ever altered his bright, sanguine nature."

When Mr. Morris came home from India on furlough in 1829, he brought John as an infant with him, and on his return in June of 1831 he left the boy, together with his brother Henry, under the guardianship of Mr. John Day, a civil engineer, and his wife, who lived first at 2, Pitts Place, Parson's Green, near Fulham, and then at 16, York Terrace, now merged in Queen's Road, Peckham, then a suburban village. To the former of these places Father Morris makes reference in his recollections. "When the wheel of time had made many a turn, and I had been appointed priest of the mission of St. Thomas', Fulham, I sallied forth to look at my new parish, and without the least expecting it, I came suddenly upon this very Parson's Green. Without knowing quite where I was, I said to myself, 'There must be a pond down in that corner'—and so there was, sure enough, though it was disappointingly small. And there was the house where I first went to school as a day boy. How little I remember about it all! I have, it is true, this most august reminiscence, that when, one day, Eliza Butterfield, our devoted and faithful nurse, was convoying my brother and myself along the Bishop's Walk, the footpath between the Thames and the Bishop of London's garden, we met an elderly gentleman in puffy lawn sleeves, on his way, I suppose, from the church to the Palace, who held out his arms so that I saw oceans of lawn, and then I heard a very pompous voice say: 'And whose nice little boys are these?'

" I was eight years old when life there came to an end, and I was sent to school at East Sheen, so that I must have been three years at Parson's Green, and for the whole three years pretty nearly the only thing connected in the most distant way with religion that I can remember was the pat on the head I got from Bishop Blomfield's soft hands. Yes, there is one thing. The Days were Dissenters, but we were regularly sent off to church, convoyed by Eliza Butterfield. The one thing I had to do at church was to remember the text and repeat it when I got home. I can recollect sitting the service out, with all the patience I could muster, and asking occasionally when the text was coming. Then I was nudged and told to look out, and I listened with all my ears for this blessed text and its reference. One Sunday I came home, and the text had fled. Chapter and verse had gone, and I was astounded when Mrs. Day told me that if I could give her a word of the text she would find it. She fetched Cruden's *Concordance*, and when the text was somehow identified, I looked on the process as a conjuring trick or a piece of witchcraft, so unaccountable did it appear.

" I may have been set to learn Collects, and I certainly had to learn my Church Catechism, but I have not the remembrance of a particle of religion. My morning and evening prayers of course I had to say, but I do not know whom I said them to. When very young I have been told, ' Come and say your prayers to me.' I may have been taught that God heard them, but I cannot recollect a single thought about God during all those years of my life.

"And when I went to Dr. Pinkney's at East Sheen, things were no better. On Sundays we had to stand in one large circle all down the dining-room to say our Catechism. The boy who was asked, ' What is your name ? ' blushed as he uttered his Christian name, which never appeared at any other time, and for the moment he felt no gratitude to the ' godfathers and godmothers who gave him this name.' On Sunday afternoons we had prayers in the dining-room, and we all sat at the dinner-tables during the Church service. On Sunday mornings we were marched to Mortlake Church, where we had a pew in the corner of a gallery, from which we could see nothing and hear nothing. Our amusement was to climb on one another's shoulders and see how high we could write our names."

Although recollections penned after a long interval of years are sure to receive their colour from the mature man's point of view, and can scarcely enable him to live over again in all the details of his once childish feelings, yet Father Morris has in the above picture very suggestively touched one or two points that indicate the way in which amongst Protestants religion used to be presented to the minds of children. It may, however, easily be that he is a little too caustic and denunciatory as to the absence of all religious impressions from his own mind when a small boy. His brother, Henry, is strongly of this opinion, for he writes : " I think that John has underrated the teaching and influence of Mr. and Mrs. Day. I can only say that I owe them a great debt of gratitude. When I left them, I being then ten, I loved the Lord with my whole heart, and I owe the foundation of my faith to them. I cannot

imagine that they never spoke a word about personal
religion to John, when they continually dwelt on it
with me." Different minds are even in their earliest
youth diversely affected, and some more quickly feel
the want of that definite and incisive teaching by
active and personal training which especially charac-
terizes the Church's spiritual education of her children.

After being at Temple Grove, East Sheen, John
Morris was sent to Harrow in 1838, when at the age of
twelve. There he remained only one year, during which
he was placed in Mr. Drury's house, taking school rank
in the Fourth Form. He tells against himself two
stories about his life while at these schools, and they
are given here as showing that he had to the full
all a sharp schoolboy's natural self-conceit, being at
the same time conscious of it himself and ready to
own to a little of the same characteristic even in after-
life. "Boys," he writes, "are naturally cruel, taking
pleasure in others' pain. I have no doubt that I was
as bad as my neighbours, but I remember my own
pain better than theirs. One day two big boys came
up to me in the playing-field, and pretended to be
very friendly. At last they were quite sure I could not
walk about the field blindfold, and say from time to
time what part of the field I was in. I of course was
equally sure I could, and allowed myself to be blind-
folded and led about. It ended by the bandage being
taken from my eyes, and I found myself up to my
ankles in a mud-heap. To take off my attention while
we were walking about, they led me on to say what
I had got 'at home,' and I remember bragging and
boasting of I know not what, and those two mischievous
guardian angels fooling me to the top of my bent.

"Oh, the spirit of vainglory that there was in me!
My moral code told me not to tell lies, and this moral
case arose in my mind and I had no one to put it to.

' Was it a lie if I said I had a pony at home, and a bullfinch, and some breeding canaries, and a Newfoundland dog, and an avenue of elms, and a lawn sloping down to the river, because there were these things in one or other of the friends' house I went to visit in the holidays?' The explosion of conceit ended in the humiliation of the mud-heap! But I remember that what I felt the most was that those two boys had shammed sympathy, and had got out of me home secrets, which were kept only for the confidences of the most intimate friendships.

" Smoking, of course, was forbidden at Harrow, and therefore equally of course we smoked. When I was going home on one occasion, I must needs show off my new accomplishment. I went to London by rail from Harrow—the London and Birmingham Railway was only opened at that time as far as Watford—and then on by the Greenwich Railway as far as Deptford. Thence I walked home to the Days, who lived at Peckham, and through the streets of Deptford I marched with my cigar in my mouth. It was a rare thing then for a gentleman to smoke in the streets, and an unknown thing for a boy to do so, and the women came to their shop-doors to look at me as I went by. When I came back to England from my tertianship, I was sent to give a mission at Deptford some forty years after this boyish escapade; I went to the same station and walked through the same streets, and the whole scene came up vividly before me. I had probably never thought of it in the interval.

" Talking of my conceit, I have a story to tell that I shall never find a place for elsewhere, I suppose. When I came from Rome a young priest in 1850, I have no doubt I was perfectly prepared to set every priest in England right. I do not exactly remember ever trying to do it with Dr. Husenbeth of Cossey, but at our first meeting I cannot have left a very favourable impression upon him; for forty years afterwards, turning over the leaves of a collection of letters addressed to Canon Tierney, I came across one from Dr. Husenbeth, the postscript of which said: '*Entre nous*, J. M. is a conceited puppy.' It was delightful to see oneself as others saw one long ago, as in an old daguerreotype; and it was pleasant to know that I had succeeded in overcoming the good old man's antipathy, for we were very good friends for many years up to the time of his death.

" I need not linger on my reminiscences at Harrow. I left it without regret. Indeed, when the letter came that said that I was to go to India, I wrote back, ' Hurrah for India ! ' It was a very critical moment in my life. On the one hand, it spoiled my education. My brother and I had a tutor sent out with us, a very clever man beyond a doubt, but a wretchedly bad tutor, and under him I learned very little. I thus never was properly grounded, and I do not know the commonest things. I do not even know the Latin grammar. But, on the other hand, I was thrown henceforward almost altogether with grown-up persons, and I imperceptibly learned to think for myself. I attribute my conversion in the providence of God to having been thus taken from school. I should have run in the rut with other boys, and never have entertained an independent thought.

" I am afraid I brought with me from Harrow nothing but evil. I had not been there long enough for it to develope any manliness in me, as the Public School system has a wonderful power of doing, when a boy has gone fairly through it. Nor did it create in me any habit of work or desire of learning, nor did it teach me anything useful. There was a French master whom the boys laughed at, and modern languages formed no part of the school course. What would I give now if I had then been thoroughly taught French and German !

"And as to religion, I have no remembrance of a single thought of God all the while I was at Harrow. We must have had some domestic prayers at my tutor's that I never attended to. In my time the school went to the parish church on Sundays, where we had a gallery to ourselves. Of services or sermons I remember nothing. The Vicar was a Low Church clergyman of the name of Cunningham, whom I was once taken to visit by some relations; but neither he, nor my tutor, nor anybody else ever spoke to me about religion, and I was a regular little pagan, knowing of course that there was such a thing as the Christian religion, and having a few of its stock formulas by heart, but as ignorant of our Lord and His Spirit as if I had been born in the heart of China."

It cannot be denied that this description of the absence of all spiritual training from Protestant public schoolboy life, together with its general effects on by far the larger number of boys, is in the main truthful. There always have, however, been many bright exceptions both as to the lads themselves and their masters, and especially of late years, along with a good deal of false show, a genuine interior religious spirit has been instilled into their pupils by tutors of a like mind.

On September 4, 1839, John Morris, accompanied by his brother, sailed for India in the *Duke of Argyll*, under the charge of the Rev. John Griffiths, of Christ Church, Oxford, afterwards a chaplain in India, and reached Madras, January 19, 1840. He went at once to Ootacamund, where he remained in his father's house, now the Club House, till November, 1841.

Although Father Morris' reminiscences do not assist us in carrying on the narrative further, his brother,

Mr. Henry Morris, has very kindly contributed some most interesting recollections which he himself has written.

" The object which our father," says Mr. Henry Morris, " had set before himself in having us out, was, that we might all know each other, and that he might, as he wrote, draw us forward and show us how we ought to behave from the example and society of our seniors. He was most anxious that this should in nowise interfere with our studies, and during the year that he was with us our lessons were continued pretty regularly, but when he was gone the regularity relaxed. Our tutor was a man of very versatile genius, and could do almost anything except teach persistently. Sometimes we were worked very hard, and then picnics and excursions were the order of the day. Sometimes we joined a shooting-party, at other times we went to the opening of a stone cairn, or made an expedition to a neighbouring mountain."

So the days ran on, pleasantly enough for the boys, who on their ponies and with their guns went through a great deal of experience, which is invaluable for the formation of character, but does not help much to the acquirement of positive knowledge. Dr. Jerdon and Mr. Samuel N. Ward, two of the leading naturalists of that day in India, took a friendly interest in them, and from the former John acquired some knowledge of ornithology, and took great pride in his collection of birds' skins, of which he obtained and cured a considerable number.

Meantime their father grew more and more dissatisfied with their tutor's mode of teaching. Mr. Griffiths, accordingly, left them in July, 1841, and his place was taken for the time being by the Rev. John Challis Street, one of the East India Company's chaplains, who had come to stay at Ootacamund on furlough.

A great intimacy sprang up between Mrs. Street and Mrs. Morris, and it was settled that next year the children should return to England under the guardianship of the Streets, and that there John should go to a tutor to prepare for Cambridge. They sailed in the *True Briton*, February 6, 1842, and reached Plymouth in the beginning of June.

Being Devonshire people, Mr. and Mrs. Street took a house at Plymouth, and afterwards one at Stonehouse, near that town; and here for the next three and a half years the brothers and sisters found a most happy home, until their mother returned from India in 1845. During almost the whole of this time young Morris was going as a private pupil to the Rev. Henry Alford, Vicar of Wymeswold, not far from Loughborough, who was then rising into notice as a poet and preacher, and became better known afterwards as Dean of Canterbury, and commentator on the New Testament.

"We knew," writes Mr. Henry Morris, "several of the families residing in that neighbourhood. The family which I remember most clearly, consisted of a widow lady and her three daughters, and my brother became much attached to the eldest of them. But the persons to whom he owed most in the way of refinement and piety were Mrs. Street and our Aunt Sarah, our father's youngest sister, and the wife of Western Wood, afterwards Member for the City of London. Mrs. Street being much attached to my brother, exercised over him a very salutary influence, which later on took the general direction of restraining him from the extreme views on the Tractarian Movement, which she saw him rapidly adopting.

" The first marked event in my brother's life at this period was his Confirmation on August 24, 1842. We were at first staying in the upper part of Plymouth, and attended Charles Chapel, the incumbent of which was the Rev. G. F. Whidborne, who prepared him for this sacred ordinance. He was deeply impressed by the instruction of this good man, and was greatly encouraged by his sympathy. I have before me a long letter to our parents begun on August 25th, from which I make the following extracts: 'Do not think,' he said, after mentioning the fact of his Confirmation, 'that I underwent it as merely a form; but pray believe that I have felt and understood what I have been doing, and that I have, through God's grace, made the resolution of amending my past life and of living up to my professions. Some boys said that they would not undertake it, because they knew that they would never be able to keep the promises that they would then make for themselves. But this I thought, and still think, was a very wrong light in which to take it, for it can add but little to the obligation of keeping that promise, which is already so great that it can scarcely be added to, while by not undertaking it they cannot expect to have so much grace from God to assist them to keep it. For the imposition of the Bishop's hands is the means appointed by the Apostles themselves for receiving that grace; and consequently that any one, having within himself the full resolution to keep it (viz., what our godfathers and godmothers promised for us at Baptism), not in his own strength, but in Christ's, and earnestly desiring and praying for pardon for his past sins, and grace to help him for the time to come, may worthily receive this rite. There is another reason why I have wished to receive it, and that is, that I might worthily be admitted to the Sacrament of the Supper of the Lord. For being here in a state where we certainly need every possible help to keep us in the right path, I hope and trust that this may also prove a means of grace to my soul. My dear papa and mama, I know that I have always been the subject of your prayers hitherto that I might see the truth as it is in Jesus. Oh! do I not much rather need them now to be kept steadfast in the faith?'

"Another passage may be taken from this letter as being an indication of his character: 'I am sure you will be glad to hear that I am wearing off my uncomfortable shyness, which I remember you used not to like at all. I can now speak to a young lady and look at her when she speaks to me, without turning as red as a turkey-cock, and feeling as uncomfortable as possible all the while. You need not, however, be afraid that I shall go to the opposite extreme. I shall take good care of that. You will perhaps notice that in this letter I have repeated your names very often; I intend to do so for the future, for it feels so much more as if I were talking to you."

It was not long after his writing this letter that the time came for his beginning his private studies under Alford.

To have had such a man for tutor would have been fortunate for any one, and his father's choice soon became especially welcome to young Morris, for similarity of tastes and feelings led to a close intimacy between them. A heavy trial in the death of Alford's son, Clement, gave him an opportunity of showing his attachment, and in effect we find the afflicted father reckoning the "Christian kindness" of his pupils, first among the blessings which tempered the bitterness of his cup of sorrows. Morris, who had been present in the sick-room till the last, kept all through his life a copy of verses on the child's death. In estimating the development of his character under Alford, an episode like this must not be neglected, for it expresses better than words could do how eminently satisfactory their intimate relations were.

He looked up to Alford with the sincerest respect, and that the "little pagan" of Harrow days should, soon after coming to Wymeswold, give up all idea of the legal profession which he had previously intended to embrace, and should aspire to enter the ranks of the Anglican clergy, affords a striking indication of the strength of the new influences by which he was now being moulded. Though he had been badly grounded in his classics, he began to show such signs of ability that he was thought sure to obtain the much-coveted prize of a scholarship at Trinity.

Two influences of a more special character, those of the Tractarian Movement and of the Gothic revival, now gained hold of his mind. The former of these had then reached its height. Tract No. XC. had been published the year before he went to Alford, and Pusey's sermon was condemned the year after his arrival, so that the whole country was full of the subject. That Morris was naturally inclined to throw himself warmly into the movement, every one who knew him would easily surmise, and to this inclination there was now to be added the weight of Alford's influence, of which it may be said, that it was then very advanced even for a High Churchman.

There is, however, some difficulty in speaking positively of Alford's position. Advanced though he then was, in later life he veered round greatly towards the Evangelical side. But this was after his pupil's reception into the Church; before that, his Catholic friends actually hoped for his conversion. To judge, however, from the letters and journals quoted in his *Life*, he was more of a sympathizer with than a participator in the movement. On the one hand he seems to have read Tract XC. without displeasure, a sufficient indication of the progress of his views, while on the other, he never appears to have felt a disposition to follow the subject to its further issues. His mind was occupied with his pupils, with problems about the text of Scripture, with his parochial work and his family, and there he seems to have rested.

Subsequently he began to feel the cold breath of unpopularity on account of such High Church views as he had adopted, and his consequent resolution does not strike us as remarkably noble-minded. He writes: "We must have more of the serpent and less of the dove in future. . . I believe very great caution is necessary. I am disposed to draw in, I freely acknowledge it. I have not altered, but the times have. Would you blame the traveller for wrapping his cloak around him in the storm?"[1]

This was, as we have said, after Morris became a Catholic. At the time of which we are now speaking, he was honestly outspoken in condemning the popular but fallacious assailants of the Oxford party, and such strictures often influence young minds more than direct instruction.

How much, then, of the Tractarianism, with which we shall soon find Morris entirely engrossed, he owed to his tutor, and how much to his own independent reading, can hardly be now determined. A general idea of what he learnt from the former may, however, be inferred from a remark which he once made to the writer of these lines, on our happening to come upon a statue of Alford in Canterbury Cathedral. "When I went to him I don't think I knew anything about the Church. I left him convinced that there was one, and in nine months I had joined it."

The second great influence, besides Tractarianism, which at this time began to mould Morris's character, was the revival of Gothic architecture. Alford's good taste led him to welcome the movement cordially, and

[1] *Life*, p. 151. Letter to Elizabeth Mott.

his pupil threw himself into it with enthusiasm. An excellent opportunity for developing this taste was offered when Alford commenced the restoration of Wymeswold Church. Mr. Pugin was the architect employed, and although their actual intercourse appears to have been slight, the impression which that remarkable man made on Morris was very considerable. Nor is this to be wondered at. If Pugin, as is now generally admitted, did more than any one else to break down the hideous ideals that were in fashion early in this century, and to draw our philistine countrymen as a body to appreciate somewhat the beauties of good Gothic, it is surely no marvel that he should have enkindled in a kindred spirit a lasting admiration for the best traditions of his art. So impetuous did Morris's enthusiasm now become, that one may suspect it had often a decisive influence in determining the degree of Catholicity in the symbolism which Alford then admitted into the church, but which was afterwards cast out of doors. Before that imperious nature, indeed, the future Dean often seemed in the unwonted position of being less ruler than ruled.

The greater part of his free time was devoted to his hobby, and he took but little part in games. A lady who remembered him at this period, describes him as being "as steady as Old Time," and some of his fellow-students devised for him the nickname of "Old Father Morris," which in view of his future career, is certainly curious.

His brother's recollections of these days are interesting. "During the holidays, besides boating excursions and social engagements, my brother and I took long walks in the vicinity of Plymouth. He introduced me to Bloxam's *Gothic Architecture,* and I suppose there was scarcely a church within the distance of ten miles, which we did not visit, and very enjoyable the trips were. He was specially fond of rubbing brasses, and many a brass did I help him to take in this manner. Even when I was alone in other parts of the country, I fell into the habit of rubbing brasses for him, and he gradually got together a goodly collection of these ecclesiastical relics, which he eventually gave to a friend at Cambridge."

When Morris's father heard of the enthusiasm of his son for his new amusement, he was not only displeased, but wrote denouncing it in strong terms. His son, however, defended himself warmly. "And now, my dear father," he says (April 26, 1846), "as to my hobby for seeing and examining old churches, architecture, and so on. I must say I was very sorry when you thought it necessary to characterize the only amusement or recreation I care to take as 'tomfoolery.' I am not aware that it interferes with my work; and surely, *as recreation*, it would be difficult to fix on one less expensive (if travelling, which is quite another thing, be not considered), or one that leads more to the cultivation of good tastes. You will doubtless be amused at my warmth in defending my pursuits, but really I have been so accustomed to congratulate myself on the great superiority of my amusements over those of the generality of my compeers, who think of nothing but boating, or hunting, or shooting, or fishing, that I was surprised to hear them blamed."

"The gradual change in John's religious views," to return now to his brother's reminiscences, "was as discernible in his letters, when we were separated, as in his conversation and employments, when we were together. It was noticeable even in the books he gave me as birthday or Christmas presents. The first of these, which I retain to this day, is Paget's *Tales of the Village.* Then followed other little volumes by Paget,

Gresley, and other Puseyite writers of tales—a department of literature which had no small influence in
moulding public opinion.

" On September 30, 1844, he wrote to me in answer
to certain questions I had put to him, and his letter
abounds in phrases which show the extent of the change
that had taken place in his opinions since Evangelical
impressions had been made on his heart at the time of
his Confirmation. Even the capital letters which he
uses tell the same tale. ' No one,' he writes, ' will
ever lose any Grace or Favour with God from having
been obedient and having submitted his will to that of
others.' ' Only pray be contented with Christ's " light
and easy burden," of " believe only and be baptized ; "
that is, of a life of Faith in His Holy Church ; and
throw aside entirely from your mind the burden of
man's inventions, " grievous to be borne," of waiting
for conversions, movings of the Spirit, and the like.'
Referring to the Sacrament of the Lord's Supper, he
writes : ' Remember what it is ; our dear Lord's words,
This is my Body—my Blood," the words of Holy
Mother Church, " The Body and Blood of Christ, verily
and indeed taken and received by the faithful in the
Lord's Supper." And if it is so awful a guest you are
about to entertain, pray look on it with the solemnity it
calls for. Remember you must be constant there, not
one day staying, another time turning your back on It,
but love It and think on It always as your rule in
everything, and remember that it is a Blessed Sacrifice
—one which represents Christ's Sacrifice to God, which
implores the benefits of Christ's Death from God, which
applies them to the worthy receiver. And it is likewise
a Sacrifice of praise and thanksgiving, and a votive
Sacrifice, in which the Communicant presents himself,
soul and body, a sacrifice acceptable, well-pleasing unto
God.' ' My letter,' he added, ' has been written after

Mr. Alford's advice. He is a good friend to you, and I hope you will see him at Christmas and thank him yourself."

"The prospect of seeing Mr. Alford at Christmas is further alluded to in a letter of October 6th. 'Church principles and practice are the principal topic of conversation. The church here is getting on delightfully, the tracery in the new windows is so delicious. By the way, I am becoming quite an ecclesiologist, and go about examining churches with the greatest zest and pleasure. When do you expect your Christmas holidays to begin? I am, I hope, going with Mr. Alford, on my way home, to see Glastonbury Abbey and Wells Cathedral. We break up about the middle of December, is that sooner than you will? I hope you can come too, for I do so much want you to know Mr. Alford. You would like him so much, besides the pleasure the church-seeing would give us both in such good company.' To the best of my recollection, however, the promised visit was frustrated, and we went by sea from London to Plymouth as we usually did.

"In the same letter, referring to my anticipated Confirmation, he added, 'May God Almighty in His own good time bring you into full membership with the Church Catholic, the Communion of Saints, the Blessed Company of all Faithful people.' In a letter on the same subject of November 9th, he adds, 'I hope you will try to make use of our Holy Mother's days, making use of her days of Fasting, for works of spiritual, if not also of carnal mortification, and that you bear in mind the godly order in which her Festivals recur, remembering on each of them, the great event or person each commemorates, and on each Lord's day, remember that as Christ died and rose again, so, as we were baptized unto His Death, we should also die unto sin and rise again unto holiness.' "

Mr. Henry Morris's reflections on these letters must be given in full, for while they do not represent what Father Morris's own subsequent judgment would have been, nor perhaps that which many of his readers will form, the view they set forth must be carefully borne in mind by all who wish to realize the story in its fulness, for Mr. Henry Morris's view is, no doubt, that which was taken of his brother's actions by his family at the time.

" I have given these extracts from my brother's letters for the purpose of showing how surely and steadily Puseyism was growing in his mind. Each time we met, some fresh phase of it appeared. The chief thing which impressed itself on my mind, was his excessive veneration for what he called his holy Mother, the Catholic Church, and the degree to which it seemed to have overshadowed the pure, personal love to the Lord Jesus Christ Himself that he had formally possessed. The manner in which he pressed this view on me was very earnest, and he seemed pained when others urged on me the contrary view. He received, it is true, some encouragement in his opinions from certain of our relations, and there was no check upon them when at home, except the gentle remonstrances of Mrs. Street.

" But I am bound to record my conviction, that these extreme High Church opinions were the result of Mr. Alford's influence and training, and although the incident of his change in his religious views is treated in a very reticent and delicate manner in *The Life, Journals, and Letters of Dean Alford,* any one who carefully studies that volume cannot fail to see that this event was the turning-point in the Dean's own life. It also clearly proves to me that Tractarianism, and its descendant Ritualism, logically lead to Rome."

We have already referred to Pugin as one of those who probably had much to do with the development of John Morris's architectural tastes. One of Pugin's gifts, which gave great force to his pleadings in favour of a return to higher ideals, was the cleverness of the sarcasm he could pour on the effete fashions, then reputed to be orthodox. Morris caught the inspiration, and, by the kindness of his brother, an interesting proof of this can be given from a lecture entitled, *A Paper on Memorials of the Departed*, written apparently for some village club about midsummer, 1845. This paper gives us the first sample of his literary style, and throws a strong light on the progress of his mind in religious matters. "*Old* Father Morris's" tone is preternaturally grave, so that the composition reads more like a sermon than a lecture. Yet an amusingly boyish trait in the composition betrays itself in his frequent lapses into extremes of thought and language. A man who cuts his name on a monument is "a beast," and on page six we find a climax of horrors ending with "heresy, impiety, presumption—from which good Lord deliver us," an exclamation which was trenchantly scored out by his tutor.

How he would have smiled at the following prophecy, if it recurred to his mind when writing his *What I Remember*. He has been describing monumental brasses, "on the glories of which we could expatiate for hours," and then continues: "The money that is now laid out on a hideous tablet of pagan device, deforming and injuring the church, would buy a very nice pious brass that should be an ornament to the church, and should last ten times as long. For the days must soon come when these pagan things will

be turned bodily out of the church, and broken to
pieces with indignation, while the graves of those will
be much honoured who have set a good example in
being the first to revive this Christian monument."

The subject of the address was of a class familiar
to the revivalists of Gothic architecture, and was
evidently suggested by some of Pugin's works. The
ugliness and bad taste displayed in the memorials of
the dead then in vogue are contrasted with the beauty
and propriety of older Christian monuments, and a
return to the ancient models is earnestly advocated.
Square gravestones should give way to crosses, mural
tablets to brasses, and pagan to Christian symbolism.
Originality is not wanting in his handling of the theme,
and there is plenty of incidental proof that his visits to
Haddon Hall, to Westminster Abbey, and St. Paul's,
and to other churches in all directions, had been made
in a spirit of observation unusual in a youth of eighteen.

The following extract will illustrate our meaning ·

" In a church in Leicester is a tomb with a sculpture
of our Lord ascending into Heaven and delivering the
keys of the church to the late Vicar, a recognition
indeed of one of the Church's doctrines, but not in the
most humble manner possible, for it would apparently
make the clergyman commemorated equal to the
greatest of the Apostles. But the very worst thing
I ever saw, and one worse than it I trust I may
never see, is, alas! very much nearer to us than
Leicester. If you enter the chancel of Bunny Church,
the first thing you see is the altar thrown far forward to
admit a very high railed vault to occupy its place, above
the top of which the heads of the very beautiful seats,
that once were used for the clergy officiating at the
altar, may yet be seen. A flight of steps takes you
to the top of this abomination, and lo! there, very

nearly over the place once hallowed by the holiest of Ordinances, stands a great marble image of a man in the attitude of wrestling. As it is not at all improbable that some of you will doubt of so enormous and so awful a profanation of the holy place, I would advise such to go and see for themselves, and until that horrid profanation is removed, let us never reproach others with bowing down to a graven image. Before this thing communicants must kneel. Let us pray to God to remove such a disgrace from a Christian land. Verily it is an abomination of desolation standing where it should not. The inscription on this thing (I dare not call it a monument), is quite in accordance with the design. Not one word of Christianity occurs in it, and thus it is even worse than pagan, for pagans would have left their worldly occupations and vanities aside, and would have mentioned their own though false religion. Besides this inscription, there are some Latin verses telling us how the man was at last thrown by the Wrestler Death, after throwing every one else. Two sculps in the marble tell the same tale, for the one represents him as wrestling with Death, and the other as lying at full length having been thrown by him.

"Let us turn as a relief from this most painful subject to the inscriptions we ought to place upon the tombs of our brethren in the faith. As we said, the lowly prayer for Mercy is the most appropriate; indeed, as a publication of the day has well said, 'No epitaph can be Catholick, unless it includes a distinct prayer for Mercy.' I trust it is not necessary for me to remind you that Catholick is but another word for Christian, 'the Catholick Faith,' which we profess, is the Christian Faith; and so when we say that no epitaph is Catholick without a distinct prayer for Mercy, we mean that the epitaph of every Christian must include this prayer."

Shortly before this paper was written, Pugin had invited his friend, Mr. Ambrose Lisle Phillipps, who afterwards took the name of Ambrose Phillipps de Lisle, of Gracedieu, to see the alterations at Wymeswold, and introduced him to Alford and his pupils. Mr. Phillipps in his turn invited his hosts to come to Gracedieu and see the newly built abbey church of Mount St. Bernard. The invitation was accepted by Alford, who went accompanied by his two pupils, Mr., afterwards Sir John Willoughby Jones, and the young John Morris. The visit was a very agreeable one, as Mr. Phillipps, himself a convert, took a lively interest in all the ecclesiastical, artistic, antiquarian, and architectural questions, which were engaging the attention of his guests from Wymeswold. Before they left they paid a visit to the abbey church, and heard the Divine Office sung in choir, in the first Cistercian monastery which had been established in England since the Reformation.

In a subsequent controversy Alford deprecated any special importance being attached to this visit, saying truly enough, that many others besides himself had "gone, gazed, and returned," without being shaken in their Protestantism; nor indeed does it seem to have had any immediate effect on his pupil. Such at least was decidedly Alford's view; for immediately afterwards, as he says, "when the time of his going to Cambridge approached, I wrote, as my custom is, a detailed character of him to his college tutor at Trinity. In that letter I stated that should he, as I anticipated, pass through the University with credit, and take Orders, he would prove a valuable minister of the Church of England, from the depth of his attachment to her, and his freedom from those Romish errors, which in these days we are called upon to combat."[1]

<hr>

[1] *The Times*, November 6, 1846.

All this may be true, but a period of doubt was almost immediately to set in, during which the remembrance of that visit and the recollection of the monks and of their music would come back like a vision of peace; and in later life Father Morris is reported to have said that the chanting which he had then heard, had no small share in his subsequent conversion.

CHAPTER II.

JOHN MORRIS went up to Cambridge in October, 1845, carrying with him the high expectations which Alford had formed of his future progress, and the proud hopes which his father entertained of his distinguishing himself at the University. His stay there was destined to be brief, though pregnant with important issues. It resulted in a cruel disappointment to his father, while it permanently affected his tutor's position. As regards himself, it ended in his embracing the true faith, and receiving the further great grace of a vocation to the religious life.

Before he had time to settle down in his rooms in the New Court at Trinity, the whole country was talking of John Henry Newman's reception into the Catholic Church. Thousands of Anglicans besides Morris felt that their own adherence to the body in which they were born might soon become a point for serious consideration, and they set about examining anew the grounds of safety for their own position. In Morris's case, the Anglican theory of the Church, to which he had hitherto clung, began slowly to lose its force with him. At first, indeed, with inborn loyalty, he tried his best to preserve his confidence in the beliefs which he had so ingenuously accepted. His state of mind at that time reveals itself in a series of letters, which he wrote from Cambridge, to Mr. Ambrose Lisle Phillipps, and which show that he held out as long as he conscientiously could, against the ever deepening conviction, that the Roman Church was after all the one and only Church. The first letter here given bears date:

"Trinity College, XXII Sunday after Trinity [Oct. 19], 1845.

"My dear Mr. Phillipps,—You may perhaps remember that when I last had the pleasure of seeing you, you gave me your kind permission to write to you. I little thought then that, before I should be able to avail myself of it, the heavy loss, which we have been expecting so long, should have fallen upon our Church. The Church of England has lost one of her most deeply learned and most holy sons, one who was once her most zealous defender ; for really, the loss of Mr. Newman is so great, that it makes one forget the many who have gone with him. Humanly speaking, it is the greatest blow the Church has ever had. . . . I do trust and believe that he will not, as so many that have left us have done, now turn against his Mother who has until now nourished him; but rather I hope that he may be an instrument in God's hand for drawing the two Churches nearer together, and I pray that we may live to see the day when both he and we shall be in the same communion, not by changing from one to the other, but by the union of our two Churches into one holy fellowship as they were in before.

"What a beautiful and affecting letter is Dr. Pusey's in the last *English Churchman*, every word of it speaks to one's heart. It certainly seems, as he says, that God is taking from us all human causes of hope, that His work amongst us may be more manifestly from Him. How truly he says our hope must be in earnest prayer; and I cannot help considering with him that the occurrence which has so grieved me is an answer to the earnest prayers of your Church, and a judgment upon us for our lukewarmness in prayer.[1] I wish there were a society to pray for the reunion of the Churches formed of members of both Churches; there are such societies in both the Churches, but this should be one in which we could meet on common ground, which might be a common bond between us.

" I much fear that you will think that I have written too freely, and on subjects too high for me. I have but written my own impressions, and I should be very glad to know how far you think with me. Let us at least pray ' that all those who profess and call themselves Christians may be led into the way of truth, and hold the faith in unity of spirit, in the bond of peace, and in righteousness of life.'

" Believe me, dear Mr. Phillipps, to be most sincerely yours,

" JOHN MORRIS.

" I value your little book very much. It is very beautiful."

Mr. Phillipps's " long and interesting answer " to this letter, unfortunately, no longer exists. He had discussed the matter with several of the Oxford leaders, and afterwards published an account of his views under the title of *The Future Unity of Christendom.*

At a time when this very question of reunion between the members of the different religious bodies in England is being so widely discussed and so earnestly

---

[1] Father Morris's own earnestness about prayer is not only seen in these selections from his letters, but also throughout the course of his general correspondence. Thus he urged upon his younger brother that he should pray for the success of his examinations at Cambridge.

longed for, and even recommended by the Holy Father himself to the prayers of all earnest-minded people, there is especial interest in reading the fervent aspirations after union in faith and in prayer which are still more strongly expressed in the following letter from the approaching convert to his friend, exactly fifty years ago :

"Trinity College, Nov. 13, 1845.

" My dear Mr. Phillipps,—I think I am correct in believing that your heart is in unison with ours in praying for the reunion of Western Christendom, for the repair of the breaches thereof; and that whatever seems to interfere with this great end is a cause of pain to you as well as to us. A point which seemed to me to involve this is the one to which your letter first alludes, Mr. Newman's re-Baptism. I was very glad indeed to learn that the conditional form, 'If thou art not already baptized,' was really inserted, and used at his and other similar cases of Baptism.

" I do not think I can quite agree with the second part of your letter, which refers to Mr. Bennett's letter in the *English Churchman*, accusing Mr. N. and his associates of schism, on which you say that if it be schism to leave the Anglican for the largest branch of the Catholick Church, then the Anglican must be a schismatick and dead branch of your Church. I must confess, I by no means see this. The 'Anglican Theory of the Catholick Church' has always been in my eyes this : that the Roman Church is the Catholick Church of Italy, the Gallican of France, the Greek Church of its nation, and the English Church the Catholick Church of England. And I have never been able to regard the Roman communion in England otherwise than a part of a foreign Church abiding in this land, through that Church indeed communicating with the Catholick Church, but as by no means being the Catholick Church *of England.* And I cannot consider it fatal to this theory to style joining their communion schism. For that there is schism between ourselves and you, as well as from the Greek Church, real horrible schism, is too plainly and fearfully apparent. For instance, a true son of the English Church going into France, believing deeply our theory of the Catholick Church, feels deeply pained at being cut off from all the sacraments of the Gallican Church, for I believe she would not admit him until he acknowledged his own Mother Church heretical, which, if a 'loving son,' he could of course never do, and his heart would as much revolt from intercourse with Protestants there as with Dissenters here. Must not he feel this to be schism indeed? Really, except on British ground, such as Ambassadors' chapels, &c., he is cut off from the Bread of Life altogether, for if he is consistent with his theory, he can (as I believe) have nothing to do with English congregations in Catholick towns abroad. He must content his soul with the publick prayers and the use of the Church's temples. She will give him no more.

"I believe this to be the only consistent Anglican theory of the Catholick Church. But it involves this belief—nay hangs upon it—that the English Church is the Catholick Church of England—the representative of the Mother of Saints of old—fallen, alas! *through us, our faults and our sins;* yet by God's grace arising, to fill one day, we trust and pray, her ancient position [see Dr. Pusey's dedication of his translation of Avrillon's *Guide for passing Advent holily*], to spread her branches through the length and breadth of her land—and one day, how earnestly do we pray, again to include as of old all who profess and call themselves Christians in this country, to be again, we pray, recognized as a sister by all other Churches, and to be again a glorious, fruit-bearing branch of the One True Vine. Unless we believed this earnestly, if we could call our Church: 'The Protestant Church,' and yours 'The Catholick Church' (as Mr. Oakeley does), how could we in good faith restore our ancient churches. What a bitter mockery would the effigy of a St. Clement, Bishop of Rome be, or a St. Gregory, Apostle of the English, or any of the tens of thousands now being erected to remind us of the Deeds and the Faith of Holy Men gone to their rest, unless we from our hearts believed that they in their day were members and are members of the Church of which we are members now—wretched, miserable successors of theirs in truth; but yet we trust by that same grace and Mercy which raised them where they now are, to be one Day admitted to a low station of the same glorious company with themselves. Again, how could we without very great sin do, as we trust to have grace given us to do next Sunday, partake of the Body and Blood of our Lord, had we not earnest Faith in our hearts that the Priests who from the Altar of our College Chapel will feed us with the food of Angels, are the very Successors of those Apostles to whom our Lord said: 'Do this in remembrance of Me.' Would it not involve *a sin* to go there with the slightest doubt on our minds of their right to give us the Bread from Heaven? What have we done, what has our Church done, that other Churches should have thought right to cut us off from their Communion and Fellowship? Does not our Church wash her sons in the Life Giving Stream? Does she not feed them with the Bread of Life? Does she not give them when troubled the 'Comfortable Word' of Absolution? Has the three-fold Apostolic lineage been broken? Has she thrown away from her the Catholick symbols of Faith?

"Why will you not feed at the same Altar with us? Why not say the same words with us? Think the

same thing with us? Be our brethren? We are all
striving to go to one Place, why must we go different
ways thither?

"I trust, my dear Mr. Phillipps, you will pardon me
if I have written too boldly or strongly to you, or
spoken my thoughts too plainly, but the kindness of your
letter tempted me to it, and must be my excuse.

"If we think the old thoughts, walk in the old paths,
tread as nearly as our imperfections will allow in the
steps of the glorious saints of old, we may trust at length
to be inclosed in the same Holy Faith and Fold, and at
length received into Paradise as children of Christ's
Holy Spouse. May God mercifully grant it for His
dear Son's sake. Amen.

"Meanwhile, until this happy day shall come when
the son of the Roman and the son of the English
Church may as of yore walk in the House of God
together as friends, let us put away as far as in us lies
all that may defer (for I trust by God's grace nothing
can finally prevent) our happy reunion.

"Yours most faithfully,

"JOHN MORRIS."

A break in the correspondence with Mr. Phillipps
occurs after this, and less serious matters call for
attention. Morris was most anxious to do well at
his studies, and therefore started his reading with a
Mr. Keary of Trinity as his classical tutor. Towards
the end of November he became acquainted with the
late Mr. F. A. Paley, whose name, sure to be respected
at Cambridge for the sake of his illustrious grandfather,
was now becoming known on account of his excellent
editions of Æschylus. The acquaintance seems to have
originated in the interest which they each took in
ecclesiastical antiquities. Paley was then one of the
Honorary Secretaries to the Cambridge Camden Society,

amongst the members of which were numbered most of the Cambridge High Churchmen, and Alford had been elected a member at the commencement of the year. Shortly after this, however, and not long before Morris came up, the Society nearly foundered, owing to the tide of unpopularity which was setting against the High Church party. As it was, a considerable number of the more dignified members, headed by two Bishops, seceded, and by the end of the next year the Society found it more expedient to change its name and place of abode, and commenced in London a new life under the name of the Ecclesiological Society.

It does not surprise us to find in the December report, the first published after the secessions above alluded to, the name of "John Morris, Esq., Trinity College," on the list of Ordinary Members. No doubt he attended their meetings with interest, and found amongst the members many friends, nor would he have refused to take his share in the troubles which befell the Society at large, because of the religious spirit in which they were supposed to have pursued their anti-quarian hobbies.

About Christmas he was at home again. The family, however, had moved from Plymouth to the neighbourhood of Portsmouth, and his kind friends the Streets had returned to India. His mother had come over to look after the household, and his father was expected back erelong in England. The new home on Portsdown stood upon the northern slope of an open grassy upland, above the great sea-port. He returned after a fortnight to Cambridge, and it may be inferred that anxiety about religious matters prevented his enjoying the vacation as much as he otherwise might have done.

There was, however, another and a mundane cause of anxiety. Like many other young men of his age, he

D

had got into difficulties as to the expenditure of his money allowance, and frankly discloses his troubles to his father in the following letter.

"January 17, 1846.

" The principal object of this letter is, however, to talk to you of my expenses. As soon as I arrived here, I got my tutor's account, and it was so very much heavier than I had expected that I was quite frightened. I kept it and thought over it some little time, and now have determined as by far the best plan to write a full account of everything, and send it out to you. I have accordingly written as full and minute an account as I could, . . . and I am going to ask you to deduct the heaviest expenses from my next year's allowance. Even with that deduction, I am satisfied, it will be amply sufficient for all my wants. The other item, which I am to explain, is one for which I am heartily sorry. I only wish I could recall it. You have heard of my passion for brasses. In my admiration for these, and while revelling in the supposed bottomlessness of £250 a year, before I came up here I most foolishly ordered a small brass to be made, with the desire of encouraging the restoration of these most beautiful ornaments. Mine consists of two little budding crosses, most exquisitely worked with an inscription, and it is to the memory of my little brother and sister. I hope you will not be angry or sorry at my having done this; it was most foolish of me, and I had no business to have done it, at all events without consulting you or my dear mother, . but now I want you to deduct the £25 for it from my next year's allowance, and to give me leave to have it laid in Wymeswold church. . . .

" I am exceedingly glad that I have written out all that account for you. It is quite a weight off my mind.

"I have now nothing more to add, my dear father, but that I am, with that only exception, quite happy and well, and hard at work. I am very sanguine I shall get a first class at midsummer, which will entitle me to a prize. I most sincerely trust I may; but I bear your proverb in mind, 'by exertion, not by wishing,' and I am determined you shall have nothing to complain of in my progress for the two next terms."

His father answered in March with an appropriate scolding, not only for being "so foolish and extravagant in buying useless and expensive brasses," but also for "subscribing £10 to Mr. Alford's church." Having completed his not undeserved strictures, he praises his remembrance of "my Persian adage," and his application to study, and concludes, "Let me assure you, my dear boy, of my sincere and ardent affection for you, and that I fully appreciate your desire to do right. If I have been obliged to censure you on one point, it is for your good, and in hope that a word now may save us both from greater unhappiness hereafter."

But matters of far greater import were taking place at Cambridge than those treated of in this correspondence. Between Morris and Paley fresh bonds had grown up, which were destined to affect deeply the futures of both. The intimacy of antiquaries had been superseded, first by the formal relation of tutor to pupil, and then by the confidences of mutual friendship. "I have been," wrote Paley, "one of Mr. Morris's principal friends and companions, from a certain congeniality of sentiment as well as from the great regard I have had for his character," for he was "well informed and sensible, . . . and of a highly religious and devotional turn of mind."

Perfect intimacy being thus established, they were

not slow to discuss *the* question of the hour. "On my first acquaintance," says Paley, "I at once perceived that his mind was thoroughly conversant, and even engrossed, with the unhappy controversy about Romanists and Protestants," and "we often and freely conversed upon that subject of deep interest to us both." "Finding him fully alive to the interests of the question, and fully acquainted with the ordinary topics of controversy, I made no reserve at all of my own sentiments. I never concealed from him the difficulties which prevented me from wishing to join the Roman Church, nor, on the other hand, the sympathies I entertained for not a few of its practices and even doctrines."

These details are taken from Mr. Paley's letters to the *Times* after Morris's reception into the Church, and although there is no indication that the younger man learned any specific Catholic doctrine from his senior (indeed the latter believed that he held all the articles of the Catholic faith before they met at all), he probably did learn from him to be more and more independent in making his choice between the contending claims of Anglicanism and Rome.

Paley, it is true, "earnestly and seriously expressed his solemn conviction of the extreme danger of haste and rashness in judging; and invariably spoke of the vast difficulty as well as presumption of a very young man deciding on such a tremendous point of religious faith." These representations, however, were not likely to have the same weight with one of Morris's temperament, as the threat of damnation when invoked by Alford on all who should be found guilty of the sin of schism. Yet it was to Alford that the young man turned first and most filially in his doubts.

As early as the previous November, he had set the state of his mind before his old master. "That day," said the latter, "was the beginning of a long and painful correspondence between us." It speaks, indeed, well for Morris's docility that he should have persevered as he did in this "painful" process. He also carefully read Alford's *Earnest Dissuasive from Joining the Church of Rome*, which was published at this time, and was especially written, the author tells us, to meet "Morris's own case, and the state of society which his letters described."

Though Alford says that he received Morris's "warmest thanks" for this paper, and an expression of the hope that "it might do good, for it was much needed at Cambridge," it soon became evident that the check to his Romeward tendencies had been but transient. On the 18th of February he wrote to Mr. Phillipps, much impressed by the stream of converts who had been steadily following Newman into the Church. "I am afraid my hopes of the restoration of unity have become weaker, for if such a man as Faber, who while he was with us, was surely with us in heart and soul, can now speak as he does of the English Church, I am afraid our hope of reunion is very small. I am very glad to see your little work on the Gregorian musick announced as soon to be expected;[1] I trust it may help the return of the good, old Church musick, in which saints and angels have delighted, and may assist in giving the death-blow to the modern flippant, almost profane musick, which usually reminds me of extempore prayers, for they seem equally irreverent modes of approaching the Lord.

"I hope Mr. Alford is prospering in his good work of restoring his church to some faint similitude of its mediæval glories; I have some hopes of being able to pay him a visit about Easter, and I expect to find the work very far advanced. I wish most heartily it were not quite so nearly a solitary instance amongst us."

[1] *The Little Gradual* (Toovey) which appeared in 1847.

His next letter to the same, dated March 22, after referring again to the proposed journey to Wymeswold, adds: "I hope to give myself the pleasure of calling upon you and Mrs. Phillipps, and once more hearing the Gregorian tones of the monks of Mount St. Bernard. I have heard no musick since I left Leicestershire to be compared with that."

To Wymeswold he went that Easter, on what was destined to be for him a critical visit. Religious high festival was being held on the occasion of the re-opening of the church. Many members of the High Church party were present, and some noted preachers. Alford sincerely hoped and Morris still desired that he might find at such a time and in such a gathering some person or principle to confirm his failing allegiance to Anglicanism. "He was very wavering, when he came to us at Easter," wrote Alford, "and I had several long and serious talks with him, and vainly hoped I had removed his doubts."

Alford's hopes were not so much vain as fatuous. He had solved Morris's doubts, but in a sense entirely opposite to what he had intended. When he returned to Cambridge, Mr. Morris informed Mr. Paley "that he would not consult an Anglican again, but would turn Romanist at once."[1]

The difficulties which now held him back were not so much doctrinal as domestic. He knew too well how it would grieve his father and mother. His mother was suffering from weak health and low spirits, and hardly had the strength to bear the shock which his conversion must give. His father, after years of absence, was actually on his way home, fondly hoping for the joy of having around him a united family. "At Easter his grief was dreadful," as his Aunt Sarah

---

[1] "Another Member of the Church of England," October 29, 1846, to the *Times.*

described it to his mother. "He kept dwelling upon the anticipated trial to you and his beloved father, constantly saying, 'What can I do? I must not put my soul in jeopardy even for a beloved parent's sake. Though I would gladly die rather than cause my dear father and mother this trial, I must profess what I believe to be the truth, let what may happen.'
I tried [continues his aunt] to point out the sin he was committing, but alas! without success, and the only thing I could get was the promise that he would take no decided steps till his father came home."

Easter Term began that year at Cambridge on April the 9th, and by the 29th he had made up his mind that a Catholic he must be, and this intention he communicated to Mr. Phillipps.

"+ Trinity College, St. Peter Martyr, April 29, 1846.

"My dear Mr. Phillipps,—I think it only due to the great kindness with which you have taken an interest in me, to be the first to tell you that, by God's grace and good favour towards me, I have at length resolved to submit myself at the first opportunity to the Holy Catholick Church. . . . I have been gradually discerning this ·to be my duty, and I cannot be too thankful to God for having of His great mercy given me grace to make this resolution while my life is as yet unspent, that I may be enabled to spend my energies in His service, within His Holy Church, and thus retrieve as far as in me lies the faults I have committed in rebellion against His Church from my Baptism until this day.

"I have not, I trust, hastily made up my mind, but I have reflected and prayed much and earnestly on this most important subject; and I think I may say that since October last my mind has been, with of course occasional relapses, made up that it is impossible for a

Church to be at one and the same time separated from the Catholick Church and yet a branch of it, and therefore ever since then I have seen the utter untenableness of the argument which speaks of 'Romish schismaticks.' I have been more and more brought to see that the Church of which I am yet a member has been separated from Catholick unity, and that, as a necessary consequence, to remain in her communion must be dangerous if not absolutely sinful. I have struggled strongly against these views as undutiful to my Church, and therefore wrong; but they have gradually forced themselves on me, and I am now so fully persuaded of their truth that, were it in my power, I would at once make my submission to the Catholick Church.

"The change of my belief, too, in doctrine has been very gradual. At first I used to reject the doctrines of the Intercession, and therefore the Invocation of Saints. Nor did I believe in the true doctrine of the Real Presence of our Blessed Lord in the Holy Eucharist; in the efficacy of Absolution, and therefore of an Indulgence; in the utility of Prayer for the Faithful Departed as either rejected by my Church, or at least as contrary to her spirit. When they forced themselves upon me, approving themselves true and Catholick, I used to attempt to reconcile them to the language of my Church, though I fear it occasionally was at the expense of my honesty. . . . But as I have been more and more enabled to see that the Roman Church is the Catholick Church, so I have also seen that what she authoritatively teaches as doctrine is to be believed as THE TRUTH. This I do most heartily believe, and therefore, acknowledging her to be the Church, I have thrown away my private judgment and unhesitatingly believe all she bids me.

"I have now spoken, but very imperfectly and briefly, of my mind; let me now speak a few words of the circumstances by which I am bound. I am not sure whether you are aware that my dear father is in India. We expect him home in the month of August, and until then I feel myself bound to remain in my present position, lest any step of mine, however consonant to my own feelings and desires, might have an evil effect upon my dear mother's health. Further, my good father has always looked forward to my passing through a prosperous course at Cambridge and then entering the ministry of the English Church. All his hopes and views in me must be disappointed, and, grievous as it seems, by me his eldest son; yet love father or mother more than Christ I cannot, lest I be found not worthy of Christ. I cannot therefore expect, I have no right to expect, that my father will do more for me than he has done. He has gone to a very large expense for me, an expense he can ill afford with his family of twelve children. What I am to do to support myself I know not, but I doubt not Providence will provide a way for me, according to that our Lord said: *Quærite primum regnum Dei et justitiam ejus: et hæc omnia adjicientur vobis.*

"You will be doing me a real kindness, my dear Mr. Phillipps, if you can suggest to me any means of employing myself to the glory of God and the good of His Church, by which I may relieve my dear parents (if indeed I have any right to expect them to help me at all) of the weight of my expenses. As I used to look forward to the Anglican priesthood, so for some time past I have anticipated the privilege and honour of being ordained a Catholick priest; but I must fear it is but an empty dream, not likely to be realized. However, if it be God's will, He will make a way.

"I am afraid I am wearying you with my long letter; but, as you may imagine, sympathy is scarce here, and I am only too happy to talk to any one who will

sympathize with me. I should be very glad to hear
from you if you will have time to write to me.

"To conclude. I have two things I feel most strongly
—the first is that the very thing which others most
object against me, my youth, is really and should be
the cause of the greatest thankfulness to God, for
having of His goodness shown me the Ark while my
strength to serve Him in it is unwasted, and by an
early conversion to save me so much the more rebellion
to be repented of; and, secondly, I feel more and more
my extreme ignorance, so much so that I think I ought
to kneel at the feet of some learned priest as a cate-
chumen before I am admitted into the Church; and,
lastly, since there never was a time in my life when I
less saw my way before me than now, so, I hope, there
never was a time in my life when I put more trust in
God to provide for me and to lead me aright than I
do now.

"Pray give my very kind remembrances to Mrs. Lisle
Phillipps, and, my dear Mr. Phillipps, ever believe me
to be

"Yours most faithfully and gratefully,
"JOHN MORRIS.
"+ SS. Philip and Jacob, AA.MM."

Almost immediately after the despatch of this letter,
Morris discovered that Dr. William Wareing, Vicar-
Apostolic of the Eastern District, happened to be in
Cambridge on a visit, and had been introduced to his
tutor, who gives this account of what followed: "On
the next day, a party of several was formed, among
whom were two Roman Catholic priests. As a matter
of ordinary courtesy, as well as of interest to my pupil,
I introduced him (as one of the party) to the Bishop.
. . . This . . . led to an invitation to meet the Bishop
at tea the same evening, and hither we both went.
Here my pupil had some further conversation with the

Bishop." The subject of that conversation was Morris's reception into the Church, and they seem to have discussed the two principal objections, which were the absence of his father from England and the destruction of all worldly prospects involved in his leaving Anglicanism. The Bishop apparently did not resist his desire to wait for his father's return, and promised to give him a scholarship at the English College, Rome, in case such a course should become advisable.

Mr. Phillipps was not slow in congratulating his young friend on the resolution he had taken, but urged him to join the Church without delay. Mr. T. W. M. Marshall, with whom at the instance of Mr. Stokes, Morris had interchanged a few letters on the subject of "Mariolatry," concerning which he long had a lingering difficulty, wrote in a like sense about the same time. Even if received, his reception might be kept private until his father's return.

Morris communicated this to the Bishop, and the feast of the Ascension was finally settled as the day when the step should be taken.

The privacy which Phillipps had recommended, meant that this resolution should be kept from his mother, then in weak health, and should only be revealed to his Aunt Sarah, to Alford, and to Paley. Alford immediately communicated the secret with disagreeable consequences, to which we shall have to return. Paley says: "The very night he went to be united with the (Roman) Church, I implored him at length and with every argument in my power, either to postpone his intention, or at least to set the whole case—his youth, his absent father, his want of reading and spiritual counsellors—before the Bishop, if perchance Dr. Wareing should not see (which did strongly occur to my mind) the absolute duty of waiting for his father's return to England at least."

But Morris was convinced, and feeling that all
further delay would be against his conscience, set off
for Northampton and was received into the Church by
the Bishop on the 20th of May, being Wednesday, the
eve of the Ascension, 1846. On the morrow's feast he
made his First Communion, and received Confirmation
next day in the Bishop's private chapel. One little
incident which happened there may be mentioned, as
an instance, by no means rare, of a comic element
entering into an action of the greatest gravity. The
only other person to be confirmed besides himself was
a maid-servant, and while the two sat side by side on
two chairs in the middle of the otherwise empty chapel
to receive the Bishop's homily, which was delivered to
them with as much solemnity as if a large congregation
had been present, the ludicrous aspect of the scene
suddenly suggested itself to the young undergraduate
so forcibly that he was seized with a fit of laughter and
nearly choked himself in his efforts to suppress it.

As the result of Alford's disclosure of the step that
had been taken, a storm of indignation was raised
against the young convert. It would seem, however,
that, in view of his leaving the University almost at
once, no public measures of reprehension were actually
taken. Happily the peace which followed conversion
enabled him to bear all with patience, and the last
three weeks of his stay at Cambridge, despite the
frowns of former friends and uncertainty as to the
future, were passed with great equanimity; indeed, to
judge from the following letter to his friend, joy and
satisfaction seem to have predominated in his soul.

" + Trinity College, June 10, S. Margarita, V, 1846.

" My dear Mr. Phillipps,—Every day that I live I
feel more and more the blessed privilege to which I
have been admitted; every day do I thank God for His

grace towards me. And let me also now thank you most heartily, my dear friend, for the part that you have had, under God, in my conversion.

"It was my wish to have taken your advice and not have informed my mother of the step I had taken until my father's return, but I did not conceal it from Mr. Alford or my aunt, and Mr. Alford wrote to inform my mother. You will perhaps anticipate that this wish of mine has become the subject of severe obloquy; in fact they seem to regard my case as one of such great iniquity that apparently it is to be made public as a beacon to prevent others following in my path. I know that God will turn all human frailties to the advance and good of His Holy Church. I have had a great deal to.contend against, which had I been yet a Protestant, remaining amongst the waves of confusion, would have been very distressing to me; but since my home is in that house which is founded upon a rock, the rains descend and the floods come, but I am unmoved, for my anchor is buried deep in the true foundation.

"I am going home to-morrow, the feast of Corpus Christi, and I hope to hear High Mass in London. I am afraid that my next few months at home will be barren and dry, for my dear mother thinks it contrary to her conscience to give me leave to attend the Holy Sacrifice, but my course is much less difficult now that my being a Catholic is known. I should be delighted to hear from you, if you have time to write to me occasionally. I am afraid that utter want of intercourse with Catholics may be prejudicial to me, but God can supply every deficiency. I should like very much to be enrolled in your Sodality of the Living Rosary, and to take part in any other devotions you can find me.

"I fear I shall have little to do for the next three months, I then expect my father home and hope to receive permission to go to Rome, to the Eternal City, the spiritual μέσον γᾶς μέλαθρον, the *Beatorum Aposto-lorum Sacra limina*, to prepare there for that noblest of all services, the restoration of England to her former beauty—to spend and be spent in the great cause of England's conversion—which may God forward in His own good time. Amen.

"Pray give my kind remembrances to Mrs. Ambrose Phillipps, and believe me, dear Mr. Phillipps, to be

"Your affectionate brother in Christ,

"JOHN MORRIS."

Thus closed John Morris's career at Cambridge. It had lasted only one short year, yet that one was indeed fruitful in results. His education was of course still far from complete, but foundations had been laid which would render him afterwards conspicuous for precision and accuracy, qualities which Cambridge is ever justly proud of imprinting on the minds of her students. In religious development the year had been more effective still. Education at home and with a private tutor had fostered the innate piety and exquisite reverence of his character, without suffering them to be fettered by the conventions which prevent ordinary schoolboys from displaying any further interest in religious matters than that sanctioned by the public opinion of their fellows. Alford's High Church ten-dencies, on the contrary, led his pupil to be willing to carry out a principle to new conclusions, and not afraid of adopting fresh views if such seemed the logical outcome of those already received. Hence his rapid advance towards the Church, which, however, while under his tutor, he had not seriously thought of entering. At Cambridge a further development takes place. He sees Newman and others leaving Anglicanism, and in the more independent atmosphere he now breathes, the idea of going and doing likewise takes possession of his mind. He steadily considers the reasons for and against the step to be taken, and consults those sure to hold him back much more frequently than those who might urge him on. But ere the year was out, he perceives clearly the direction in which his convictions are leading him, and advances at the call of conscience with admirable promptitude and vigour, ready to bear with firmness and resolution the troubles that befell him in consequence.

Besides prematurely disclosing his secret, Alford removed from Wymeswold Church the brass which Morris had erected in memory of his brother and sister, and sent back his subscription to the restoration of the fabric.[1] If he spoke in public about the conversion, it was only, it seemed, in order to turn away unpopularity from himself at the cost of Morris's other friends. The trial to one so affectionately sympathetic towards his friends, as Morris ever was, can easily be imagined.

But this was a small matter compared with what he suffered at home. He had long foreseen the effect it would have upon his mother, now depressed as she was with feeble health. The knowledge of the fact of his conversion, together with all its circumstances, inflicted, says his brother Henry, " a crushing, life-long sorrow, from which she never fully recovered." John came down to see her for a day or two, and then returned to Cambridge on Tuesday, May 26th. After putting his possessions in order, he went back to Portsmouth, where he remained for the greater part of June, July, and

---

[1] Father Morris in his recollections adds : "I then took the brass to Northampton. It is in the Cathedral there now set against the wall. It used to be on the floor in Bishop Wareing's time, and the soldiers from Weedon Barracks with their hob-nailed boots scratched it so every Sunday, that I wonder it has survived."

August, with his mother and the rest of the family, awaiting his father's return. His brother Henry was absent at a tutor's, preparing for the entrance examination at Haileybury.

It was well that he had at heart a store of peace and strength when he left Cambridge to meet his mother, desolate and distracted as she was by what she considered her son's "sin and delusion." On August 24, 1846, John wrote to his father the following touching and affectionate letter· "When you read these lines you will be in England, what you have looked forward to for so many years will be accomplished, and the happiness you have been fondly anticipating will be marred by one blot, and that blot I am. Were it not that I fully believed that I have done and am doing my duty towards God, I should have no comfort, consolation, or hope. I acted simply with the desire, as single-hearted as my nature would permit, of doing God's will, and, as my intention was pure, He will not desert me in the day of trial. One thing only I ask, not that you should think me right, but whether misguided or no, at least sincere. This, however, I need not ask—no one will refuse me this; no one can think that I would throw away all my earthly happiness except to secure my soul. Nothing but the belief that *that* was in danger would have made me lay aside everything I have hitherto held nearest and dearest—affections in which my heart has delighted. God knows how little I value my life in comparison with your happiness—but my soul, that I could not risk."

Painful in many ways must have been the subsequent meeting, where the feelings on both sides were so highly charged. But the peace of conviction, which, as we have seen, grew strong in young Morris's heart from the moment of his conversion, prevailed.

Dr. Virtue, the Bishop of Portsmouth, for forty years an intimate friend of Father Morris, informs me that the latter, not long before his death, while stopping at Portsmouth, pointed out the church where he had gone to Mass in the summer of 1846. He added that at that time his father had discussed various plans to prevent his bad example from affecting the other children, amongst which were projects of sending him into business in China or India. The firm by which he was to have been employed had nearly completed their agreement, when they discovered the fact of his conversion, and straightway rescinded the arrangement, after which his father gave the desired permission to go to Rome. Father Morris added that all the while he had felt quite confident about the result. If God wanted him to be a Jesuit, He would work out His design as easily in China as in England.

The history of the working out of that design is the story of the life of Father Morris, which must be left for another place. The episode we have been considering, needs for its conclusion only a few words about those left at Cambridge.

On the 18th of June a paragraph appeared in the *Times*, copied from the *Cambridge Advertiser*, announcing the conversion, and adding that " stringent measures are, it is said, about to be adopted in order to stop any further movement in the same direction. In particular it is rumoured that Mr. Morris's tutor has called upon the authorities to institute proceedings against a resident Master of Arts of another college, well known for his classical attainments, on the ground that he is suspected of using his influence against the Establishment . At the present stage it is unnecessary to publish the names of the persons alluded to, although they are pretty well known to those who are conversant with the internal administration of our colleges." No

E

such steps against Paley as Alford here calls for, appear to have been taken during the long vacation ; but when the scholars began to return in October, a letter appeared in the *Times*, signed by " A Father,"[1] urging that paper " to hold up to the scorn and indignation of every virtuous mind" the conduct of the " Resident M.A.," whose name was also now made public. The *Times*, of course, rose to the occasion, and strongly urged Paley's expulsion and disgrace. Then the *melée* became general. Paley retorted on Alford, who returned to the charge, assisted by several correspondents of similar sentiments, while " A Father" accused Dr. Wareing of offering his convert a "dispensation" to sham being a Protestant after leaving the communion of the Church of England; and suspicions and insinuations were freely thrown out against Pugin and Phillipps and the Cambridge Camden Society. " The conduct of the agents of Rome," said Alford, "in this and other lamentable cases, has rendered it our duty, even in ordinary intercourse, to suspect and distrust the most amiable professors of their faith."

Poor Paley suffered most, for he was made "the victim," as the *English Churchman* truly said, "to the paid Protestantism of the men who do the 'ecclesiastical' for the daily press." He was turned out of his College, and his career in the University was seriously, though not permanently, injured. For the rest, it will suffice here to say that Mr. Phillipps, in a local paper, disposed of Alford's charges made against him, and that Mr. Pugin answered that he had no merit or share in the conversion whatever, as he and Mr. Morris

---

[1] "The letter of 'A Father,'" says Mr. Henry Morris, "was written, with our father's sanction, by our uncle, Mr. Wood, for they considered that the conduct of Mr. F. A. Paley in the matter deserved to be brought to the notice both of the English public and of the authorities of the University of Cambridge."

had had no other communications except those connected with the erection of the memorial of the latter's brother and sister. Dr. Wareing remained prudently silent until challenged by " A Catholic " to contradict the rumours current about his having granted a dispensation to his convert to sham Protestantism. To this he answered (November 6) that Mr. Morris, "in returning to his home, was not required to trespass unnecessarily on the feelings of his mother, by avowing his change of faith and claiming the public exercise of it. He was left to the performance of his religious duties to the best of his power privately, and in this I ' acted' solely with a view to spare the feelings of a beloved mother, till the return of his father, to whom he was prepared to state respectfully his change of religion."

After this the subject languished, but it was revived again at the time of the " Papal Aggression " scare, when Mr. (afterwards Sir) W. Page Wood, the Solicitor General, in a speech during the debate on the Ecclesiastical Titles Bill (February 10, 1851), gave a cleverly distorted description of Father Morris's conversion, omitting however all proper names. Father Morris, a connection of the speaker, was present at the debate, in company with his friend, Mr. Robert Berkeley, of Spetchley, who informs me that, when Page Wood had finished his inaccurate presentment of the case, Father Morris turned round and remarked with characteristic energy, " I would give my two eyes and my two ears to answer that man."

We will conclude with a pleasanter episode about Dean Alford, with which we shall be glad to leave him. Morris and he met, and this is the description of their meeting, which Alford sent home to his wife: " Morris and I had luncheon together, and a two hours' talk about the whole matter. I am very glad that this has been so, for it has given me the opportunity of healing wounds, and removing misapprehensions, which although kept in the background by his affection for me, were evidently still existing. We also had much talk about the Church of Rome, and our different but now perfectly intelligible positions; his, that of traditional sacramental transmission of Christianity; mine, that of individual guidance by the Holy Spirit, the promise of the covenant irrespective of any external form of Church. Certainly no two positions could be more opposite, and no two more without hope of any approximation.

"He is the same kind, earnest fellow as ever, full of energy and affection."

JOHN MORRIS IN 1846

The inscription in the lower left-hand corner runs · "M R.G del 1846, in Roma "

To face p. 52.

CHAPTER III.

THE ENGLISH COLLEGE, ROME.

REFERENCE has been made in the last chapter to the probability that Father Morris would be enabled to carry out his strong desire to make his studies for the priesthood at the great centre of Catholic teaching and authority, and so we are prepared to find the scene of the next chapter of his life laid in and about Rome itself. He was among the first to set an example which almost every convert has followed since who has had the opportunity of doing so and has felt himself called to the ministry. We learn from his own reminiscences, published a few years ago in *The Month*, and reproduced here by permission, that he arrived in Rome during a very memorable year. These reminiscences will be found most interesting and descriptive throughout, and they describe no scene or event more pleasantly than they do Father Morris' own most genial character, just as he was at that time :

"My first journey in Italy was during the autumn of 1846, the year in which Pius IX. was elected Pope. A large party of us travelled from Lyons to Rome in a *vettura;* and thus we passed right through Italy in the way in which the country and the towns could best be seen. A driver at Lyons contracted to take us with the same carriage and horses as far as Genoa in a given number of days. His contract included our lodging and our keep at the hotels on the road, and a very good arrangement it was. The hotel-keepers were most anxious to stand well with the *vetturino*, for fear lest he should take his passengers to a rival house; and the passengers, if they were not contented with their rooms or their meals, remonstrated not with the hotel people but with the driver, a word from whom set all things right. For people with but scanty knowledge of the language of the country the arrangement was excellent, as it saved them from the tender mercies of landlords whose *maximum* and *minimum* prices were widely different, and who looked on foreigners as fair game. To have had to chaffer over prices day by day would have counterbalanced most of the pleasure of the journey. At Genoa we contracted with another *vetturino* to convey us in like manner to Rome, and Rome we reached on St. Charles' day. I can still see the bay leaves and red hangings outside the Church of St. Carlo in Corso, as we drove down that famous street in the dusk of the evening, holding our breath at finding ourselves in Rome.

"A few days afterwards Pius IX. took solemn possession of St. John Lateran's, his Cathedral Church; and thus we were in time to see a Papal *Cavalcata*, the last equestrian procession in which a Pope has passed in state through the streets of his city of Rome. The procession on horseback looked as though it had just ridden out of a mediæval picture. The cross-bearer was there on the white mule, but the Pope was in a state carriage with two Cardinals, and the rest of the Sacred College awaited him at St. John Lateran's. But the prelates and officials were all on horseback, some of them old men who looked nervous in their cappas and tasselled hats, though a groom walked on each side of their horse's head, and some of them young men, especially the Chamberlains of *Cappa e spada* in

their velvets and chains and frills, who seemed to wish
to show off their horsemanship—

> The left heel thrust insidiously aside
> Provoked the caper that it seemed to chide.

"Ah me! I have arrived at Rome in a great hurry,
and I have begun my story at the end, instead of the
beginning, of my first journey. Well, I was eager to
see Rome; and much as I enjoyed each of the thirty
days of that delightful journey, I longed to be in Rome,
the only place in the world, I remember thinking, where
all men of every nation under heaven can feel themselves at home. But though I have no intention of
writing a diary, long after the events, or of binding
myself to the order of time, still I must go back to the
beginning and set foot on the Continent afresh as I
then did for the first time in my life.

"With Dr. Ferdinand English, then Vice-Rector of
the English College at Rome, and afterwards Archbishop of Trinidad, I left England, happy to be under
his convoy on my way through countries of whose
languages I could not speak a word. It is an awkward
position, even with a kind friend at your elbow. I
remember my astonishment at a *table d'hôte* when the
waiter, after announcing the name of a dish, heard my
civil *Merci*, and whisked the dish away as I held out
my hand to help myself. We learn by experience and
by nothing else, I suppose; yet more than once since
then I have had trouble to check that ready *Merci*,
which means No.

"Dr. English and I joined the rest of our party in
Paris. I knew none of them before, but I was happy
to have had the chance of making such friends. One
was bound to the English College like myself, Frederick
Neve, afterwards its Rector, and ultimately Provost of
Clifton. He had been a country Rector before his

conversion, and he was considerably the senior of all
of us. The rest of our party were ladies. One was
an artist, who many years later entered a convent in
Italy. Then there were three sisters, two of whom are
classed in my mind as the cleverest and brightest
women I ever met. One was a widow, having with
her a little child, and that child and I, the two youngest
of the party, are now its sole survivors. The second
of the sisters was that ideal Religious for whose coming
Mother Margaret O'Halloran waited in faith, as all
readers of her charming Life will remember. This
fellow-traveller of mine became ultimately Mother
Margaret's successor as Provincial of the Sisters of
the Third Order of St. Dominic ; and the third of the
three sisters entered the same Religious Order, and
died there soon, of consumption, from which she was
suffering during our journey. Those fellow-travellers
of mine were as nearly perfect companions as I could
have wished for. · There was not a heavy moment
during the whole month. It was well it was so, for
the *vettura* was tightly packed, one only being in a sort
of *coupé* with the driver, and all the rest finding room
inside. How we did it I cannot imagine, but it was
done, and as we had but five-and-twenty miles or so
to do each day, it was for no very long time. But we
had been through a discipline that reconciled us easily
to any tight packing in the *vettura*. We had travelled
to Lyons in the *diligence*, and its discomforts were not
easily to be forgotten.

"My first acquaintance with the *diligence* was at
Boulogne. The railway from Paris was only open as
far as Amiens, and the *diligence* took the passengers
from Boulogne to the rail. A cumbrous machine it
was—a coach in the middle, with an omnibus at one
end and a *coupé* at the other, with the *banquette* over the
coupé, and the luggage piled high, all over the top.

The first journey was pleasant enough from Boulogne to Amiens, in the *coupé*, where one could see everything. The first start was very amusing. The great hollow-backed Flemish horses were linked to us by ropes for traces, and to English eyes long ropes they were. When the signal was given to start, away went the six horses as it seemed in every direction but the right one; however, the driver was skilful, and his whip brought them all to order, and away they started at a heavy jog-trot, with all their bells tinkling, along the first stage towards Amiens.

"But leaving Paris and finding our way to Lyons was a very different thing. We got into the *diligence* at Paris, the *diligence* was then driven to the railway-station, and the whole affair, with all its passengers in their places, was lifted by a powerful crane off its perch and wheels, and deposited on a railway-truck, and so conveyed to Orleans. This was then the end of the line, by no means the well-known *Chemin de Fer Paris-Lyons-Méditerranée* of our time, in those days not begun. At Orleans a crane hoisted us up once more, the horses were already harnessed to a perch and wheels, we were swung round to it and fastened on, the coachman climbed up into the *banquette*, cracked his whip, and we were off. This time I was in the *rotonde*, as the central coach was called, one of six, in the middle place, with nothing when I fell asleep to lean against except my neighbours, who did not like being leaned against, and, to crown it all, in an atmosphere of garlic to which I was not accustomed. Think of the worst third-class railway-carriage that ever was, and compare it with this horrid thing at first-class fares. Or think how you leave Paris nowadays by the mail train in the evening, and wake the next morning at six as the train runs into the Lyons station, where a wash awaits you, and *café au lait* that would refresh the weariest traveller. Then we had four days and four nights of it, from Orleans to Lyons: the road the roughest *pavé*, straight as an arrow, with the everlasting poplars on either side, and not a thing to see. With every bone in my body aching, I can still recall with gratitude the blessed sensation of finding oneself between clean sheets in a Lyons hotel.

" The starting of a *diligence* was a very solemn affair. French officials are not given to hiding their light under a bushel, and an official with loud and imperious tones shouted aloud the names of the passengers in the order of the seats for which they were booked. I little knew what I was in for when I was summoned to the middle place in the *rotonde*. Talking of the start of a *diligence*, I remember hearing that the great Anglican Dean, Dr. Hook, had booked a seat for himself, and the official stentoriously summoned ' M. Voltaire' to take his seat. No one answered to the name, so the place resounded with the cry, ' M. Voltaire ! M. Voltaire ! ' At last it occurred to Dr. Hook that he had, English fashion, given his name as Walter Farquhar Hook.

" Leaving Dr. Hook at Leeds, where he was when we were at Lyons, we set our faces for Italy in a *vettura* that was chartered to take us to Genoa. It was an enjoyable change after the wearisome *diligence*. If there was anything interesting on the way, we could stop our driver and see it leisurely. The day's journey was never long enough to be fatiguing. We arrived always in time to explore a new place, unless we had started late because we had preferred a morning, as well as the evening before, at some place that took our fancy. And while we were on our way, the conversation to me, a young convert who had hardly spoken freely to a Catholic before, was simply delightful.

" We crossed Mount Cenis, long before the tunnel or even the singularly ingenious Fell railway was thought of. Oxen helped us up, and when we got to the top of the pass and had settled down into our place again in the *vettura*, away went our driver with his sure-footed pair of horses full tilt down the splendid road, swinging round the corners and swaying over the precipices, till at last the courtyard of the inn at Susa received us, and we felt that indeed we were in Italy. And in this leisurely delightful way, we passed from town to town till at last we arrived in Rome.

" Thus we had time when we reached Terni, to go and see the falls. Does any one go to see them now? One look I had at them from a point of view that put me into some danger, and it gives me a creepy feeling to think of it now. I had separated myself from the party, in search of some better position from which to see the waterfall, when I found a sort of promontory projecting out towards the face of the fall. Down this I went, its face getting steeper and steeper, and the grass more and more wet with the spray, till at last I began to slip. It did not take long to swing oneself round and to begin to crawl back on all fours; and thankful I was that I could go up, instead of continuing to slip downwards into the waterfall itself below me.

" The two things in this journey that have made the deepest impression in my memory are what we saw at Assisi and at Monte San Savino. Assisi ranks in my mind as second only to Loreto. The records are worthy of the places, and the places are worthy of the records—St. Francis and St. Clare and their lovely histories; the Porziuncula in the plain, the Sagro Convento like a mediæval fortress on the hill-side, and the Carceri in its solitude up on the mountains. The places telling their deathless tales of the past, and the past all but brought into the present by the sight of the places.

" The Porziuncula, a tiny church with a great

Basilica built over it, resembles greatly the Santa Casa in the Basilica at Loreto. On the gable of the little Porziuncula is the fresco by Overbeck, representing St. Francis receiving that unexampled Indulgence from our Lord, which all the world over can now be gained in Franciscan churches on the anniversary of that vision, and in the Porziuncula itself every day of the year. Against the wall the door is fastened that St. Francis has many a time opened and shut. Hard by is the cloister, from the midst of which he took the three roses in the winter, by which Pope Honorius was to be assured of the truth of his vision. And here around us is the plain where the five thousand friars assembled in General Chapter during the lifetime of their holy founder.

" We leave the delightful Porziuncula, and there on the left, at the extreme end of the town of Assisi, is the Sagro Convento, built on arches, and towering up grandly like the noble place that it is. The Obser- vantine Friars had charge of the Porziuncula, the Conventuals were here at the Sagro Convento, from which and from other great convents they derived their name. The church may be said to be in three stories. The upper church is the lofty and magnificent Basilica, showing what Gothic architecture should be in Italy. The windows are narrow, to exclude light and heat, and the abundant wall-space is covered with splendid frescoes. The church beneath this is not lofty, being, indeed, the crypt of the Basilica, but it is well lighted for a crypt, and Giotto's frescoes are delightful. The chapel where the body of St. Francis rests has been comparatively recently excavated and decorated. It is not in keeping with the two splendid churches above it, but the eye is not much attracted by ornament, nor is taste a matter of criticism, when one is conscious of the nearness of such a treasure as the body of

St. Francis of Assisi. This is the ancient place of execution, where St. Francis begged that he might be buried amongst the malefactors, and its old name of Colle dell' Inferno was changed by Pope Gregory IX. into Colle del Paradiso.

" But the Carceri leaves an impression on the mind perhaps deeper than either of these charming sanctuaries of the poor man of Assisi. Its name of ' the Prisons ' dates back to some former use, prior to the time of St. Francis. As it stands now, it takes you back to the days when the Friars Minor first began. The whole place is as it was when St. Francis left it, except that St. Bonaventure added a little nave to the chapel. There is the coffin in which St. Francis used to sleep. There is the tree where he preached to the birds. There is the bed of the stream that he bade to cease flowing, for it was undermining the convent. There is the little refectory, with its poor rough table for sole furniture, and its bench round the walls; and there is its earthern floor where Francis cast himself on his face one Christmas night when he had been listening to the story of the Nativity, and, able to contain himself no longer, broke out into that cry of his loving heart ' What! Thou my Lord, so poor, and I in such luxury!'

" The body of St. Clare had not yet been discovered. Gregory XVI. had ordered a Commission of Bishops to search for the body of St. Francis, and a similar Commission was appointed by Pius IX. to excavate the resting-place of St. Clare in the Church of San Damiano, and to disinter her precious relics. My dear friend, Dr. Louis English, had the good fortune to be at Assisi at the time, and the three Bishops who had charge of the search for the Saint's body, permitted him to be present and to be one of the first to see and venerate the sacred body of that faithful disciple and daughter of St. Francis.

" Assisi is a place to tarry at, but I have a longer word to say about a striking sight that we saw on an earlier stage of our journey. We stopped at Cortona, and when we had visited the shrine of St. Margaret, the penitent Saint, we turned aside out of our road to Rome, in order to visit a village called Monte San Savino. We were attracted thither by what we had heard of an Ecstatica who dwelt there. It was in her favour, we thought, that she lived in an out-of-the-way village like this, for if the object had been to make money by showing her as a sight, she would have been put where visitors would be frequent. The accommodation in the village inn was of the poorest. Dr. Neve, I remember, slept on a table, and the ceiling of the room in which I slept was so black with flies that I got up in the dark for fear they might awake while I was still in the room.

" The family of the Ecstatica did not impress me very favourably, but perhaps it is hardly fair to them to have carried away an unpleasant impression from mere looks. I gathered that we were very unwelcome to the mother and brother, which at all events did not look like imposture, and certainly the constant intrusion of visitors must have been very trying to them. But nothing could have been more impressive or more edifying than the Ecstatica herself. I have always been glad that I went to see her, and that, I gathered, was the feeling of us all. It was a Friday morning, on which day of the week she was allowed to have Mass celebrated in a room separated by folding-doors from that in which she lay. The parish priest said the Mass, and as it could not have been said without the Bishop's leave, the fact that it was said gave us confidence. As the Mass went on she flew into ecstasy again and again. She had been confined to her bed, we heard, for many years, and fainted when she was lifted from it for the bed to be madé; yet when the ecstasy came on her, she simply flew into a kneeling posture on the foot of the bed. It was so sudden and so rapid a movement that when one saw it first, it was very startling. It was as though she had been shot from a càtapült. Each ecstasy lasted but a very short time, and then she very slowly and quietly subsided, her head touching the pillow, and her arms, which had been extended as she was kneeling, meeting at the same moment across her breast. This was repeated several times during the Mass, and I particularly noticed that as the priest turned towards her with the Blessed Sacrament for her Communion, she flew up to her kneeling posture at the *Domine non sum dignus.* I wondered how she would be ready to receive Holy Communion, but the priest was by her side, making the sign of the Cross over her with the Blessed Sacrament exactly at the moment when her head touched her pillow. Instantly she flew into ecstasy again. After Mass it was remarkable that she turned in her ecstasy towards the neighbouring church, and we heard afterwards from the priest that when there was a procession of the Blessed Sacrament through the streets, she would move in her ecstasy, always turning towards our Lord. It struck me as very remarkable that when her ecstasy was towards the church, and she was kneeling therefore on the side rather than on the foot of the bed, on her subsidence to her recumbent position, her head invariably reached exactly the same place on her pillow each time. The slowness of movement with which she fell back was most striking, and of course she had no assistance from her hands, as her arms, which had been outspread as she knelt, just as slowly crossed themselves as she gradually lay down.

" One or two of our party knew enough of Italian to talk to her, but my ignorance of the language was complete, and I did not exchange a word with her. When we sallied forth from her house, we were waylaid by a gentleman of the village, who told us that he had an interesting museum of Etruscan antiquities, and begged us to come and see it. We went in with him almost mechanically, our heads full of what we had seen, and as soon as we could get his attention off his treasures, he was eagerly asked what he thought of the Ecstatica. 'Oh, she is a good girl, she is a good girl,' said he, evidently surprised that we should think more of her than of all sorts of precious relics of Etruscan workmanship. We left him, saying to ourselves that to call her 'a good girl' was to say a great deal. If she were a good girl, then she was not an impostor.

" I may add here a story that I was told of her some three years or more after this, and as I heard it in Rome and in Florence, and to the best of my belief independently, I was led to think it true. A young artist was sent to see her by some one who wanted a picture representing her in ecstasy. He was to be present at Mass in her room, as others were, and from memory afterwards he was to do his best to paint her likeness. The people about were in the habit of having recourse to her prayers and consulting her, especially in times of doubt and trial. Her answer to them was always modest and humble, to the effect that she knew nothing about these things that they asked, but that if God in her prayer should choose to tell her anything about them, she would let them know. This young artist was an unbeliever, and he said to his friends before he went : 'I have a question to put to her that will test her; but I do not mean to let any one know beforehand what it is.' He went to Monte San Savino, saw her, and put his question : ' There is an intimate friend of mine whom I have not seen for some time; shall I ever see him again?' After her usual answer he went away, and on his returning to her she said to him : ' You did not ask me that question because you wanted to know, but only to test me. But God has told me to tell you that you certainly will see your friend again, if you lead the life you are leading. He is in Hell, and you know it, for he committed suicide.' The artist fell on his knees by her side, and then rising, ran off to the neighbouring church to make his peace with God."

This delightful journey, all after his own heart, formed a fitting passage from the troubles and excitement of controversy, and the many trials attending his conversion, to the charming peace in which he was to spend the next four years. These were destined to have a lasting effect on his after-life, but they were to be spent in retirement, study, and spiritual training.

Every one who wishes to approach the priesthood fitly prepared must allow full time for calm study and earnest prayer, that his mind may be matured in a thorough understanding and appreciation of Catholic doctrine, drinking in at the same time the true spirit of the priestly life under such influences as those which Father Morris so well describes. We can also trace the development of his devotion to art and antiquity, to ceremonies and holy functions, to friends and country, as well as to Indulgences and works of piety. In fact, we easily recognize the working of the same mind that even in advancing years preserved all the vigour of these early enthusiasms.

In the spring of the following year, after the young student had well settled down in his new life at the English College, he wrote a letter to his staunch friend in which he contrasts his present peace of mind with his past anxieties.

F

" + Coll. S. Thomæ Anglorum de Urbe,
"Fest. S. Georgii, M. [April 23], 1847.

" My dear Mr. Phillipps,—I am afraid I must have seemed very ungracious in not having answered your kind letter sooner, but I trust you will excuse me for I have very little time unoccupied to write, for, as you know, time in a Catholic College is not quite the same as at Cambridge, calls first for one duty and then for another summon you away and leave you anything but the unbroken time one has been accustomed to. I must thank you very heartily for the very kind interest you have taken in me, and at the same time I must tell you how sorry I am for the treatment, I do not know that I ought not to say persecution, that you have endured on my account; it has thrown another item into the scale of gratitude that I owe you.

" Almighty God has been very good to me, and fulfilled the dearest wish of my heart by placing me in a Catholic College to study for His holy priesthood; this is what I used to look forward to and long for, though it seemed hopeless and unattainable when I was going through the struggle of my conversion; and afterwards, when my dear father was debating plans of sending me to China or to India, I felt quite undisturbed, for I was sure God would find means of making me a priest if He wished it, and now I am here. I am studying for the priesthood with the great advantage of being in Rome, learning in its genial atmosphere to uproot all remnants of the poison of Protestantism, and in its place to implant all the feelings and practices of our holy religion, carried to its own fair limits and not stunted by the withering cold of an almost overwhelming heresy. Besides, here we are under the Holy Father's own eye, his more immediate sheep, with his blessing continually resting on us, and we are in the midst of martyrs and apostles, and surrounded by all that is holy

" I have not told you of the privilege we had of receiving Holy Communion from the Pope's own hand and of assisting at his Mass. There was a feast at the Seminary with which we are connected, in honour of a miraculous picture of our Blessed Lady, and His Holiness observed it by coming there to say Mass, and to give Holy Communion to all the students of the Seminary. I suppose there has seldom been an opportunity that would better remind one of the Last Supper, than an occasion when the Vicar of Christ distributed with his own hand the Bread of Life to a number of young disciples, all trusting some day to become priests in the Church of God. Afterwards, we were given a place near the Pope at breakfast, and had a beautiful opportunity of seeing him. We are, of course, loyalty itself here to the Chair of St. Peter, and really, apart from all spiritual claims, the name of Pope Pius alone, to whom all Europe is beginning to look, is almost enough to bind one to it. May we not hope for the very greatest results from his pontificate? God grant that the conversion of our own dear land may be one.

" Few sights have so stirred up my soul as the Solemn Pontifical Mass at St. Peter's on Easter Day, and the Pope's blessing afterwards. I have now seen the Papal blessing three times, from St. John Lateran's, the Mother Church of the Earth, on the day of the Possesso, and from St. Peter's on Maundy Thursday and Easter Day. I must not, however, remain on one subject, or I shall not tell you half what I wish to say.

" I have twice had an audience of His Holiness and I missed a third, namely, one which Mr. Ryder got up of converts only. I dare say you have heard that he

counted seventy-five or seventy-nine converts in Rome
during Holy Week, about half of which number were
presented in a body. This number of course does
not include those who have visited Rome, but who left
it before Holy Week. Their being so numerous shows
how false the supposition is that the adoption of
Christian art and similar principles alienates men from
the Holy See, for what but affection for the Supreme
Pontiff could have brought them here. Mr. Pugin is
now in Rome. I saw him two or three days ago. He
intends, I believe, to spend about a week here and then
go on to Assisi, Perugia, Florence, &c., where certainly
he will find more remnants of Christian art than Rome
can show, although, especially in monuments and
crypts, &c., it is by no means devoid of them. He was
delighted with the crypt of St. Peter's, where he was
yesterday (April 27), crowded as it is with Christian
objects, though of course it is impossible to say as much
of the great church above it. The profuse waste of
money here on this most wretched style of architecture
through the four hundred churches of Rome, has excited
his indignation greatly. I believe he intends to visit
Overbeck on Sunday, and I should very much like to
go with him, to see together two of the greatest men
of the present generation. I am delighted to say that
Mr. Pugin is a great deal better, he will I trust return
to England made quite well by his tour. . . .

"Mr. Newman I have often seen. He is prospering
and has just now been joined by nearly all his friends
from Maryvale. So far from that absurd story in the
English papers being true, the Pope has a great liking
for them, and has promised to provide them with a
house to go through the novitiate of the Oratorians of
St. Philip Neri. I am delighted at the thought of
St. Philip's glorious patronage and apostolate being
brought to England. He will work wonders for us.

" The Basilica of St. Paul's, now in progress, is a most disappointing place, not badly described as a mixture between Noah's Ark and a railroad station, and this to cover the tomb of St. Paul. Well we must hope for better times for Christian art in Rome; at present, taste in sculpture, building, painting, and I suppose I may add music, is as low as it can be. The revival must come from England I am sure. It never-theless gives one hopes when such a man as Overbeck is encouraged, and a place cannot always continue enamoured of Pagan art that contains such a store of beauties as the Christian Museum in the Vatican. When you write to me, pray tell me how art is advancing in England, I shall be very anxious when I return to see what advance it will have made in three years. I hope to return about Easter in the year of Jubilee, and I expect to receive the tonsure and minor orders next Whitsuntide. Pray for me that I may be less unworthy of such holy things. .

" I have seen Mr. Coffin frequently. He is staying with the Passionists at SS. John and Paul, until Mr. Newman's Order gets into operation. He looks very well in his clerical dress. Pray give my kind remembrances to Mrs. Ambrose Phillipps, and ever believe me to be, my dear Mr. Phillipps, *vostro affeziona-tissimo in Gesù è Maria.*

" JOHN MORRIS.

" *Mi raccomando alle sue orazione e santi sacrifici,* as the good people here say."

The development of character of which this letter reflects the first stage, proceeded silently and steadily during the ensuing years. On the 13th of May, he took the so-called " mission oath " to return to England and labour on the mission there. After that he received

at due intervals the minor orders and subdiaconate at
the hands of the " Illustrissimo " Giuseppe Canali,
Patriarch of Constantinople, in his private chapel, and
the diaconate (in 1848), as afterwards the priesthood
from Cardinal Patrizi in the Lateran Basilica.

Of the revolution of 1848, and the siege of Rome in
the year following, he seems to have been a comparatively distant spectator, for, owing to the good
management of Dr. Grant, the students of the English
College were kept at as great a distance as possible
from disturbances, which might otherwise have been
long fatal to all spirit of study. When, therefore, active
operations round Rome made the English College an
impossible place for studying in, he sent them, in
lay attire, on the 29th of April to their villa at Monte
Porzio. He then hoisted the Union Jack over the
College, and remained there, with one student as a
companion, all through the siege. The building was
hit six times during the bombardment, but the damage
done was slight. The danger from the besieged was
no doubt greater than that from the besiegers, but
Dr. Grant's courage and tact triumphed over all difficulties, and he succeeded in preserving not only the
papers and property of the College, but also the records
of the Inquisition, which had been entrusted to his
keeping by the Pope.

Meantime, the students at Monte Porzio had had
a share in the general distress. Provisions became
exceedingly scarce, they were in perplexing ignorance
of the progress of events, and there were frequent
alarms of the approach of fighting. These, however,
were but small inconveniences, and, all things considered, their escape from annoyance was very complete.
A professor from the Propaganda took refuge with
them, and under his guidance studies continued without
intermission. Dr. Grant managed to send them out

letters full of fun and encouragement,[1] and after three
months they were able to return to their home in the
city. It is somewhat remarkable that the only reference
to these times in Father Morris's recollections of "Italy
before the Railways,"[2] should be a description of the
recovery of the head of St. Andrew, April 5, 1848.

Some mention of Father Morris in 1849 is made in
the journals which the Rev. John Wynne kept of his
travels in Italy with his friend, the Rev. T. W. Allies.
Both were then in Anglican Orders, though soon to
join the Catholic Church, Mr. Wynne in April, and
Mr. Allies in September of the year 1850. The former,
having obtained his degree of Doctor of Theology
in the Roman College, joined the Society of Jesus in
1857, and after filling various posts died at Beaumont
on Tuesday, October 17, 1893, only five days before
Father Morris himself. The two friends reached Rome
in August, 1849, and on the morning of August the 9th,
"We went," to quote Father Wynne's journal, "to the
Vatican with Dr. Grant and Mr. Morris." How the
introduction to them had come about, does not appear,
but intimacy soon followed. Father Wynne continues:

"In the library they showed us an illuminated Virgil
of the fourth century, which satisfies me that the
ancients must have been our masters in this as in every
other art; also a Dante illuminated by Julio Clovio
and Pinturicchio, a most exquisite work upon large
vellum executed for the Dukes of Urbino; and Cardinal
Mai's manuscript copy of the *Republic* of Cicero, recovered by the use of acids after having been obliterated
in order to receive on its surface a copy of St. Augustine
on the Psalms. On some of the pages both works

---

[1] See *Thomas Grant, first Bishop of Southwark.* By Grace Ramsey,
pp. 81—84.

[2] *The Month*, August, 1890, p. 520.

coexist and show the process of restoration. After walking through the library, and wandering among antiquities and art, both Christian and Pagan, of the highest order and most interesting periods, which gave rise to many observations and discussions, we returned to the English College. Here we dined in the refectory. One of the students was reading aloud in Latin when we entered, but was desired to cease, in order to allow conversation. . . .

" After dinner we adjourned to the library, where there is a good working collection of books, but of a rough character in general as far as exterior is concerned, the College not having laid out much money in choice editions. Here coffee and rosoglio were served. Conversation soon took a controversial turn, the principal point urged against us, the necessity of a proposing cause for the support of a true faith. Though we should of course admit (those at least of us who style themselves Catholic) the principle which they assert, we undoubtedly have a real difficulty and are thoroughly pushed into a corner when we have to apply it. Mr. M—— was good enough to copy an extract from Bellarmine[1] on this subject for my consideration and edification; it certainly touches questions which have been forced upon my mind a good deal of late.

" The students seem to hold Perrone in cheaper estimation as a theologian, than I should have expected. They say he is neither very profound nor original, and that the chief cause of his great celebrity is his having written a theology embracing almost all the range of the subject. They seem to consider Passaglia as their first man; he also is a Jesuit. The Society of Jesus possesses all the first men in science, the Collegio Romano is entirely under their management. They give the Roman Jesuits the same character that I have

[1] *De Grat. et Lib. Arb.* vi. 3.

heard from Catholics elsewhere, an extreme simplicity and want of the worldly cunning for which the vulgar hold them notorious. They gave several instances of this conduct during the late revolutions, which told against the popular notions of them. The unpopularity of the Order is fully accounted for by their strict Rule and the anti-political..influence of such a body in the exercise of direction of consciences.

"They spoke of Newman as having adopted the Oratorian Rule on account of his character being too much set and matured to fall into a very strict and absorbing Rule without difficulty.

"There appeared to me a Benedictine character about the English College, or rather, what I should suppose a Benedictine character to be when in action. Their hours are not so early, their habits not so ascetic, their time not so rigorously disposed of as in St. Sulpice and the French Seminaries, and the system seems altogether more elastic.

"I think this is wise; and I see two reasons for the difference. First, the French Seminaries are intended to educate the whole priesthood of the province in which they are instituted, but the English College aims rather at keeping up a perpetual leaven of the ancient traditional spirit; the students are therefore of a more intellectual and select grade, whereas the former must from their Rule admit minds of the most ordinary stamp in respect to ability. Secondly, the numbers are far greater in the French Seminaries, the English College numbering only twenty to thirty at a time. .

"After dinner we went into the chapel for a few minutes, where some Latin prayers were said for the conversion of England to the One Catholic Faith. Dr. Grant is an able and clear talker, and having had much to do with converts appears to know thoroughly the weak points of the Anglican communion and the

nature of its difficulties. He pressed us hard on one or
two points, and never lost sight of these in the direction
of his conversation during the rest of the day. After
coffee we went to the Lateran, having first visited
a new chapel they are decorating with designs by a
nephew of Cardinal Weld,[1] and seen Mr. M—— and
Dr. G—— in their own rooms."[2]

Father Wynne's journal further records that Dr. Grant
acted as their guide on one or two other occasions
during their short stay in the Holy City; and for the
15th August there is this entry: "Took leave at
English College, great kindness shown. MS. written
by Dr. Grant, &c., present from Mr. Morris." Wynne
wrote to Morris from Naples, and so commenced a
controversial correspondence of which three letters
written by the latter have been preserved. Considering
that he was then only three-and-twenty, they must be
commended for the facility and precision with which
they handle a large subject. An accident threw them
together again as Mr. Wynne and Mr. Allies were
returning home, and they continued their discussions.
On this occasion Father Wynne remarked, as we shall
see in the following entry from his journal, that he
did not consider Mr. Morris as ready as Allies in controversy. This may or may not have been correct, but
even if it were so the previous opportunities of both
would easily account for it.

"*September* 5.—We had a motley party on board
the *Tancreda*, a Greek merchant from Beyrout, a Spanish

---

[1] This nephew of Cardinal Weld was Mr. Charles Weld, of whose work in
the Lady Chapel of the English College Father Morris was very proud. He
gave a full description of it in a letter to Mr. Phillipps, dated October,
1850.

[2] *Journals*, pp. 23—28.

gentleman returning from the East, a Franciscan monk going back to Genoa, Italian Liberals refused admittance at Malta by Sir Richard More O'Ferrall, exiles from Rome flying from the returning Cardinals, priests in disguise who had been driven from their cures by the recent persecution of all that was priestly, and now returning to see how matters stood and to resume their charges, a party of French people, guests of the Captain, and Messrs. M—— and H——[1] from the English College at Rome, who came on board at Civita Vecchia. . . . Messrs. M—— and H—— have finished their education at Rome and have just been ordained priests, they are now returning to England to be employed in missions, full of zeal and prepared for a life of action and ministerial labour, and showing signs of excellent spirit. Mr. M—— had written a letter to Allies at Naples with a view to his conversion, and followed it up by some advances to him in person. His conversation, like his letter, showed an excellent heart and sincere charity, but he was no match for A—— in controversy."

There is a slight error here. It was Father Hawksworth who had been ordained and was returning to England. Mr. Morris was accompanying him on the way, though not yet ordained priest. That great dignity he received a fortnight later. How deeply this sacred charge impressed his whole life, his notes of retreats and other outpourings of his soul abundantly testify. We read the expression of his feelings at the time in the following letter to Mr. Phillipps :

"Monte Porzio, October 12, 1849.

" My dear Mr. Phillipps,—Although I have been so long without writing to you, I have by no means forgotten the kind interest you used to take in me, and I

[1] Father Hawksworth is meant by this initial.

am sure that you will be glad to know that I have
received that dignity to which I have so long aspired.
I was ordained priest in St. John Lateran's last Ember
Saturday by Cardinal Patrizi, Bishop of Albano and
the Pope's Cardinal Vicar. It has been by no means
one of my least pleasures to reflect that now at last I
have it in my power for the first time worthily to repay
all the kindness that my friends have heaped upon me,
and as when I was received into the Church, your name
was one of the first that rose to my lips as a friend
for whom I was bound to pray, so now I have thought
that I could not do less than place you once for all in
my *Memento*, which is, as it were, the entrance to the
Treasury of the Mass, where God allows me to put in
my hand and draw out treasures, freely to scatter on all
around. I cannot tell you the consolation I feel in my
ordination. If it were nothing else, the celebration of
Mass is such a priceless blessing that I have nothing
but itself that I can offer in thanksgiving for it; it
hallows everything in the day, and calms my soul in
such a way that I am reminded in resting upon it of
the privilege of my holy patron, St. John, at the first
Mass that was ever celebrated. You will, I know,
sympathize with me, for *you* were, I think, the first to
point out to me where I could find that which would
really satisfy my soul.

"Poor Rome, it is sad to see its streets and holy
buildings thronged with foreign soldiers instead of
ecclesiastics or religious as formerly, and I fear the
harm that has been done, especially to young men, will
hardly ever be cured. The city itself has suffered
nothing at all save from the Republican Government,
there is no trace whatever of the siege except at Porta
S. Pancrazio and the neighbouring villas and vineyards.
The French in Rome behave in a very exemplary
manner, as I heard a priest say once, they are *come tanti*

Seminaristi. Of course many of the large convents are filled with them. The Gesù is half occupied by them while the sons of St. Ignatius have already returned, at least some twenty of them, to work for the Rome that has so ill requited their zeal. Our own College was struck during the siege by five or six pieces of shot or shells, one of which entered, but did little damage. St. Thomas has been a good Patron to us; thanks to him, we are perhaps the only ecclesiastical house that has not been in some way or another molested. We also were threatened, but he protected us. . . .

" The Prior of the Camaldolese near us told me a curious thing the other day when I was with him. He said that they had occasion to open their burying-place to bury a lay-brother, when they found the body of another lay-brother quite entire, Fra Placido, who was buried in 1831. They are all great saints. Several grand things happened during the siege. Some Republicans went to the convent of the most austere Order of nuns, the Sepolti Vive. The Superioress came out with a crucifix in her hand and spoke to them so severely of the judgments of God that they went away quite abashed. The Vicar-General of Frascati refused to allow the Governor to be present at the *Te Deum* on the Pope's restoration, although he had received the French orders to do so."

We may here insert a lively sketch, drawn by an eye-witness, of that vivacity of character for which Father Morris was at this time conspicuous. His fellow-students at Alford's had nicknamed him " Old Father Morris," but during his student-days in Rome, he would seem to have far more deserved the title of " the youthful." Those who only knew him later on in life, when years, ill health, and long subjection to religious discipline had modified his ardour or directed it into fixed channels, will perhaps be surprised at some of the following traits.

"My first meeting with Father John Morris took place in the spring of 1850 at the English College, Rome. It was the custom at that time for some of the students to make use of the Vice-Rector's room as an evening study-place, and I well remember how Father Morris would now and then break the silence with some enthusiastic exclamation. Two things seemed chiefly to fill his mind and heart: the happiness of being a priest and the privilege of living in Rome. Being fresh from a public school myself, I was particularly struck by the continuation of his public school boyishness of manners, yet withal his intense realization of the supernatural. It is needless to say that never before had I come across the like, and I do not think that I have ever met with it since. The graces of the priesthood and of the Holy City appeared to him to be almost sensible, and in speaking of them his voice would at times rise into a scream of delight.

"These two characteristics had not left him when he returned, in 1853, to be Vice-Rector to Dr. Corn-thwaite, although perhaps his boyishness was, for a time at least, somewhat overshadowed by what I may call a "cock-sureness" in his conversation. This may have arisen from the important position which had been in the meantime assigned to him in the diocese of Northampton. But be this as it may, his over-confidence gradually gave way, first to a marked, and then to an extreme deference to the opinions of others; only to be broken at rare intervals by quickly-suppressed signs of impatience or half-smothered laughter, with just a flash of fire in his eye, when he found that his opponent had overstepped the boundary-line of fair argument. His intense realization of the supernatural and the unseen seemed only to have increased.

"How can I forget the vivid way in which this was brought out during the pleasant excursions and pilgrimages which he made with parties of the students to places of religious interest and well-known shrines, and which he has recorded so brilliantly in the pages of *The Month*?[1] As we visited them on foot, taking in every lesser shrine and place of interest on our way, it seemed to me as if Father Morris were personally introducing us to the saints whom we had come to visit, as to his own familiar friends, and as if he had some personal claim on the home of the Holy Family, so familiarly did he speak of them and to them, so intimately acquainted he appeared to be with all concerning them, so vividly present did he bring everything before us. It was clear that even then it was no effort to him to live ever in the presence of God and of his holy ones. At other times he would read to us passages of his *Life of St. Thomas of Canterbury*, in which, as he thought, he had happily caught some trait of the blessed Martyr's character, and then he would ring out the words with that sort of scream of delight, of which I have already spoken.

"It was chiefly through Father Morris's influence with the Rector and the Cardinal Protector, Cardinal Ferretti, that the English College students were transferred from the course of the Roman Seminary of Sant' Apollinare, to that of the Collegio Romano. That in so advising Father Morris merited well of the Church in England, will not, I think, be disputed by those who are able to form an impartial judgment of the state of studies in Rome between the years 1850 and 1856. For there can be but little doubt that, although there was here and there a professor of great merit at the

---

[1] These will form the subject of our next chapter.

Sant' Apollinare, the lectures of the professors of the Collegio Romano, taking them as a body, were of a higher order.

"Another feature of Father Morris's vice-rectorship was the untiring zeal with which, in the midst of his other duties and occupations, he kept up his study of Canon Law, and his attendance at the meetings of the Congregation of the Concilio. Yet he always had time to attend to the difficulties and wants of the students, and in so doing seemed to lay aside every other pre-occupation.

"I cannot conclude these memorial notes of Father John Morris, without adding my testimony to that of so many others who have borne witness to his unfailing sympathy for those who were in trouble, or were passing through some great tribulation or temptation. I know that to one who was in sore straits he was ready, more than once a week, to come many miles simply to take a walk with him and cheer him up. He was a priest, who never turned away from a sinner or wearied of being kind to him, being ever ready to bind up his wounds and pour in the wine and oil of his Lord's sympathy and love. Above all, he never despaired of any one, but hoped even against hope that by God's good grace and Mary's prayers the victory would be gained. . . . Truly may we say that the last words which he ever uttered on earth, were the setting of God's own seal on the works that follow him."

After the example of the writer of these pleasant recollections, we will, before accompanying Father Morris to England in 1850, complete what little we have to say of his second residence in Rome, between the years 1853 and 1856.

Being happy in his Superior, the incidental evidence of this and the following chapter will abundantly show

how happy and hearty was his intercourse with the students over whom he was placed, in spite of certain natural difficulties, which were of course always in existence, and which we can estimate more exactly later on.

Something must also be said of the occupations with which he filled up the intervals not required for official duties, as it was thus that much of the most important work of his life was accomplished. The main direction of these studies, as we have already seen, was Canon Law, and he had soon acquired a sufficient reputation to be entrusted with several commissions, as when he helped Mr. Frederick Lucas in the drafting, translating, and revision of his long "Statement" to the Holy See. He was offered the post of Secretary to the Second Council of Westminster, but the expense of returning to England prevented his acceptance of the appointment. Before this he had been instructed by Cardinal Wiseman to petition that the Venerable Bede should be recognized as a Doctor of the Church. He drew up a form for this purpose, and obtained the signatures of all the Bishops who came to Rome for the definition of the Immaculate Conception in 1854. The cause was then consigned to Mgr. Minetti, Sub-Promotor of the Faith, "who has made me," wrote Canon Morris, in May, 1855, "promises of expedition. I shall be agreeably disappointed if the event proves them to have been true." In fact the matter still hangs fire.

Another undertaking then entrusted by the Cardinal to Father Morris has made more satisfactory progress; indeed it is one with which his name will ever be closely linked. He was commissioned to request the Congregation of Rites to grant the privilege of a feast-day, with a special Mass and Office, in honour of the English Martyrs, as a step towards their canonization.

G

This petition, however, and several others of a like nature, all drafted by Father Morris, were at the time rejected by the Congregation of Rites, who steadily refused to allow the least relaxation of the strict laws that regulate the "promotion," as it is called, of servants of God to the honours of the altar. Father Morris, therefore, had to go on searching for yet further proofs of the reality of their claims to be considered martyrs. His labours, and those of others who generously supported him in the cause, were, as we know, crowned by the decree of our reigning Pontiff, and have resulted in the widely extending interest and reverence with which our sixteenth and seventeenth century martyrs are now regarded. The course of this development will form the subject of a separate chapter.

We shall conclude this present one with some extracts from three letters addressed to Mr. and Mrs. Scott Murray in 1853; the first of these being a few words of introduction for Dr. Louis English to present to them.

"*July* 4, 1853.—I write a line or two to introduce to you the future Archbishop of Westminster. I dare say you remember my theory as to the classification of our great men:

"Class I. 1. Father Newman. 2. Dr. English. 3. Cardinal Wiseman.

"Class II. Vacant.

"Class III. Father Faber, Macmullen, &c.

"I hope that Dr. English may leave an impression upon you in conformity with all this, but I dare say he will want drawing out. At least this I can say, that you will find him an original and a deep thinker, whenever I measure myself beside him, I am proud of being his intimate friend."

"*November* 1, 1853.—I am just come home from the Morning Capella at the Quirinal, and am going to the afternoon one soon, so that I shall not be able to despatch all at once. I am so glad to see our Cardinal in his place in the function. He is looking very well. Oakeley was there also and in raptures, as indeed he has been ever since he came to Rome. He spent the whole day in St. Peter's twice. Last Sunday I saw him there at the Beatification of Blessed Andrew Bobola. The Cardinal says he will be getting up a Beatification at St. John's, Islington. The poor Cardinal hurt his hand by a fall from a chair, the legs of which broke off as he was standing on it hunting a gnat. He was consequently unable to give the *fervorino* and General Communion at S. Carlo as he had engaged to do. To-day, however, he said Mass. The *crocifisso* over the Mamertine Prison worked some miracle or other a while ago and so the people got up a devotion to it. They had a triduo there which did so much good that the Jesuits thought it was a pity that more should not be made of it, so they borrowed the crucifix, took it in grand procession to S. Carlo in Corso, and preached a mission, which was to have ended last Sunday, but which I hear is to be prolonged for another week. The church is full of devotion all day. Rome altogether seems in a very satisfactory state. There were great crowds at Blessed Andrew's Beatification. There are plenty of *ex votos* round Blessed Peter Claver's picture in the Gesù, and I hear that his canonization will not be difficult. . . .

"Manning is to be back here very soon. I wonder whether the Holy Father will tell him to come back again when he goes to England next summer. Cardinal Wiseman is going to ordain in our chapel a number of our students, and Howard is to have the tonsure and minor orders at the same time. He is very anxious to have the subdeaconship at Easter, after which he visits England, I believe. I dare say he may have some difficulty about it, for Mgr. Talbot wanted his cousin to be ordained subdeacon before he had finished his first year's divinity, and the Cardinal Vicar refused. .

"You must tell Mr. Murray that I said Mass for him on St. Charles' day, though I had a great temptation to say it for our students who are in retreat. He must see that as he has diverted a Mass from them, he must say some prayers for them to make up. The men are very edifying and have gone into a retreat with all their hearts, and Father Mignardi, who is giving it, is very grand and quite deserves his great reputation. He was ordained priest in 1814 by Ven. Mgr. Strambi, the holy Passionist Bishop who gave his life for the Pope's. . . .

"Father Etheridge is here, and I have seen something of him, and like him more the more I see. I think his appointment as *Assistente* for England a matter most important to religion, for he is a thorough Jesuit and would be glad to see the English Province rival the Roman. I am thinking of attending a course of Canon Law lectures or something of the sort this year, if it can be done without interfering with my own proper work here at the College, and think I must go through the examination for faculties, though the English have plenty of confessors, and I hardly know Italian enough for a Roman confessional, still it is a step in the right direction. I enjoyed the vacation at Monte Porzio very much, and it did me a world of good. It gave me an opportunity too of seeing something, though not as much as I wished, of the men

"Every one in England is raving about Father Faber's new book—*All for Jesus*. Birks has sent me a copy, and it really is very fine. A large edition was exhausted in a month. He must truly be a saint. I am going, or rather I am going to try, to go to Casamare in the spring, when the Abbot is going to translate the bodies of some most interesting martyrs of whom I have no room to tell you now, and then if you were here we might manage to go together to Sezze as well. Oh, ho! too delightful a dream to be realized, for this is a work-day world and there is plenty to do in it and no time for holidays.

"*November* 24, 1853.—The Synod has appeared, and is very grand indeed, and will be truly a reformation when carried out. The Cardinal has received me very well after the first time or two. Now he is very kind. He is in tremendous health and spirits. He had a grand ordination last Sunday. He ordained in our chapel two priests, four deacons, two subdeacons, and five minors, amongst whom were Wynne and Howard. The Abbot of Mount St. Bernard's is here, and Cardinal Wiseman is to bless him solemnly on St. Thomas Apostle at St. Gregory's Church. Manning is to preach and the function altogether to be a great affair. The Cardinal is to give a set of Advent lectures at St. Andrea delle Fratte, which will doubtless do good. He is at present at Monte Porzio with Stonor, who is mending rapidly and wonderfully. Poor fellow, he has had a very narrow escape. . "

CHAPTER IV.

HOLIDAYS IN ITALY.

1853—1855.

ONE may have been acquainted for years with a man in the ways and habits of his business life, as doctor, for instance, or lawyer, an employer or employé, and yet have a very incomplete knowledge of his true character until one has seen him amongst his amusements. The remark is perhaps more true of priests than of any other class, and certainly Father Morris was no exception to the rule. The present chapter, therefore, will be found to contribute very much to the knowledge of the whole man as he was really in himself, not only during any passing phase of his youth, but as he remained till the end. He was an ideal companion for a holiday, brimful of interest in all that he saw, and able to impart it to others through his admirable power of conversation.

Father Morris wrote an account of the first of his holiday rambles through the country in the letter which is given below: his subsequent expeditions are well told in the articles which he contributed to *The Month* in the year 1890, under the title of " Italy before the Railways."

1.—A VACATION RAMBLE IN 1853.

" English College, Rome, November 24, 1853

" My dear Mrs. Scott Murray,—I am sitting up with a poor sick man in the College, which gives me a

delightfully quiet time while everybody else is in bed
to prove my gratitude for your fine long letter just
received by writing you an account of my expedition
this vacation. You must know then that we started
from Monte Porzio one Sunday afternoon in September, being the feast of our dear Mother's most
charming name. We were six in all: myself the only
priest, two deacons, two subdeacons, and a minorista.
I may presume that I need not describe myself, and
yet without a faint reference to shorts and a straight
cut coat, you would hardly picture me as I was. Add
also the idea of a very thick stick with a pound of lead
in the head thereof, and pockets distorted with an
ungainly fulness, and I am satisfied with my own
portrait. Then comes the deacon, our senior student
and technically 'the Dean,' a young gentleman whom
the change from Stonyhurst to Rome has precociously
raised to a wonderful corpulence. He is imperturbably
good-natured, suffers somewhat in walking from the
weight he carries, and as he enjoys (which few men do)
chaffering with Italian hosts, and therefore bears the
purse and beats down the bills and pays them, he is
invaluable on an expedition. Next is an Ushaw man,
the other deacon, a good fellow, given to singing un-
weariedly, and all along the road organizing songs and
catches, and even when whispering roaring stentoriously.
He sets an example of jolly patience in mishaps, rendered the more evident by a solitary instance of grumble
when, in a barber's shop, where we were shaved in
public with all the world for spectators, he who was
shaved last declared 'he wouldn't be scrub again.'
Third comes a young convert, known to the newspapers
as 'the Rugby boy,' the sharpest fellow of the party,
no doubt, and singularly resembling Father Faber.
Fourth, the property of the Bishop of Northampton,
a man who I rejoice to think will be the death of the

good Bishop, for if I shook his nerves by talking and preaching fast, this man will be the death of him outright. Lastly, an Oscotian, thoughtful, gentlemanly, having a turn for philosophy, and a habit of pursuing his own train of thought under surpassing difficulties. This description of the *dramatis personæ* is intended less as a preface than as a running accompaniment to the whole journey, to interpret everything as their conversation did to me.

" On the Sunday afternoon then we, the six above described, started on our way. Our baggage produced unnatural-shaped pockets and nothing more, except, indeed, one man, who was daring enough to carry his furniture in a white handkerchief. We had therefore no superfluities, and that in the very widest sense which the word will bear. The sky was overcast and threatening, if one ought not rather to describe it as a cessation of rain, for the morning had taxed our resolution by making us prepare to the sound of torrents of rain. The first thing we had to do was to say the Litany and *De pròfundis* going down the steep and stony Porzio hill, a devotion appertaining to our expeditions from time immemorial. We struck across the Campagna, through ruins and past a frightfully odoriferous sulphur lake towards Tivoli. In a smoky *osteria* we got a glass of wine, surrounded by so many dogs that the more nervous of the party were in dread. The way uninteresting, except from the great chance of a storm of rain, which with our wardrobes would be a serious matter, was beguiled by the composition of English sapphics on the plan of the ' Needy Knife-grinder,' originated by a contribution in that metre from one of the party (the Rugby boy of course), to a newspaper I started called THE PORZIO POST. Ascending up to Tivoli, said the Rosary, or rather tried to say it, for I laughed like a child the while. However, our Blessed Lady did not care, and she or the Holy Souls kept off the rain. Safe at ' The Sybil,' a sort of place rarely to be found in Italy and nowhere to be enjoyed as at Tivoli, a hotel where you get really good food.

" Monday at Tivoli. Said Mass in an astonishing chapel, being the old Temple of the Sybil, now St. George's. Having found the sapphics very tiresome, everything that was said running into them, made a memento to forget them. Succeeded pretty well. Breakfast wonderful, real tea and two noble trout. All in fine feather except the Bishop of Northampton's man, who says with wonderful rapidity, ' V'ry ill, v'ry ill 'deed.' After a glimpse at the falls, off for the day's work, to wit, Subiaco by the mountain road. Prayers as usual, people taking off their hats to us as if we were on a kind of pilgrimage. Hard boiled eggs rather the worse for carrying. Two roast fowls tied up with string spin as they are carried as if the sun were finishing the roasting. The sun piping hot, and white handkerchiefs universally worn under hats, which gives the party a nunnish look. Christened the Dean ' Rev. Mother.'

" The first fifteen miles splendid road, constantly rising among mountains, but without much climbing. This walk a great deal of Scripture quoted, but on the whole rather profanely. Dinner at Gerano at foot of mountains, on the twice-roasted fowls and hard-boiled eggs, in an *osteria*, amidst plenty of natives, with whom we fraternized. We got rather the worst of one or two encounters of wit. Could not persuade ourselves to eat some snails we were offered. In Gerano is a beautiful Madonna, a masterpiece, which in the great Revolution was brought from Rome for safety, and the Geranesi, taking a great devotion to it, would not let it go back again. It is not often that so beautiful a picture works so many *grazie*. The sick man went to the doctor, who gave him some coffee, and recommended an ice at Subiaco. Hired a donkey for him, and proceeded.

"Now a regular climb, a mountain-pass, the path nothing but the bed of a torrent. The Oscotian tied his Roman collar to his button-hole, and then lost it, and henceforth is a marvellous figure in a black silk hand-kerchief. This bit of road seven miles, and very severe walking, but gloriously beautiful. Passed through the town of Subiaco (of which Cardinal Andrea is now Abbot,[1] the Pope used to be) to the Monastery of Sta. Scolastica, two miles further. Here the Abbot Casaretto unfortu-nately was away, but we were hospitably housed by the Master of Novices. The monastery very remarkable, a sort of little Propaganda, some little black fellows and little English mixed up with the Italian Reformed Benedictines. Stopped there two nights, and treated like princes. Indeed, we have discovered that the truest, readiest, heartiest hospitality was always to be found in any of the offshoots of the Benedictine Order.

"Said Mass first morning at St. Benedict's Cave, and the other at high altar over relics of SS. Benedict and Scholastica. A famous crypt, with splendid frescoes, which has been used as a charnel-house, is well restored. Subiaco, however, is indescribable, and ranks in interest next to Assisi.

"The two monasteries are a mile or two above the town, up in a charming valley of their own, fragrant with memories of St. Benedict; the upper monastery, the Sacro Speco, and the lower and larger, Santa Scolastica, and in both the holy patriarch of Western monks has never ceased to live and breathe. In old time there must have been a dam across the valley, which made the lake whence the place derived its name of Subiaco. It was the lake on which, by a miracle

1 That is, the abbacy is held *in commendam*.

unexampled since St. Peter, as the Roman Martyrology says, St. Maur walked upon the water. There are some beautiful things at St. Scolastica's, for instance, the mediæval fresco in the canopy of which we have King David counselling custody of the tongue, and beneath, St. Benedict, with his finger on his lips, bidding us act on his counsel. There is the chapel, interesting to an Englishman, built by Abate Casaretto to house the relics of Venerable Bede, with his *Semper legit, Semper scripsit, Semper docuit, Semper oravit* carved in the four corners. There is the garden where St. Benedict cast himself into the thorns, beautifully and symbolically all roses ever since. And at the glorious Sacro Speco, there is the cave where St. Benedict lay hidden from the world, with the great rock overhead, threatening the house beneath, but upheld ever, so that it should be a shelter and not a menace. The church there with its various levels, and the devout faithful going up its stairs on their knees, are a sight never to be forgotten. One thing that adds immensely to the sense of beauty is that as you go down the steps which lead from the church to the holy cave, you have on one side the rough rock untouched, on the other side the walls covered with ancient and most interesting frescoes. Not an easy place to tear yourself away from is the Sacro Speco at Subiaco.

" Wednesday started, overwhelmed with kindness, with plenty of letters of recommendation, guided part of the way by the village Hercules. Our way lay up the beautiful valley, along the Arno to its source, which was very fine and interesting. On to Guarcino, where we had an introduction to the Canonico Patriarca, canon of their collegiate church, whom we disturbed from his siesta about mid-day. He was very kind, and gave us all he had, our appetites astonishing the household. A lump of butter brought from Rome, and

evidently a luxury, was not spared. He expatiated on
a pointer, which he called a dog with two noses, which
belonged to his nephew, the canon of a neighbouring
collegiate, whose gun was in the corner of the room.
On to Trisulti, character of the country changing, and
becoming much more rugged and wild. Subiaco to
Guarcino seventeen miles, then to Trisulti, ten. Trisulti
is a *certosa*, and a fine one, the Novitiate to S. Maria
degli Angeli, and head place hereabouts. Arriving tired,
the lay-brother trotted us about to see everything to
such an extent that we were fit to die for lack of food.
By-and-bye it came, but owing to their solitary system,
it was cold and cheerless.[1] The church was beautiful
and clean, as every *certosa* is. One wall occupied with
the martyrdom of the English Carthusians. I said
Mass after a Carthusian, who lay upon his side.
Thursday afternoon, left Trisulti, beginning to suffer
from abstinence-food, and walked twenty miles to
Casamare. Lost our way, and arrived at a place called
Civelli, anglicized 'Chiffels.' Here we with some
difficulty got into a Redemptorist house, and eat the
supper of the Religious. They are just on the confines
of the Neapolitan States, a mountain-path leading into
the kingdom, so that they are obliged to be particular.
We were guided to Casamare in the dark by a lad
whom I questioned and cross-questioned on his catechism, and he answered wonderfully. He had been
taught well by a Redemptorist of Civelli, a house, by
the way, founded by St. Alphonsus.

---

[1] Writing later in *The Month*, Father Morris implies that the cheerless-
ness of the meal was rather due to their over-fatigue than the diet in itself :
" At Subiaco, I remember, there was a guest who had travelled the other
way, and came from Trisulti. I said to him, 'They never allow meat
within their gates on any occasion, do they?' His answer was, that they
provided you so well with meagre food, that you never thought about meat.
Pane stupendo, he said, *acqua magnifica*, and so on with a string of epithets
that experience soon told us were well deserved."

"Casamare is very fine, and most interesting, a splendid old Gothic abbey, with a fine church. It is a Trappist house, with a Camaldolese Abbot, the dearest old man, for whom we all formed a great affection.[1] The Abbot was powerful enough to get us from the nearest Neapolitan authority a sort of passport which enabled us to go to Monte Cassino. We had still meagre fare, and on Saturday marched thirty[2] miles to S. Germano, the last ten or twelve in heavy drenching rain, the only time we suffered from the weather in a fortnight. The greater part of this day's march was along a straight, unvaried level road, but still it was interesting, as being within the Kingdom of Naples, which we had despaired of entering without passports. With no other adventure than the severe wetting, we reached S. Germano. 'We had to go to bed at an inn whilst our clothes were dried. For a fire to dry them at, we could of course have nothing but one of those wonderful Italian fires, made of the very lightest possible fuel, which blazes up and scorches your face, and then speedily dies down, and leaves you to throw on more twigs, almost at once.'[3]

"The next morning we climbed up the weary three miles of hill to Monte Cassino, where we stayed till

[1] Writing in 1890, Father Morris added : " Pius IX. sent him there, I suppose, because the Trappist monks had no one amongst them fit for government, but it looked curious to see the Camaldolese habit on the Abbot and the Cistercian on all the community. . . . He was what the writers of inscriptions in the Catacombs would have called *Anima dulcissima.* The memory of him has remained as deeply impressed on my mind as that of any one I ever met, and for thirty-five or forty years I have kept steadily to my side of a bargain we made to name each other in our *Memento* at Mass. I have had the best of that bargain, I know, though I am sure that I must have said many more Masses than he, for he was my senior by many years, and long ago God must have taken him from the evil days that were to come on the Religious of Italy."

[2] Probably twenty, not thirty, was intended ; in *The Month* he calls the distance eighteen miles.

[3] Added from *The Month,* p. 331.

Tuesday. I do not attempt for an instant to describe it. Perhaps you have seen it. If you have not, and sit down patiently under the thought without an effort to do so, you never deserve to see anything beautiful again. For a little while, the church shook my allegiance to Gothic, for it is the very perfection of its style in marbles and painting, but it ultimately confirmed me in my ancient fealty, for no large church could be built and as perfectly finished, and but few little ones could approach this. It proves that to make the style a rival to Gothic, it must be finished as Monte Cassino is, which can very rarely be the case.

" On Tuesday we began our return, leaving Monte Cassino by the road which leads down towards St. Scholastica's ancient nunnery, now their Grange, by the place where the Saint got the rain through her prayers. Back by the same road, we stopped at a wayside chapel, where the hermit in charge, a poor, but very devout man, gave us grapes. His chapel was dedicated to St. Eleutherius, an Englishman, who cures hydrophobia. On past Arpino, Cicero's birthplace. We did not leave the Kingdom of Naples, but after a twenty-six mile walk, lodged at S. Domenico di Sora, being a filiation, or Priory of Trappists, dependent on Casamare. We passed hundreds of people coming out of paper-mills and other manufactories, which are conducted under the Bishop (who is a friend of the King) on most satisfactory and Catholic principles. At S. Domenico, a wonder-working image of the Saint, who was a Benedictine in those parts, and who cures the bites of snakes. The church Gothic, but spoiled. The Prior very old and hospitable, but irresistibly odd. He tried to say the long grace for our dinner, but forgot it, and was prompted by a lay-brother (a German convert of some fifty years), and made a mess of it, which set me off, what with the hunger and meagre diet, into a long and loud fit of laughter, which the old man bore very well. The night was passed somewhat wonderfully in Trappist cells.

" The next day we contented ourselves with going to Casamare, eight miles. I on a donkey, as the day before I had worn my feet out. Thursday, we went six miles to Veroli, where the collection of relics is most magnificent. Glorious holy Cross in old reliquary, head of St. Mary Salome, and many others, and to me most interesting of all, a bust (very good) containing a relic of our St. Thomas. The canon curato showed us a picture of the Madonna which had lately done great things, talked, &c. He also recommended us to go to Sezze to see the Saint who knows all sorts of things. We will hunt him up when we go to Casamare, and see if a bit of St. Thomas cannot be got from them. Thence to Fichiena, which is a Grange subject to Trisulti, Carthusian, and very hospitable—fed on frogs. The Bishop of Terracina was there, on his way to Guarcino to pontificate on their festival, and he was accompanied by the young canonico, who owned the gun and the dog with two noses, a very smart young gentleman. Thence through Ferentino to Anagni, where we lodged with Augustinians, a very funny place, two Fathers and two Brothers. Meagre again. At Anagni next day went to Cathedral, the floor of which is a perfect specimen of an old mosaic floor. In the sacristy, on a picture, is an inscription of May, 1325, saying that there were there relics of St. Thomas of Canterbury, who went thither to the Pope, was made a canon of the church, and whose cave they show, though we did not then see it. On Friday, passed S. Maria di Paliano, a Passionist house, through Paliano to Genazzano, where is our dearest Lady of Good Counsel. Slept there that night—tired of meagre food, so broke the fast—and next morning, said Mass at the sanctuary.

Saturday by way of Palestrina, which is always interesting, returned home shortly before the *Ave* on the
feast of Our Lady of Mercy; on one of whose festivals
we had thus begun and ended our expedition.

"Our total distance was two hundred and ten miles,
walked in nine days: away from home thirteen days,
slept two nights only in hotels, to wit, the first and last,
and expended three and a half scudi apiece. Sanctuaries
visited were Cave of St. Benedict at Subiaco, Tomb
of SS. Benedict and Scholastica at Monte Cassino,
S. Domenico di Sora, Veroli and Our Lady of Good
Counsel at Genazzano. I may add that my shoes,
being English, were the only pair that were thoroughly
sound and whole on returning home. There, I think I
have a right to ask whether you do not call that something like an excursion.

"Now, as it is nearly two o'clock, I will write
Mr. Murray a note, then call the good man who
succeeds me in watching this sick person, and then I
shall go to bed with a quiet conscience, and a conviction that if it had not been for this long evening, my
letter would never have been written.

"I am ever, my dear Mrs. Scott Murray,

"Yours very faithfully,

"JOHN CAN. MORRIS."

2.—LORETO.[1]

"We were a party of eight, seven students and
myself, who then was Vice-Rector and of course in
some sense in charge. I do not now feel quite certain
who all these seven were, but five names recur to me
readily, and of those five four are dead. God rest them.
They became zealous priests, who did God good service

---

[1] From *The Month* for May, 1890, vol. lxix. p. 28, "Italy before the
Railways."

in England. At the time I speak of I was the only priest of the party.

"We were on foot of course—the way to see the country and to enjoy what you see. We entered into the Kingdom of Naples near Sora, visiting on the way the Trappist Monastery of Casamare, to which I will return in some other expedition. I think it was on this occasion that we were led away under a sort of arrest by a Neapolitan soldier on the frontier, who marched us into Sora to give an account of ourselves. We passed a comrade of his on the road, who asked him, 'Whom have you got there?' Our escort answered, *Gli inglesi, che 'fanno la loro solita passeggiata*—'The English, out for their usual walk.'

"We made our way with little adventure past the Lago di Fucino, then a fine lake, which long ago Prince Torlonia drained and converted into cornfields, as an investment for his money. All I remember of our lodging there was an altercation with the people of the inn who charged us heavily for having provided a full meal for a large colony of their fleas. Their prices were impressed upon me as exorbitant by what happened when next we were housed in a wayside inn.

"We came down upon the Adriatic, and emerging from the Kingdom of Naples, we re-entered the Papal States at a little town called San Benedetto. There were houses and inns by the side of the road, which ran along the beach; but behind these houses there was a steep cliff, and on the top of this was the parish church and the chief part of the town. Our custom was when we entered a town where we were going to sleep, to depute two of our party to settle about rooms, food, and all we needed, while the others amused themselves as best they could. This time I think they bathed in the Adriatic, while Dr. Roskell and I went off on a tour of inspection in the upper town, before

H

we settled on our quarters. In the middle of the *piazza* before the church, the parish priest was talking to a layman. We went up to them and asked the *parroco's* advice where we should lodge. 'This gentleman is the very man for you,' said he; and away he went, leaving us with his friend the layman.

"We immediately found that we were in strong hands. 'Come with me,' he said; 'you are very fortunate in having found me. I am the very man for you.' He said so much in praise of our good fortune, that I said to Dr. Roskell, 'I wonder whether he is an inn-keeper himself,' and under this impression I told him that we were extremely obliged for the trouble he was taking, but that he must distinctly understand that we meant to judge for ourselves. He dropped his congratulations, but continued to lead us to one of the inns on the roadside opposite to the beach.

"We went in with him, and he said to the landlady, who was as obsequious to him as possible, 'Show these gentlemen your beds.' 'Are you content?' he said to us.' 'Are they clean? Is everything to your liking? *Cinque bajocchi*—twopence halfpenny a piece.' We had not grumbled at four times that elsewhere, and at once we saw that things were looking well for us this time. 'Fetch a *foglietta* of your best wine,' said he. 'There, taste that, and don't forget the taste of it, for you must not be put off with any other. So much the *foglietta*, and no more.' 'And now,' he said to the landlady, 'what will you cook their dinner and serve it for?' 'So much; very good, now come with me, gentlemen, to the butcher's and we will buy your meat.' On our way to the butcher's we were as civil to our powerful friend as all the Italian we could muster between us enabled us to be. The meat was ordered and paid for, and the bargain made that the butcher should send it to the inn forthwith; and then our patron, taking off

his hat, and saluting us with a low bow, said, ' To-
morrow morning, gentlemen, before you start, I shall
do myself the honour of calling upon you' When
we got to our inn, the landlady, who naturally did not
look best pleased, said, ' Do you know who that was
you brought in here with you?' ' No,' we said. ' He
is the Commissary of Police.'

" Next morning our good friend the Commissary
paid us a formal visit. His services to us were not yet
ended. He said, ' Gentlemen, you are on your way to
Loreto. You have forty miles to go along the Adriatic.
There is nothing to repay you the fatigue of walking.
If you will like to ride, there is a return *vettura*, which
will hold you all comfortably, and if you will follow my
advice you will take it. You can have it at half-price.'
We consulted together and accepted the offer, and we
left San Benedetto in state, our friend the Commissary
accompanying us to the door of our nice two-horse
carriage, and we taking off our hats to him as much
as ever we could.

" Our *vetturino* took us safely and quickly to Porto
di Fermo, just half-way to Loreto. There he very
naturally told us he would have to stay a while to
bait his horses. We, nothing loth, turned out to look
about us. At the time he told us, we returned to
him and found another and very inferior carriage, and
what was worse, another passenger already in possession
of a back seat. Eight Englishmen, each one with
a determination not to be done, were not likely to
acquiesce; and so, passing over the change of carriage,
we objected very distinctly to the extra passenger. Our
driver was not going to give way, neither were we, so
we told him that he had broken his contract, we were
not bound to pay him anything, but as he had brought
us half way we would pay him half that had been
agreed upon, and we would finish our journey on foot.

He flared up into a great rage and said he had two sons, and that the three of them had knives, and we should not leave Porto di Fermo alive. We on our side laughed, and told him that eight Englishmen with sticks were not afraid of three men with knives, so he might do what he liked.

" As the man would not take the money we offered him, we looked round and saw a little *gendarme* not far off, so we called to him to ask where the *Gendarmeria* was. 'Ah,' he answered, *non mi impiccio in queste cose—* 'I don't mix myself up in things like that.' 'You foolish fellow, do you suppose that, in a little place like this, we cannot see the Papal flag hanging up to mark the place?' So leaving the passenger sitting in the carriage, and the driver storming and fuming, we went in search of the *Gendarmeria*, and found it in a minute. Asking to see the commanding officer, we were shown upstairs, and there we sat, all eight of us, in a circle round the lieutenant of *gendarmes* in his *sanctum*.

" The sense of the ludicrous struck us forcibly, but we did our best to be as grave as the dignity of our officer required, and so we told him our story. The lieutenant then went to the head of the stairs, and cried out, ' Antonio !' The answering voice at the bottom of the stairs was that of our little *gendarme*, and the words it said were those we had heard it say before, *Oh, signore, non mi impiccio in queste cose.* The police force, under the command of our lieutenant, seemed to consist of our little *gendarme*, whose one idea of his duty was not to mix himself in what promised to be disagreeable. Not this the idea of our lieutenant, who drew himself up to his full height—he was a tall, handsome man— and with the most melodramatic air I ever saw, let fly at the small *gendarme* down the staircase the noble sentiment, *Quando la patria commanda, ciascuno obedisce,* which means something like Nelson's famous ' England *

—only here it was another *patria*—'expects every man to do his duty.'

"The little *gendarme* not doing his duty, we got tired of expecting him to do it, and I suggested to the lieutenant that the *vetturino* would doubtless accept the money from him, and we with good conscience could then go on our way to the Holy House. The man took the money, of course ; and we, with a *Buon giorno, signore,* that did not amuse him, and a *Buon viaggio, signore,* to our intended fellow-traveller, started off, at four o'clock in the afternoon, to walk our twenty miles to Loreto.

"Our young lieutenant said that it would be safer for us if he went a mile or two with us, but we soon found out that there was something he wanted to say. *Lor' signori*, he said to us, belonged to a College in Rome: that College had a Cardinal Protector : that Cardinal Protector had influence, and could get a poor lieutenant of the *Gendarmeria* transferred from a miserable station like Porto di Fermo to something better. We, on our parts, were civility itself, but we never promised that. 'Porto di Fermo, *Signor Luogotenente,*' we said, 'was one of the most delightful places we had seen. How happy the lot of a lieutenant of *gendarmes* who was quartered there! And who so likely to distinguish himself for his good offices to travellers as our excellent friend?' The more he pressed the Cardinal Protector upon us, the more we gave him of the praises of Porto di Fermo. And so at length he left us, our civility having lasted out beautifully, in repayment for the service he had done us.

"On the way there was a large house with five windows on a floor facing the sea. At a well near it a servant was drawing water when we came up. We asked her to get us a glass that we might quench our

thirst, and as we were talking to her, the centre window
opened, and at it appeared two dear old ladies, who
asked us whether we should not prefer a bottle of wine.
The first bottle was succeeded by another, and we
stood there under the window, holding converse with
the good-natured old bodies, who told us that Cardinal
Piccolomini came to them every summer—Cardinal
Piccolomini, who was half an Englishman, for his
mother was a Jackson. *Una grande'famiglia, non è vero?*
la'famiglia Jackson, as I once heard the good Cardinal
say.

"It was time to step out, for twenty miles was a
good walk after four o'clock in the afternoon. And
unfortunately Dr. Meynell—there were, I think, three
in the party at least who afterwards became doctors of
divinity, and I use their titles here by anticipation—
Dr. Meynell broke down, and Dr. Roskell and I had
almost to carry him up to Loreto. On that expedition
of ours each one of us broke down once, and once only,
and never two on the same day. I remember my
breakdown perfectly, how I sat by the wayside on
a heap of stones till a wine-cart came by that gave
me a lift to the next village, where I hired a mule.
For Charles Meynell we could get no help, so he put
an arm round each of our necks, and made believe to
walk between us. The last two or three miles up to
Loreto were all uphill, and the clocks were striking
midnight as we three got in. The others had gone
ahead to order supper, and to get a mustard bath for
Paul—so we called him, for his name was Charles.
How he screamed, poor fellow, as the circulation of
the blood was restored! He was all right the next
day, and never broke down again. That supper after
midnight was of no use to me, for I would not have
missed saying Mass at the *Santa Casa* on any account,
so there was nothing for it but to go supperless to bed.

"Three days we spent at Loreto, and they were delightful. The *Santa Casa* for devotion surpasses anything I know in Rome. *Verbum caro hic 'factum est,* 'The Word was *here* made flesh,' comes home to you with extraordinary force. The altar of the Annunciation outside, the altar with the famous image of Our Lady of Loreto within, the many lamps always burning, the earnest devotion of the innumerable pilgrims, the Masses succeeding one another without ceasing for hours and hours, the magnificence of the gifts in the treasury, the sculptures of our Lady's life casing the Holy House, the stones within, the very stones of the Holy House of Nazareth, witnesses of the Hidden Life of the Thirty Blessed Years—it is like a pilgrimage to Nazareth and more, to visit the *Santa Casa* at Loreto. Pilgrims enter the vast Basilica which covers the Holy House, shouting *Evviva Maria e Chi la creò !* It matters not what else is going on. The cry of the pilgrims rises up, as though the joy of entering there was irrepressible, and they could not conceive that any one at that moment should have any other thought. They have brought with them from their distant homes special clothing to be worn only in their visit to the Holy House, and then to be put by for them to be buried in. When they go out of the church they back out, as from the presence of Royalty. They go round the Holy House on their knees, and often on bare knees, and they have worn a deep furrow in the marble pavement. And every one in the vast Basilica attends to himself and to his own devotion, while the Canons are singing their Office in the choir, and confessors in dozens of confessionals are hearing the pilgrims' confessions, and Holy Communion is being given to hundreds, and processions are going away and processions arriving. Such is my impression and recollection of Loreto. It was a charming thing of an evening to see the sanctuary closed. A Canon mounted up over the altar to dust and then to cover the statue of our Blessed Lady; and as he went quietly and slowly through his work, he said the Litany of the Blessed Virgin, all the people answering him, and he added many *Aves* for all sorts of intentions, public and private. This is the origin of our familiar Litany of Loreto, and all its loving invocations spring from the tender thoughts respecting our Lady entertained in her chiefest sanctuary by those who were engaged in this homely and domestic service to her.

" I have a tender remembrance of our sweeping out the Holy House on our knees, by permission of the Capuchin Fathers, who then had charge of the sanctuary; and we went round outside on our bare knees as other pilgrims did. The groove that had been worn by the knees of innumerable pilgrims had, at least in one place, a very sharp edge, and when I came in contact with it, the pain instantly threw me forward on my face.

" We spent three days in Loreto, and that was just the number of times that a priest, visiting the place in pilgrimage, is allowed to say Mass for his own intentions. After that he must accept an alms, but there was nothing to prevent his giving his own alms, and so securing his own intention. But the alms he gave was larger than he received, for the ecclesiastical authorities had decreed that the alms for a Mass at Loreto should be three pauls instead of two, as elsewhere in Italy, that is a franc and a half instead of a franc; and one-third of the sum was devoted to the Basilica.

" The great church erected over the Holy House is the only public church in all Loreto. It contains a multitude of altars, and the Masses said there, besides those celebrated in the sanctuary, are very numerous;

and as there is no other church, all the inhabitants have to come here to attend Mass. This is done to maintain the dignity of the *Santa Casa*, and to keep the people about it. The story runs that a good man once set to work to build a church in Loreto, and when it was done he offered it to the Bishop for consecration. The Bishop sent him into retreat to find out whether it was our Lady's wish it should be consecrated, and the end was that it was given to a religious house to serve as its domestic chapel. The moral seems to be to consult the Bishop, and even to go into retreat, before you build your church.

"The morning we left I crept into the church as soon as it was opened, long before daylight. The lamps before all the altars that line the nave showed the way to the sanctuary of our Lady. I entered in, and early as it was, Mass had begun. I was able to go to Holy Communion, though I could not wait to say Mass; and I leant against the hallowed stones of those walls to make my thanksgiving. That man is happy who has had the privilege, once in his life, of visiting the Holy House of Loreto.

"On our way home we paid a visit to two Saints. One was St. Nicholas of Tolentino, of whom I only remember that little tiny biscuits were blessed under his invocation. The other was St. Joseph of Cupertino, of whom there are a large number of memorials at Osimo. This was the Saint who had such marvellous ecstasies. When imprisoned as a trial by order of the Inquisition, he came out in ecstasy through the window bars; and at Osimo, when he looked out towards Loreto and thought of our Lady and her Holy House and the paradise it had been to her, he used to fly up in the air in his ecstasy. They show at Osimo a tree, in the branches of which he was caught on occasion of one of these heavenly flights.

3.—GENAZZANO.

" Genazzano is the place where there is the beautiful shrine of Our Lady of Good Counsel. It is just eighteen miles from Monte Porzio, and I have been there many times, but one of those visits in particular I wish now to recall. Eighteen of the students went with me, which is by far the largest party I ever had charge of. We had staying with us at Monte Porzio at that time that extremely charming man, Bishop Willson, of Hobart Town, and he said he thought us mad. Our plan was to get some supper very late and to start at midnight, to do our eighteen miles in the dark, and have our Mass at the sanctuary early in the morning before the throngs of pilgrims came. The feast of Our Lady of Good Counsel is kept at Genazzano on St. Mark's day, and in other places on the day following. The parish procession of the Greater Litanies, with its cross and purple vestments, winding its way through the narrow and densely-filled streets of the village, crowded by visitors, all bent on doing honour to our Lady, forms a picturesque scene.

" Our start at midnight, with the 25th of April just beginning, was under circumstances that seemed to verify Bishop Willson's estimate of us. It was raining and blowing all the night. Every one was armed with a torch, but the weather was such that all but one would suddenly be extinguished. Somehow one always remained alight, for the others to be speedily relighted from. We had first to get clear of our Alban Hills by narrow and wretched lanes, mere paths leading to the vineyards, and it was too dark for us to pick our way, so we had to walk straight on through pools of water. Then we had a stretch of old Roman road with its large, carefully fitted paving-stones, taking us near to Palestrina on the opposite range of hills, crossing thus the Campagna Felice. Then we turned into the hills and made our way up the long pass, leading to Cavi, where Cardinal Acton's carriage was upset, of which there is a votive picture at the shrine, representing his Eminence in short dress and red stockings kneeling in the road, making his thanksgiving for his escape, while students of the English College, who were his companions, are being hauled out of the carriage window.

"In that pass, the weather having somewhat improved, by the light of our torches we said the Litany of the Saints. And so we reached Cave, a village at no great distance from Genazzano, just as the aurora showed us that sunrise was not far off. The village had, as Italian villages generally have, its washing-place outside, long stone troughs, through which the water flows. Some of the more prudent ones amongst us had brought soap with them, and we stopped for a refreshing wash. Our clothes were drying on our backs, and we were looking forward to sunlight and warmth, when, as we entered the gate of Genazzano, down came the rain again in torrents. The eaves of the houses projected over the road, and it was impossible to help getting wet through and through during the last few minutes of our pilgrimage. However, we had heart enough left in us to sing the Litany of the Blessed Virgin as we ascended the steep street, and there was something outlandish enough in the sound of our English voices, to bring the people to their windows to see the first procession arrive that day.

"We went to the Augustinian convent which is attached to the sanctuary, and explained to the lay-brother that we should like to be allowed the use of the altar as early as might be, for we were so wet that we ought to start home soon. He gave us fair words and showed us into a room, where there were chairs enough

for us all. We sat down, and it is hardly to be
wondered at that we were all speedily asleep. I
woke up, not knowing how long we had slept, and
called out · 'This will never do; we shall get our
death of cold.' We found our way through the house
to the sacristy. I vested, set one of them to tell me
when the altar was free; and then, without saying,
'With your leave or by your leave,' took possession of
it. They all went to Communion at my Mass, and the
only mishap was that during our thanksgiving poor
Drinkwater fainted.

"We then went out into the *piazza* to get a cup of
coffee, and for the first time we fairly saw one another
in the daylight. The sleeves of our coats, made of
some alpaca stuff, had shrunk up and exposed our
wrists, so that we looked like charity boys that had
outgrown their clothes. And then we saw what had
happened when we washed our faces at Cave. Through
the night the smoke of the torches had blackened us,
and our washing had got our faces pretty clear of it,
but all round our eyes there was a circle of lampblack
that gave us the most singular appearance. We were
laughing at one another, when some English friends,
who had slept at Genazzano that night, walked up to
us in the *piazza*, and they were amused, as they well
might be, at our plight.

"Italy is not the place for breakfast, so getting what
we could, we promised ourselves an early dinner at
Palestrina, on our way back. Nina Bernardini was the
name of the good woman in whose house we were
accustomed to rest when we went to Palestrina; and I
said to her, 'Nina, I am quite certain that you cannot
give us too much to eat, so just try.' Nina started her
dinner with enormous dishes of macaroni, plentifully
covered with gravy and minced meat, an appetizing
dish at any time: and thus a foundation was laid.

She kept on bringing in a variety of things, till at last I was driven to saying, ' If you fellows will go on eating, I will carve for you.' And Nina gave me something to carve, for to my surprise and amusement, when I thought all was over, she brought in three quarters of a lamb. I did my part of the bargain and cut it up, and they did their part and eat it up; and I do not think that Nina had a scrap left of her dinner, though she had catered for us nobly.

" There were a dozen miles between us and home, and we were back at Monte Porzio in good time. No one was the worse for the drenching we had, not so much as by a cold. But the effect on me was that I took the longest sleep I have ever had in my life. After a cup of tea, I went to bed at four o'clock in the afternoon, and the next morning at ten the Rector came to my room to see whether I was alive. I had never waked nor moved, while the clock went round, and half round a second time."

4.—ON HORSE AND ON FOOT.

"Sometimes we went on horseback; more frequently, indeed always on the longer expeditions, we were on foot. One riding excursion I remember very well for its singular scenic effect. Three of us resolved on riding to a chapel of St. Michael, perched on the top of one of the mountains between Tivoli and Palestrina. We called at San Pastore on our way, the villa of the German College, charmingly situated in the midst of the Campagna Felice, the fertile belt between the Alban Hills and the Apennines. We then rode on and made our ascent very successfully on a fine afternoon, till we were within half a mile of the chapel. All at once, to our dismay, a thick cloud came down upon us and we could hardly see one another. In a few minutes we were aware that we had lost the mountain track, and we went on slowly and carefully, till at last we came to a standstill on a shelving ledge of rock, where the horses could hardly turn round. We could not see where we were, nor could we guess which way we were to go. Perforce we stood perfectly still, and there was this to be said for the Frascati horses we were riding, that they were willing to stand quiet for any length of time. At last the welcome sound of an axe fell on our ears. Shouting did nothing for us, but the axe went on with its work, it was hard to guess where; so, as the axe would not come to us, there was nothing for us to do but to go in search of the axe. It had to be very warily done, or we might make things worse instead of better; so one of our party dismounted and handed over his bridle to another, and left us slowly, under solemn promise not to go out of earshot. We kept up a steady fire of shouts and answers, until at length, to our great relief, he reappeared with the woodsman, who took us up straight to St. Michael's chapel. Just as we reached it, the clouds opened for a little, and, in bright sunshine framed in dazzling white mist, we saw into the interior of that beautiful mountain range, up the valley of the Anio, right over to the hills beyond Subiaco. It was worth passing through the clouds to have the view so gloriously enhanced by contrast, and by the unexpected suddenness with which so beautiful a prospect burst upon us. The chapel on the hill-top, we found, was more used than such out-of-the-way sanctuaries usually are; as at Michaelmas it was the custom of the villagers, for miles round, to come up there to receive the sacraments. *La Pasque di St. Michele,* they called it, and the people seem to have used it as they would their parish church at Easter. The Jesuit Fathers from Tivoli and San Pastore heard confessions there all through the night that ushers in the feast of St. Michael, and the people would lay themselves down to sleep anywhere, on the hillside, or on the chapel floor, or the altar steps, when they had been to confession, waiting for the early Masses on Michaelmas Day.

"The riding excursions were generally limited to a single day. Far more enjoyable were the expeditions on foot, when there was a new resting-place each night to look forward to. Sometimes a religious house would take us in, sometimes we tried our fortunes at an *osteria*. The advantage of the latter was that we could order our food to our own fashion, more especially at breakfast, which of course was wanted to fortify us for our day's walk. Once an excellent Abbot of a monastery received us with open arms and showed us what religious hospitality was; but all his good-will could not suggest to him that Englishmen wanted a solid breakfast and were not good for much exertion without it. Overnight we had done excellently, but in the morning, after an early Mass, and by way of preparation for a long day's walk in the mountains, the breakfast to which our kind-hearted Abbot introduced us consisted of a tiny cup of excellent chocolate, a sponge cake or two, and a glass of lemonade. We took it, promising ourselves that before we left the town we would drop in on some house of entertainment and secure some bread and butter and *café au lait*, and if possible a little meat. What was our consternation when we discovered that our Abbot was bent on seeing us a mile or two on our way! There was nothing for it but to put a good face on it, and as soon as our well-intentioned host left us, have a hearty laugh at our mishap. It was late enough before our hunger was satisfied that day, for one of the peculiarities of an Italian *osteria* was this, that there never was anything to be found in it to eat out of meal-times. So, however famished you might be on arriving, you had to wait till your meal was prepared before you could get anything to eat."

5.—Smike.

" And now I must write down something of the history of a companion of ours on many of these excursions. He was a dog, and the name we gave him was Smike. The inhabitants of Monte Porzio had an experience of him very different from ours, and they called him *Crudele*, and said he bit the children. With us he never made show of biting anything but what might be given him to eat, and there was so little cruelty in our experience of him that evidently the creature led two lives and had a dual nature. A red dog he was—a kind of terrier I was going to say, but hardly can say, as I never saw another terrier of the kind, and so, Indian fashion, I call him a pariah dog. It seemed that he had no owner, and he chose to attach himself to us. Poor beast! Our holidays must have been his little glimpse of Paradise, when he got a kind word—in English, it is true, but friendly for all that, and he answered to the name we gave him readily enough. Cruelty I take it there had been, but not on his side, and I venture to conjecture that if he snapped at the children in the village it was in self-defence. The only weapon of self-defence he ever employed against us was to say ' Owgh!' He said it loudly and sharply, and he only said it once at a time; but he said it on the slightest touch. His favourite habit was to come into our refectory—the ground-floor room that looked out on Monte Catone and the Spanish chestnut-trees—and to walk round the room under the seat against the wall on which we sat. Nobody knew he was there until some restless man would throw his heels back, and then if they chanced to touch Smike, as they hardly ever failed to do, there was no mistaking the 'Owgh!' that followed. This was his only fault, for he would trot along contentedly with us for any distance, happy to take up his quarters anywhere, and winning his dinner by the quiet way in which he abstained from begging.

"The dog did not seem to know what fatigue meant; at any rate, I never saw in him the very least sign of being tired. Once he lost us at the end of a long day's walk, and he trotted straight back to Monte Porzio without stopping, as I gathered by inquiring the time of his reappearance at the College. I think that was the day when we were mobbed at Veroli—mobbed, that is, in the friendliest way, but so surrounded by the natives that Smike lost us altogether. We had called on the Bishop of Veroli, and he asked one of his Canons to take us into the Cathedral and show us the treasury. A crowd surrounded us and pent us in to our mingled amusement and indignation. Whether it was astonishment at the discovery that Englishmen could be Catholics, or whether it was surprise at the sight of a party of young ecclesiastics who did their travelling on foot, or whether it was curiosity pure and simple, I cannot say, but we did get stared at unmitigatedly from time to time, and now and then by crowds. Once we betook ourselves to a barber's shop, to get the benefit, after the fashion of the country, of the singularly expert use of the razor that the professional shaver possesses. The room was open to the street, with broad open doors. There we gravely sat waiting our turn, while one was under the barber's hands, and the entire population, as it seemed to us, stood around speechless with delight that it had fallen to their lot to see the sight. If I were to add that it had the effect of shortening the tempers of some of us, I should probably not be far wrong.

"But Smike! What has become of Smike? I

promised myself five-and-thirty years ago that some
day I would write a memoir of Smike, and if I do not
do it now I shall go down to my grave leaving Smike's
memory unhonoured.   One single continuous story of
him I will tell, and quite enough, too, for no art can
make it short.   A party of us were going to the Jesuits
at Galloro to make our retreat there.   Smike chose to
be of the party.   As we started to make our way across
through the woods from one side of the Alban range
to the other, some one expostulated: 'Ought not Smike
to be left behind?'   I pleaded for the poor beast, that
he might have a walk, and I rashly said, 'It will be
easy enough to shut him out when we get there, and
he will go home.'   We got there, and were admitted
through the outer gate, and I went through the farce
of excluding Smike.   He took it quietly, and well he
might, for he had but to turn to the right, run a few
yards, and the wall came to a sudden end, and then
he outflanked the obstacle and met us at the house
door.   It was impossible not to have a hearty laugh at
that little arrangement, which I have seen elsewhere in
Italy, but never out of Italy.   It is the honour and
glory of the thing, I suppose, to build the gate and
a few yards of wall while all the rest of the enclosure is
practically, though not theoretically, unenclosed.

" Smike was solemnly shut out as we entered the
front door, and enjoined in our best English to go
home.   But he did not.   He waited quietly till somebody else entered, and then in he came.   He found out
my room in a moment, and expected to be made
welcome.   Well, he was not; and as I took him down
to the front door, and adjured him to depart, I read in
his face that I had not seen the last of Smike.   I
returned to my room, and began to set myself in order,
when after a few minutes there came a gentle rap at my
door, and a lay-brother silently beckoned to me to come.

He led me off to the room of an old Father, who had retired into a safe corner, while two lay-brothers on their knees were trying with broom handles to dislodge Smike, who had taken refuge beneath the bed. All they succeeded in doing was to elicit from him an emphatic 'Owgh!' every time they touched him, and then he shifted over to another corner. I snapped my fingers, and out came Smike with as near an approach to a smile on his face and a wag on his stump of a tail as he ever allowed himself. Once more he was shown the front door, and was spoken to more solemnly than ever.

"Our next move was to the little chapel, where we were to hear the preliminary instruction from the Father who was to give us our retreat. We knelt down for a little prayer first, and as I rose from my knees I heard 'Owgh!' which signified that Smike had been touched by my foot, and said so. He remained quiet enough during the discourse, the subject of which was sadly mixed in my mind with the thought of Smike. From the chapel we went to the refectory for supper, Smike accompanying us, nothing loth. We were ranged on the outside of the tables in three sides of a square waiting for grace, and Smike occupied the middle of the room, diverting himself by jumping at the flies. A tendency to laugh, when there is not much to laugh at, is apt to take possession of you sometimes when you go into retreat; and I imagine that the good Father, who came to me after supper and said, 'If you want those young men to make a good retreat, I would advise you to get rid of that dog,' had good reason for what he said. 'Get rid of him!' Of course I wanted to get rid of him, but it is easier to give advice sometimes than to carry it out. In a moment of despair I called a man and said to him, 'Get rid of that dog!' He went away leading Smike, who would have put his tail between his legs or what remained of it if it had not been so short and stiff. By-and-bye the man returned, and I asked him what he had done with Smike. 'Thrown him over the viaduct,' was the answer. Now that viaduct is a magnificent bridge of three stories, built by Pius IX., and worthy of the ancient Romans. 'Poor beast,' I said, 'I must go out and see what has become of him. He may be lying there half-dead.' Not he. The words were hardly said when Smike reappeared, as calm as if nothing had happened. What had happened I do not know, but I suppose that he had fallen on a bush or into a tree. At any rate, there he was, and there he meant to pass the night. And so he did on a chair; but unhappily for me the four legs of the chair were not of the same length, and the rattling he made woke me many times, when he was more than usually molested by the fleas, which in that country freely overrun both man and beast.

"Early in the morning I started off, with Smike contentedly running at my heels. The Collegio Pio, which since has been amalgamated with the English College, was then taking its *villeggiatura* at Genzano. I was met by the Rev. Edmund Knight, afterwards Bishop of Shrewsbury, who never yet refused to help a man in trouble. 'Take care of Smike? Of course he would,' and Smike was tied up then and there. I retraced my steps to Galloro with a light heart, and fell into the retreat, and all went well till we went down into the garden for a walk and some fresh air. Who should walk up to us but Smike? A piece of cord was fastened to his neck, showing that he had bitten himself loose. There was nothing for it but to revisit Genzano, and to express oneself with a fervour and an earnestness with which one seldom makes a petition. Dr. Knight shut him up in a garret this time, and turned the key upon him, and when our retreat was over, we went and released Smike from his.

"One word more about the dog. Smike accompanied us on the pilgrimage to Our Lady of Good Counsel at Genazzano, the history of which I have already told. But I then left out Smike's part of the story. Poor dog! it was not altogether a pleasant pilgrimage for him, and, without meaning it, he made it uncomfortable for us. When we were shown into the house of the Augustinian Fathers, he was shut out, but he found his way into the church. On our coming into the sanctuary for Mass he found us out immediately, and of course got as close to us as he could. This was embarrassing for me while saying Mass, for when I was at the book, Smike went to the middle of the altar, and when I was at the middle of the altar, Smike went to the book. At length in a rash moment Smike ventured outside the sanctuary. The picture of Our Lady of Good Counsel, with all its votive offerings, is protected by strong iron screens, and at the door through which we entered this enclosed sanctuary, there was a sentry stationed, to do honour to the festival and mount guard over our Lady. Smike wandered within reach of him, and the butt end of the soldier's musket fell heavily on poor Smike's flank. For once he did not say 'Owgh!' but the din he raised was so tremendous that I did not know whether I was on my head or my heels. I felt much as once I did at Monte Porzio, when I served as deacon at the parish church and the *parroco* sang High Mass on the feast-day of the village. At the Elevation, with the church doors wide open, a pile of fireworks in the *piazza* just outside was let off with a bang, bang, bang, that went on increasing in intensity as the closely rammed powder exploded, till at last the final explosions, all of which sounded as though they were inside the church, simply knocked you into the middle of next week, or at any rate out of all possibility of recognizing the present. Smike's howls in the church did not disturb the Italians, who took it all as a matter of course, but I was not sorry when they died away in the distance. He did not wait to go home with us that day. Poor old Smike! I hear that he has been hanged in his native village for all the crimes a dog could commit. I confess that I honour him for his fidelity to a stranger and for his gratitude for small favours, and if I have a fault to find with him, it is not want of goodness, but that he could be too good, as indeed we have seen."

6.—THE IMMACULATE CONCEPTION.

It was in Rome itself that Father Morris witnessed, at the close of the year 1854, a sight which neither he, nor any one present, could ever forget. When speaking of it as " quite the sweetest and most delightful recollection of his life," he adds, " I mean of course the definition of the Immaculate Conception by Pope Pius IX. He then continues, " It would have been a great privilege to have been present at a canonization, or at the Œcumenical Council, or again, at the Election or the Enthronement of the new Pope; it would have been a great thing to have seen the far larger number of Bishops, and to have been present when the Infallibility of the Pope was defined: yet if I had to choose one such ceremony—and to be present at one is enough for a lifetime—I should without a moment's hesitation choose the definition of the great and singular grace of the Blessed Mother of God. To have lived at the time when the Immaculate Conception was proposed as a revealed doctrine to the whole Church by the Vicar of our Lord is a happiness great enough to make life in this century more desirable than in any that have gone before: but to have been present, to have seen the Pope at such a time, and to have heard the sound of his voice when proclaiming the greatness of Mary's redemption—that was enough to make one say, *Vixi*. Every life has its culminating-point, and that is mine.

" The day before had been kept in Rome as a strict fast, and the feast of the Immaculate Conception, in that year falling on a Friday, had its abstinence dispensed. The Pope himself sang the High Mass at the high altar of St. Peter's, with all that beauty of ceremonial of which the world has been deprived since the Piedmontese entered Rome. It was as on Easter Day. I had seen the great function many a time, but it never looked grander. The high altar with its seventh candlestick, because the Bishop of the diocese was singing Mass. The throne at the far end of the choir, under St. Peter's Chair. The Pope vested in cope and tiara, carried by the *palafrenieri* in crimson between the two fans of white feathers; and afterwards for the Mass, over the sacred vestments wearing the fanon[1] and the pallium. The Cardinals, with *cappa magna* outspread as they came up one by one to do homage. Some two hundred Bishops in cope and mitre—a number largely overpassed since, but which was then beyond all precedent in our generation. The splendid *Curia Romana*, Bishops and Archbishops assisting at the throne, and glorying in being chosen for the simplest services. The most perfect instrument of music, the human voice in its perfection, needing no support from any instrument that man has made. The majestic march of the ceremonies, faultlessly performed, with the precision of perfect self-possession and familiarity. The Pope, the centre of the Christian world, as he is the centre of that great gathering, doing homage to God, and offering with solemnity unequalled upon earth the august

[1] The fanon is a double veil of four colours with gold fringe. The lower half is worn over the alb, and the upper half covers the Pope's head until the chasuble is put on, when it falls over it like a tippet. The pallium is fastened with its three pins over the fanon.

Sacrifice that every priest is empowered to offer: the Elevation at that altar in which the celebrant has the nave of the church with all its multitudes before him, the thronged transepts on either side of him, and the vast choir behind him; the Elevation therefore unlike any other Elevation, as the Pope turns round after each consecration, making the entire circle while he holds the Sacred Host on high for adoration to all around him, and in its turn in like manner the Sacred Chalice, and all the long while, the silver trumpets playing music fit for the vestibule of Heaven. The Communion too, in this unlike any other Communion, that the Pope retires to his throne at the far end of the choir, and the Blessed Sacrament is brought to him; the Sacred Host, after a fresh Elevation by the Cardinal Deacon, carried slowly by the Subdeacon, who passes up alone through the choir, all kneeling on either side, and then the Chalice, when the Subdeacon with his sacred burden is standing by the throne, elevated anew to all the quarters of the church, and brought with like solemnity by the Cardinal Deacon, who holds in his hand the golden reed through which the Pope receives a part of the Precious Blood.

" Besides the usual ceremonies of the Pope's High Mass, on the occasion of the definition all was done that is customary at a canonization. The most striking and impressive part of all is the petition to the Holy Father, made three times, *instanter*, *instantius*, and *instantissime*, in the name of the whole Catholic Church by the first Cardinal Bishop, Priest, and Deacon. On the first two petitions the Pope answered that prayer must be made for the Divine guidance in a matter of such great moment. The Litany of the Saints was sung after one petition, and the *Veni Creator* after the other; and when the petition was renewed for the third time, the Pope rose, and taking into his hands the form of the definition which was afterwards embodied in his Dogmatic Bull, read it aloud in his clear ringing tones, while the crowded church was as still as death. The Pope stood, with the large book in his hand in which the form was bound, and in the emotion that took possession of him, swung it energetically to the right and left, marking with emphasis the expressions he was uttering. The tears poured off his face as he read the solemn words of the definition *ex cathedra,* by which the conscience of the faithful throughout the world was henceforth bound.

" When the voice of the Pope ceased to be heard, the vast multitude present breathed again. Feeling had been pent up during those most solemn moments, and when the tension was withdrawn, a sort of sigh rose up all through the church, as every one breathed audibly. I was standing not far from the high altar, where I had a full view of the Pope on his throne beneath St. Peter's Chair. We were packed together closely in the dense crowd, and not far from me were two Englishmen. When the definition was pronounced, one of them said to the other, ' The only thing now remaining is for the faithful to believe it.' By an irresistible impulse I instantly said, ' Believe it, sir ? We believe it with all our hearts and souls.' Oh, how grateful I felt to that man ! The relief he gave to my heart was immense, and he little knew the favour he conferred on me. The moment in God's good providence had come when, with all the certainty of Divine faith, we knew from the unerring voice of the Vicar of Christ that God had revealed the glorious fact that the Mother of God was Immaculate in her Conception."

CHAPTER V.

1850—1861.

BISHOP WAREING of Northampton had provided John Morris, after his conversion, with the scholarship at the English College, on which he lived till his ordination. To Bishop Wareing, therefore, he returned when he came back from Rome in the summer of 1850. After acting as the Bishop's secretary for a short time, he was appointed chaplain to Mr. Scott Murray of Danesfield, who from that time forward became his most valued and constant friend, while Danesfield was more truly his home than any other house in England. Thirty years later, when Mr. Murray died, Father Morris wrote a short notice of his life in the *Tablet*.[1] He would no doubt have spoken even more fully than he did about his former friend and patron, had not the latter expressly desired that no sort of panegyric should be pronounced over him. In this notice Father Morris mentions many particulars about the place, in which he was now to pass some very happy years, and these will form an excellent background for our narrative of this portion of his life. We cannot do better than reproduce them here.

"Danesfield takes its name from a well-marked Danish encampment on one of the loveliest reaches

[1] *The Tablet*, September 2, 1882.

of the Thames, between Marlow and Henley; and Mendenham Abbey, of which little that is really ancient remains, is below the house, on the river's bank. The estate includes a portion of the parish of Hambleden, where St. Thomas of Hereford was baptized. . . .

"When Mr. Scott Murray came to live there, after his conversion, Danesfield became one of those centres of Catholic influence and edification, the multiplication of which is almost as important an element in the conversion of England as the multiplication of her priests and religious communities. This was one of the Catholic houses in which Cardinal Wiseman felt at home, and it was here that he was first received with the state belonging to his rank, on his return to England as its first Cardinal Archbishop.

"As soon as he entered into possession, Mr. Scott Murray decided to build a church, and consulted Bishop Wareing, then Vicar Apostolic of the Eastern District. The Bishop said that, seeing there were no Catholics in the neighbourhood, he would be quite justified in selecting as a site for his church the place that would be most convenient to himself. 'But I should like to place it where it would be most useful,' said Mr. Scott Murray. 'In that case, no doubt it should be in the town of Great Marlow,' was the Bishop's advice, and in Great Marlow it was accordingly built, at a distance of two miles and a half from Mr. Murray's house at Danesfield. This involved the necessity of the whole family going up and down that distance to Mass on Sundays, giving the angels many footsteps to count.

"The Church of St. Peter in Great Marlow is a little gem, designed by the elder Pugin, consisting of a nave and one aisle, a chancel, and a Lady chapel, with a tower and a spire all in miniature. The niches are filled with the figures of the patron saints of the family, and one of the chief ornaments is the beautiful family tomb, where the founder is this day laid.[1]

Not content with this beautiful church, and the priest's modest house adjoining to it which he bought, Mr. Murray in the course of time built excellent poor schools and a convent for the Sisters of Charity of St. Paul, who have now taught the schools for many years. He settled a moderate endowment on the mission, and the church was erected into a benefice by the first Bishop of Northampton, which act of erection was confirmed in a Brief by His Holiness Pius IX.

"Still Mr. Scott Murray's zeal for the glory of God's house and for the good of souls was not satisfied, and later on he established a second mission for the benefit of his tenants at Danesfield. The domestic chapel was the very last work executed by Mr. Augustus Welby Pugin, just before the sad malady came that clouded his brilliant genius. The chapel is extremely simple in design, and very striking in effect—a worthy reproduction of the style of the thirteenth century. The interior decorations were designed by Mr. Edward Welby Pugin. The chapel furniture and ornaments are in the most perfect keeping, and it would not be easy to find anywhere in England two churches that breathe the spirit of devotion more thoroughly than Danesfield and Great Marlow. Mr. Scott Murray took the liveliest interest in every detail, and they remain as witnesses to his perfect taste, as well as to the more valuable possession of a spirit of self-sacrifice and desire for the greater glory of God.

"When Mass was first said at Great Marlow, in a room that Mr. Scott Murray hired before his church was built, the congregation consisted of Mr. Scott Murray himself, the priest's sister, and one good old Irishwoman from Cookham. The mission had indeed

1 The date of publication is September 2, 1882.

grown since then. The church was consecrated in July, 1846, and the first priest was the Rev. Peter Coop. He was soon succeeded by the Redemptorist Fathers, who held the mission till 1851, in which time their zeal had succeeded in providing the little church with a congregation."

It was at this time that Father Morris took over the charge of the parish, and devoted to it the first vigorous years of his manhood. If there was no probability in the nature of things of a rapid extension of the mission, there was no remissness on the part of its pastor in preaching and organizing. The following letters manifest the spirit in which he commenced and carried on his work.

"St. Peter's Church, Great Marlow, April 3, 1851.

"My dear Mr. Scott Murray,—My first week has spent itself, so I write to report progress. I am beginning to know something of the people, and am getting accustomed to our pretty little church and its work. I came home last night very tired from my first expedition in search of a confessor. I managed to find my way to Stonor very well, but coming back I got into the woods above Hambleden, which lengthened my ride. I said Mass in the morning at Danesfield, where all the household seemed very flourishing and happy. They have been indefatigable in coming in to my Wednesday and Friday evening services. The people generally seem to like them, and my congregations have been really very good. .

"Perhaps you have heard how Mr. Harper contrived to take all the poetry out of our beginning pastoral work. He had just been ordained doorkeeper, and his first use of his new order was to lock one of the 'sheep of Marlow' into the church for the whole night. When I went into the church at six to ring the *Angelus,* I thought

I had myself unlocked the door, and was proportionably surprised to see a bonnet praying at the high altar. The bonnet edified me considerably, because after a night's vigil it did not even turn round when I entered the church. It was Charlotte Beckett, and her grandfather had sat up for her till three o'clock. She was not the least afraid, she says.

"I am meditating an improvement in the Vespers, which will I expect astonish the people a good deal. I am thinking of having a procession during the *Magnificat*, in order to incense the Lady altar. However, I have not yet broached my daring scheme to any one. . . .

"Half a dozen of the 'sheep of Marlow' have decamped: the 'sheep' being the Eatons, who live in the gardens. I see Father van Antwerpen has entered them in the Register as 'Heathens.' . . .

"Harper and myself send our respects to Mrs. Scott Murray, and I remain,

"Yours ever very faithfully,

"JOHN MORRIS."

"*September* 15, 1851.— . . . My Harper leaves me to-morrow for Hodder, and I shall be alone in my glory. I hope I may not do something desperate before you come back. Vespers went capitally last night. Samuel Harman in choir. Wray disabled. We took the alternate verses of the hymn downstairs, *Vexilla Regis*, and that too without a practice, and with very good effect.

"The meeting to congratulate Father Newman was most successful. The Bishop compared him to Tertullian, in a very good speech. The *Times* thinks the meeting was held to thank him for the *Discourses to Mixed Congregations*. There is no other news whatever. D.C.L. has got Archbishop Sumner, the Dean of

Bristol, and Lord Palmerston (who has been bishoping another chaplain) to worry. Saturday's *Chronicle* has a column of the Archbishop's journal, writ years hence *à la* Burnet, and 'mighty fine.' What a comfort there is no sin in cutting up a *Protestant* Bishop, at all events —*persequar et impugnabo.*

"Finally, I have written to Pugin about the Madonna; and in saying this I have finished my stock of topics, unless I give way to the temptation to write slang, against which I have been striving, and say, in the words of my favourite, that the 'cows is well, the pigs is well, and the boys is bobbish.'

          "Yours very faithfully,

             "JOHN MORRIS."

               "St. Peter's [August], 1852.

"My dear Mr. Murray,—What a bore it is when people are too good. Now, that good Bishop of Southwark made me write to the Bishop of North-hampton to ask *him* to bless our image, and, failing that, to give leave for his *confrère.* The answer is: 'My very dear John,—May Heaven bless and reward your kind and zealous feelings and exertions with regard to Marlow House! As to the inauguration of the image of our Blessed Lady, let *me* have that gratification; giving me due notice and letting the ceremony not take place on a Sunday. At present, I am quite unable to be absent from St. Felix on the Sunday. I beg that the Bishop of Southwark will preach, pontificate, and consecrate the altar-stones, as you request; and I feel under obligation to his lordship for his kindness in doing so. . . . Don't despair of Wycombe: when you come to have a coadjutor, you will both have enough to do.' Write to these good Bishops I must at once, but I am puzzled because I cannot talk the matter over with you first."

After discussing the various contingencies under these circumstances, he settles the matter by arranging to have two functions instead of one.

These letters certainly give us a very pleasant picture of the life of a country parish priest. So to describe his life sums up in fact all that can be said about it, except for a few less ordinary features and one public affair. The less ordinary features sprang from his marked predilection for the study of Canon Law and his facility with his pen. It was the time of the restoration of the Hierarchy, and he was employed by his Bishop in drawing up the necessary documents for the foundation of the Diocesan Chapter, and in other work of a like nature. So far, indeed, was he already trusted, that he was himself appointed canon on the 24th of June, 1852, though not quite twenty-six years of age. He also found time for literary pursuits, contributing articles to the *Rambler* on Rubrics, Canon Law, &c.,[1] and for reading with a pupil or two. He appears at this time to have taken more seriously to historical studies, of which his *Life of St. Thomas of Canterbury* was afterwards to be the first-fruit.

The one public affair alluded to, was the conflict between Mr. Scott Murray and the Lord Chief Justice of England, Father Morris's appointment as chaplain to the High Sheriff being the *casus belli*. As the event· was a significant one, we may quote his own account which was printed in the *Tablet*.

"On being appointed High Sheriff, in 1852, Mr. Scott Murray ascertained from Sir Charles Tempest, who had recently filled the same office in Lancashire, what had been the practice in that county with respect to the chaplain of a Catholic High Sheriff. Sir Charles told him that he had had a Jesuit Father for his chaplain, and so Mr. Scott Murray, fearing no oppo-

---

[1] Under the heading, "The Priest's Portfolio," 1850, 1851.

sition, took with him the priest from Great Marlow. The Assize was opened at Aylesbury by Mr. Justice Crompton. The High Sheriff took him with the usual state to the Protestant church, and then drove to the Catholic chapel, where Mass was said and a sermon preached. The chaplain [*i.e.*, Father Morris himself] was present in court and at the dinner given, according to the custom of the county, to magistrates of the shire, and all were so friendly that there was nothing to indicate that a storm was brewing. The next day the Lord Chief Justice Campbell came down, and was received by the High Sheriff and his chaplain at the railway station. Lord Campbell showed himself much disturbed, but still the High Sheriff was not led to expect what followed. The Lord Chief Justice charged the jury in condemnation of the High Sheriff, who had brought into court 'a Roman Catholic priest in the vestments of his order,' which, as may well be imagined, was not the case. The grand jury brought in a present-ment to express their concurrence in the indignation of the Chief Justice, and the next morning the *Times* newspaper published a leading article which re-echoed the thunder.

"At first public opinion was against Mr. Scott Murray, but the tide was completely turned by the publication of two extremely able letters in the *Times* which were written by the late Mr. James Hope Scott, Q.C., who maintained that the chaplain was the Sheriff's chaplain, and not the chaplain of Her Majesty's Judges. Mr. Hope Scott had, amongst other arguments, stated that the shrievalty was a judicial office, and Lord Campbell virtually abandoned the battlefield by writing a short letter to the *Times*, saying in a bantering tone that he had not been aware that he had been treating with a brother-judge. The proof of the victory Mr. Scott Murray had gained was that, when the next Assize came round, Mr. Baron Parke, afterwards Lord Wensleydale, assented without diffi- culty to the presence of the High Sheriff's Catholic chaplain, and permitted all that which Lord Campbell had objected to."

Two letters respecting the pleasant termination of this affair, addressed by Father Morris and Mr. Scott Murray to Mr. Serjeant Bellasis, who had been one of Mr. Murray's most trusted advisers in the matter, may well find a place here.

"Aylesbury, April 15, 1852.

" My dear Serjeant,—You will, I am sure, be glad to hear that everything has gone off as pleasantly as possible this Assizes. . . . I went with the Judges in the carriage from the station to the court, but Mr. Murray went alone with them to and from the church. I was in the court during the opening of the com- mission, and for the first two or three trials the next day, since which time I have left the Judges in peace. The only sign that the Chief Baron's civility was against the grain, was that he kept one of his marshals close to him while I was in court, so as to prevent me from sitting on his left, where the chaplain usually sits. Both Judges have been very facetious, beginning to cut jokes as soon as they were in the carriage. To crown all, Mr. Murray got a note from Baron Parke, in his own and the Chief Baron's name, asking ' you and your chaplain ' to dinner this evening. If any other Sheriff had had such a letter, it would have been a fortune to us during that ' unequal contest.'

" To-morrow comes the nomination for the county. After which we propose to go to Oscott to see the conclusion of the Synod. .

" Yours very faithfully,

" JOHN MORRIS."

Mr. Scott Murray's letter is as follows :

"Yarmouth, July 18, 1852.

"My dear Serjeant,— .   I was so late in court on Thursday that I got Mr. Morris to write to you before I came out. He will have told you all that had occurred up to that time. The dinner-party at the Judges consisted only of themselves and marshals, Serjeant Byles, and Mr. O'Malley, Mr. Morris, and myself. The Judges were most civil, and made Mr. Morris say grace before and after dinner, and called him Mr. Chaplain. Both Judges drank wine with him, and Pollock having forgotten to sip his wine, imagining he had also forgotten to bow, went through the whole ceremony the second time, saying it was better to do so twice than omit the usual etiquette. Altogether nothing could have gone off better than the whole thing. The Judges, Pollock especially, were most amusing. . . . There was a very small attendance of magistrates, and all went off well with them. Mr. Coles, the clergyman who preached the sermon, we found to be a great Puseyite, and he fraternized with me and Mr. Morris wonderfully.

"As for the nomination, it went off more quietly than even at the last election, and was over before two o'clock. D'Israeli made a civil bow to Mr. Morris, with whom he afterwards came in contact, but I do not think that he looked pleased at his Roman collar. I cannot sufficiently thank you for your notes and all the share you have taken in what I think we may well reckon to have been a victory.

"Believe me yours very sincerely,
"C. R. Scott Murray."

Some Catholics may not have approved of Canon Morris's having attended the court, as he did in his biretta, cassock, and Roman collar, but this quasi-public episode was itself soon over, and life in Great Marlow settled down to its usual quiet course, from which indeed it had been but momentarily diverted.

The perfect uneventfulness of his surroundings was in truth in somewhat sharp contrast with the energetic activity of the parish priest;[1] nor can it surprise us to find that, much as the Canon loved the place for what it was, he found in it limitations under which he felt uneasy. For one thing his rapidity of thought and speech prevented his keeping quite in touch with his rustic parishioners. Moreover, the desire to become a Jesuit had grown greatly in strength since he had left Rome.

While in this state of unrest, he was offered the vice-rectorship of the English College, Rome; and, for reasons which will be given in his own words, he accepted it without delay, and was at his new post before midsummer, 1853. As his own reminiscences of his happy stay there have already been given, we pass at once to his return from Rome, which we find to have been influenced by the same reasons that led to his going thither. In February, 1856, he had an audience with the Holy Father, and asked leave to enter the Society. To his surprise the Holy Father went into the case readily, promised to reconsider the question of a dispensation from the mission oath, and indeed finally granted it.

Meanwhile the Canon, expecting a refusal, had written to Cardinal Wiseman, and told him of the petition which he had addressed to the Pope, and—in

---

[1] "The energy of Father Morris was very remarkable. I once said this, or something of the sort, to him in this house, and he replied: 'Oh! it's heart disease.'" (Extract from a letter of Canon Bernard Smith, his successor at Great Marlow, and its present parish priest.)

case that petition should be refused—asked to be transferred to the Westminster diocese.

The part of his letter referring to this matter is as follows :

"When the vice-rectorship of this College was first offered to me, I did not hesitate to express my willingness to accept it, because I thought that as long as I remained at Great Marlow, the Bishop might always say with truth that he could not spare me. I thought that if a successor could be found for me there, as has been fulfilled in the presentation of Mr. Bernard Smith, and if the time should ever come, which has now come, that I could truly say that there were young men perfectly fitted for my post of Vice-Rector, then if ever, the Holy Father would allow me to be a Religious.

"If my present application is refused, I shall be glad to return to the mission.

"I feel, however, one difficulty. I should wish exeedingly to be in London. I have had experience of a country mission, and I should feel much happier in leaving College again, if I could look forward to employment in a large town like London. Such employment, the Bishop of Northampton cannot offer me, and though I am not without fear that I may be acting somewhat irregularly, I beg your Eminence will excuse me if I ask your opinion whether it would be possible for me to be transferred to the diocese of Westminster. I should of course resign my Canonry into Bishop Wareing's hands, and I should ask you to put me at the bottom of the list of chaplains of some hard-worked chapel.

"Your Eminence's obedient servant,

"JOHN CANON MORRIS."

To carry on Father Morris' history we must now trace out the different steps of his transfer to the diocese of Westminster, in which, despite Canon Morris's frequent appeals, Cardinal Wiseman seems to have moved very slowly.

The first step was to entrust to him the care of the Church of St. Thomas of Canterbury at Fulham, the charge of which he commenced late in the same year. Of the beginning of his stay there is no record, but later on, necessity compelled him to address to the Cardinal a series of letters, beginning with the following, of which only a portion is given.

"St. Thomas's, Fulham, S.W., April, 1857.

"My Lord Cardinal,—I have allowed nearly six months to pass over my head at Fulham, without making to your Eminence any report of the state of the mission. I now, however, know quite enough of the resources, expenses, and needs of the church to be able to lay them before your Eminence.

"I will begin by a petition, I think that I must ask for the assistance of another priest. In addition to the work which my predecessor had, I have the charge of the new female prison called the Fulham Refuge, and as soon as the correspondence I am carrying on with the Poor Law Board is ended, as it soon must be, I shall have a long morning's work every week at the workhouse. By half-past twelve o'clock on Sunday I have said two Masses, walked two miles, and preached two sermons, not to mention a few words after the first Mass. There are about two thousand people in the parish, and I find that when the church, prison, work-house, and schools are attended to, I have done all I can, and the people are left undisturbed in their singular neglect of religion."

The laborious work which he had to get through (three priests are now employed on this mission) began soon to tell seriously upon his health, but on the 30th of April he is able to give a better report of himself to the Cardinal: "I thank your Eminence very much for your kind inquiries after me. The inflammation of the lungs is quite subdued, and if the doctor would only let me out of doors, which as yet he will not do, I would have paid my respects to your Eminence in person."

We find him next month taking a few days' holiday with Mrs. Manning at Chichester. But his complete recovery was slow, and he was soon after again confined to bed even on a Sunday. Sickness thus made the want of a coadjutor all the more urgent, and from the tone of his letters it is evident that he felt the strain acutely. While we sympathize with the trouble which he was undergoing, we cannot but feel interested in the lively picture of himself which these letters incidentally present. Thus he writes again, April 30: "It is not because I want relief for myself so much as because through my want of strength, much work, to the detriment of souls, is left undone . . that I ask for assistance; though I confess that I shall not long be able to bear the pressure of my Sunday morning." Six weeks later he writes again explaining the reasons of his inability to do all expected from him.

"June 10, 1857.

"My Lord Cardinal,—Your Eminence's unvarying kindness to me leads me to hope that you will hear with patience a word or two respecting myself. There are some kinds of work for which I have an aptitude and preference, and some which I find very uncongenial and do very badly. I like the pulpit, I am fond of ceremonies, and to all others I prefer paper work, and especially anything connected with Canon Law. On the other hand, I am a bad parish priest. As I am of a nervous, over-anxious temperament, the sense of responsibility in the cure of souls preys upon my health; and as intercourse with the poor is against the grain, to my shame be it said, I am consequently unsuccessful with them.

" I have had occasion to write to your Eminence before, saying how incapable I felt of carrying on the mission single-handed. Will you allow me to suggest that it would be greatly for the advantage both of the mission and of myself, if another priest could be appointed for the cure of souls, and I were made his coadjutor. . .

" I think that the priest could afford to give me board and lodging in return for the share I should take of his Sunday work; and I could take off his hands the institutions of the parish, that is, the workhouse and the prison, which are duties additional to those which Dr. Fergusson had to perform. I should thus have time to preach a little in London, when I grow somewhat stronger; and I should be at your Eminence's disposal for work of which I regard the compilation of the *Ordo* as an instalment, and which in connection with the Provincial Synods your Eminence was good enough to mention to me when writing to me in Rome. I should thus also be relieved of work for which my health and temperament unfit me, which I now perform most inefficiently, and the non-performance of which renders me very anxious and incapacitates me more than four times the quantity of more congenial work. . . .

" I am afraid that all this looks like a great wish to have that only to do which I like best, and I therefore once more place myself absolutely at your Eminence's disposal, and I will do my very best over the work upon which you may decide for me.

" Your Eminence's most obedient servant,

" JOHN MORRIS."

This letter he had left at the Cardinal's house, and on his return home thought well to supplement it by another in which he says : " I hope your Eminence would not feel any delicacy at sending a priest more recently ordained than myself to take charge of the place. My half allegiance to the diocese, as it stands at present, might serve as an excuse; and if your Eminence chose to give me charge of the prison, for instance, I should be rather living with him than under him. It is, however, only the simple truth to say, that I should not feel the remotest awkwardness at being made the second priest."

Not long after this the Cardinal found means to act upon Canon Morris's suggestion, and appointed the Rev. Father Rymer to the charge of the mission, much to the delight of his predecessor, who had been gratified shortly before by the post, which most people would probably have dreaded, of editor of the *Ordo celebrandi Missam.* This is the Canon's acknowledgment of the receipt of the honour conferred.

" *April* 30.—I feel much pleased at being entrusted by your Eminence and the Bishops with a work, for which I have so strong a fancy, that of the compilation of the *Ordo.* Hitherto I have amused myself by criticizing ; I shall now have to see how I like being criticized in turn. I have the disadvantage of being almost destitute of the necessary books. If your Eminence will furnish me with the requisite information, for instance, a copy of one for the past years, I shall have much pleasure in drawing up the *Ordo* for your own private use."

So at last he is settled down at the work which he thoroughly likes, and with surroundings that were all to his taste, but circumstances soon led him elsewhere. Viscount Campden asked him to undertake the post of tutor to his son Charles, the present Earl of Gainsborough, and Cardinal Wiseman recommended him strongly to accept the appointment. Canon Morris did not hesitate to do so, though rather regarding the project as an experiment, than expecting to find that teaching was his vocation in life. In truth he was never engaged in it again. The following letter tells us, both his contentment with his present circumstances and his plan for finally returning to them.

"St. Thomas's, Saturday.

" My dear Lord Cardinal,— . . . The arrangements which your Eminence so kindly made for me at Fulham suit me exactly. I am of sufficient use to the priest not to feel that I am any burden on the mission. I have enough missionary work to prevent my feeling that I am deserting a priest's highest duties. I have leisure for the paper work, which I should be sorry to lay aside; and I am enabled to go up to the limit of my strength in desultory London work. This is precisely the state of things in which, according to my own estimate, I can be most useful. I should not easily find another place as conveniently near London, and with the actual work (and that too for the most part independent of the missionary priest) and yet with no more work than this. I consequently feel exceedingly unwilling to leave my present moorings altogether. .

" I have always thought myself very deficient in some of the qualities required for the charge of children, so that though I am quite willing to try, yet I am conscious that it is but an experiment. Lord Campden tells me that he would be content to make an engagement for a twelvemonth: this, therefore, is what I wish to propose.

"Your Eminence was kind enough to say that you would call any such engagement with Lord Campden *a visit*. That is just what I wish to call it. If they should wish it to end before the year is up, they would be at perfect liberty to say so. I will undertake to stay the twelvemonth, if they will hold me at its close as free as I am now. And I want to ask your Eminence to regard me as *not leaving Fulham*.

"Your most obedient servant,
"JOHN CANON MORRIS."

In accordance with this plan he went from Fulham at the close of the year 1857, and joined Lord Campden's household. The letters which he wrote during the year he thus spent, partly in London, mostly at Campden House, are of comparatively little service to a biographer; but one to Mr. Scott Murray, dated June 24, 1858, contains a sentence which shows that his *Life of St. Thomas of Canterbury* was making progress: "A book that would amuse you endlessly is Benedictus Abbas Petroburgensis, *De Miraculis S. Thomæ*. It is more amusing than any modern book, except Pickwick. *Salva reverentia Sancti mei dictum sit*."

The following letter to the same closes this period.

"September 6, 1858.

"The fortnight you thought of asking the Bishop for the loan of me would have been very pleasant indeed. . . . We had a very agreeable visit from the dear old Provost (Husenbeth), but he was obliged to go straight back again to Cossey, and could not take

Danesfield in his way. He said that Lord Stafford
would be sure to tell you that he never was absent on
Sunday. I like him very much. I drove him over to
Brailes, where there is an old schoolfellow of his, who
has been eight-and-thirty years and more at that
mission. Their meeting and heaps of old recollections
of Sedgley Park were very amusing. I have been
lately at Malvern Wells with the children, and (having
come back here for the Sunday) I am writing to know
what Lord Campden's arrangements are for the return
of the children. I think it not improbable that I shall
return there to rejoin them for a few days longer, but
I shall know to-night when Lord and Lady Campden
turn up, bringing I believe, Canon Oakeley with
them

" I get very good accounts from Jersey,[1] I am happy
to say. . . .

"Yours very faithfully,
"JOHN MORRIS."

Canon Morris' plan of returning to Fulham was not
destined to be carried out. Bishop Wareing resigned
the see of Northampton in February, 1858, and was
succeeded by Bishop Amherst, who recalled his subject
to his own diocese and appointed him, November 3,
1858, Diocesan Archivist, Notary, and Ceremonialist;
and he spent the next twelvemonth in discharging these
offices and that of secretary to the Bishop. The one
event of importance which took place during that time

---

[1] This refers to his own family. Canon Morris' father, who was also
a friend of Mr. Scott Murray, had died at St. Helier on the 2nd of
August, and was buried in St. Saviour's churchyard on August 7th. " I
should greatly like to see Jersey again," writes the Canon to the Bishop of
Portsmouth in September, 1884, " if it could be got at without a sea voyage.
I have only been there once, and that was to attend my father's funeral.
However, Jersey is likely to continue an island, and therefore, if for no
other reason, my wish to visit it will be inefficacious."

was the publication of his *Life of St. Thomas of Canterbury,* which we shall notice more fully in treating of his literary work.

A year was thus passed in secretarial work, agreeable to himself, but leaving little to record that is of interest to others. Towards the end of the year, however, an event took place which renewed all his previous repugnance to the duties of a parish priest in the provinces. Mgr. Eyre had retired from the charge of the church at Northampton, and, for lack of another priest to take his place, Bishop Amherst placed Canon Morris in charge of the mission. The change was the more distasteful to him as he had just before been engaged, to his heart's content, as secretary to the Third Provincial Synod of Westminster. But we may let him express his sentiments in his own way.

"Bishop's House, Northampton, September 3, 1859.

"My dear Mr. Scott Murray,—I was very sorry that I had not a few more minutes to speak to you when at the Synod, but it was like being in a factory and having to attend to the working of some great piece of machinery. I never enjoyed a fortnight more, and I am sure I derived more pleasure from the Synod than any one else. . .

"Mgr. Eyre has left Northampton, and I have consequently temporary charge of this friendless mission. I need not say that I do not like it, for the cure of souls is not my line, and it is not improved by the indefiniteness of the term, as I am sure I do not know where the Bishop is to find a man for this place. I hope that you will pray that he may find a thoroughly good missionary, for the place is an important one, and a great deal of good might be done here.

"The Bishop has started on a tour of visitation in Suffolk, and will be away all this month, or nearly so.

I am disappointed at not being able to go with him, but it can't be helped. Neither do I know how I can hope to accompany the Bishop on his visit to you, to which I have been looking forward for ever so long. I have always been afraid of this particular fix.

"With my kindest regards to Mrs. Scott Murray and the children,

"I remain, my dear Mr. Scott Murray,

"Yours very faithfully,

"JOHN MORRIS.

When a man owns himself to be in a fix, of which he has long been afraid, it is not surprising to find him taking efficacious means to avoid a like predicament in future. Hence we are prepared to hear of decided steps in furtherance of the scheme of the transfer to London; and indeed, at the very beginning of the next year, his Bishop granted Canon Morris leave to pass to the Westminster diocese.

Father Morris, however, was to retain his canonry in Northampton together with the accompanying obligation of returning for the Chapter meetings. This continued for more than a year, when, on the death of Canon Long, who had been Canon Penitentiary of Westminster, a *concursus* was held for the appointment of a successor. For this, with the leave of his Bishop, Canon Morris presented himself on September 10th, and was pronounced the "most worthy" by the examiners, of whom Provost Manning was the first. The stall was accordingly conferred upon him by Cardinal Wiseman on the 18th of the same month, and Canon Morris, after resigning his preferment at Northampton, and making his solemn profession of faith before the Chapter at St. Mary's, Moorfields, was admitted by the Provost to the possession of his canonry on the last day of the same month.

CHAPTER VI.

CANON OF WESTMINSTER.

1861—1867.

CANON MORRIS had repeatedly expressed his wish to be employed as a secretary in some work connected with London, should his desire to enter the Society of Jesus not be granted. Such desire had for the present passed into abeyance, and so he entered upon the alternative course which he had proposed. That his choice of occupation was a wise one this chapter will probably show. Not that it records many or striking occurrences; on the contrary, it places him before us chiefly as identified with his work, and a better proof of his aptitude for it could hardly be found. Since, however, it would be impossible to give a full account of that work without involving a history of the whole diocese, it has been thought better to publish certain letters which represent him to us as fully active in one department, and thus enable us to form a fair idea of his general life at this time.

When Canon Morris came to London disabilities still pressed heavily on Catholics, and a Committee had been formed to obtain redress for the poor who laboured under very irksome restrictions in the workhouses, prisons, and elsewhere.[1] The Canon was appointed

---

[1] Many priests and gentlemen joined in this good work. But they gave their aid so unostentatiously that it is impossible to find out what persons deserve to be specially mentioned. Canon Morris's part, however energetically he filled it, was of course a subordinate one. The Hon.

Secretary to this Committee, and in an article published by him in the *Dublin Review* for August, 1860, he set forth some of the grievances complained of. Certain quotations from this article will explain the object for which he was working, and will throw light on a state of things that is now, we are glad to say, considerably changed for the better.

He begins by showing that the grievances of the adult poor were then neither few nor light. The inmates of the workhouses were almost entirely at the mercy of the Guardians, whose treatment of their charges was as varied as it was vexatious. Catholics had to be present at Protestant prayers and hymns, it was rarely that they found out that they were not bound to take part in Protestant Services. As a rule no priest visited them, and if he did so, it was not until he had been formally applied for by the pauper, which application in many cases was through an excess of bigotry required *toties quoties*, before the priest was admitted to see the sick and dying. The Guardians could allow the poor to go to church, but they often exacted the most tyrannical conditions before they did so, sometimes not permitting the inmates to attend church till they had reached the age of sixty years.

Canon Morris then continues: "Hard as the spiritual lot of the adult inmate is, the lot of the child is ten thousand times worse. The present administration of the Poor Law may be fairly characterized as a system on a very large scale for changing the religion of the children of the Catholic poor who come under its operation.

Charles Langdale was its chairman, Dr. Bagshawe, now Bishop of Nottingham, Canon Macmullen, Mr. Richard Swift, Father Gallwey, and Mr. Edward Riley, were its originators, or early promoters. Lord Edward Howard and Sir George Bowyer in Parliament, and Mr. Serjeant Bellasis as a lawyer, lent it all the assistance in their power.

Thousands are thus lost to the Church and the religion of their fathers. In fact, we would ask, was any child ever known to have been through one of these workhouse or district schools, . . . and to have come out a Catholic? We sincerely confess that we doubt it. . . . Where every facility is given under the present system the children fall away when they come out of the workhouse. What must happen when no facilities whatever are afforded, or where, as in the metropolis, an hour in the week, or even less, is all that is at the priest's disposal to counteract the whole tone of the life the child leads and of the education it receives?

" We beg our readers' attention particularly to the fact that of the two thousand three hundred children in the district schools only nine ever see a priest. . The trouble that the clergy have had to go through has been great indeed, in order to obtain access to this small number. And when they have succeeded in getting all the requisite formalities accomplished, what good can they hope to do under the present system? In the great majority of cases the children never assist at Mass, hear a sermon, or enter the doors of a Catholic church. Their secular instruction is taken from books written by Protestants, and taught to them .by Protestants. They live in a thoroughly Protestant atmosphere, and the strongest influence of all to which children can be subjected—the influence of the public opinion of the children amongst whom they are—is Protestant. Nobody but the Protestant Alliance will oppose us, if we ask that Catholic children may be given into Catholic hands, and that the Guardians should pay towards their maintenance what they now cost the rates. When justice can be done without any expense, there are very few amongst us who would not be glad to do it."

K

Here was an undeniable grievance, but happily Canon Morris's concluding words proved true, and no protracted resistance was made to its correction. Yet the labour involved was not inconsiderable while it lasted. A Parliamentary Committee was first obtained to report on the proposed amendment to the Poor Laws, Canon Morris's special work being to collect the evidence that was to be brought before it. Sample cases had been selected from various parts of the country, and confirmatory evidence secured, no easy operation when the witnesses are poor and cannot be forced to attend by a subpœna. When all was prepared the matter came before the Committee. The following letter gives an account of the first day there.

"45, Devonshire Street, W., May 28, 1861.

" My dear Lord Cardinal,—It is in the early morning of the 29th in reality, that I am writing, but as the excitement of the afternoon prevents my sleeping a wink, I have got up to tell your Eminence how we got on. We started by narrowly escaping a serious calamity. Mr. Farnall came up to us and said that *he* was going on first, that he would state all our grievances for us and acknowledge them, that it therefore would not be necessary for us to bring any witnesses, &c. As clearly an official was not likely to know as much about our grievances as we, whom the shoe pinches, Lord Edward Howard stood up for having me first. I was accordingly under examination all the afternoon, and have only got through the case of the adults. I appear again on Friday with the children. We had one serious *contretemps*. I had prepared Sir John Acton to examine me, and he was thoroughly up in the case, when he was prevented from attending by a Private Bill Committee, attendance at which is compulsory. Sir George took it up, and the result was we jogged along very roughly at the start, and I was afraid that it would prove a failure: but the running improved as we warmed to our work. I will borrow a member's copy of the evidence, if possible, for your Eminence. The Committee was very civil, and though of course they consider many points as insufficiently proved, I do not think that much passed which can be used against us. Archbishop Cullen was in the room. Mr. Villiers beckoned Mgr. Manning to a good place.

" Your very faithful servant,

" JOHN MORRIS."

There is no report of the Friday's evidence, but a fortnight later, he writes that the progress of the Committee has been favourable. Mr. Villiers has conducted the examination " splendidly," drawing from Protestant witnesses " plenty of admissions that strengthen our cause." On June 19, he reports a " glorious day with the Committee." Mr. New brought out his cases " capitally," and " the master of the Marylebone Workhouse has been summoned for examination." The next report says that, when he came he " gave excellent evidence in our favour, . . . winding up with adding that the discipline would be decidedly improved if Mass were said in the house." With this the Catholic case before the Committee was concluded " most satisfactorily," in Canon Morris's opinion.

The progress of the amendment in Parliament corresponded with its prosperous start in Committee, and the measure desired became law in the course of the ensuing year, Canon Morris having plenty to do meanwhile in supplying the Catholic members with the necessary information. The work grew under his hands for another reason.

One good work often suggests and paves the way for another, so here while one Committee was advocating

the claims of workhouse children, a second Committee
was being formed to advocate measures to improve the
spiritual condition of Catholic prisoners. Canon Morris
was again offered the secretaryship. "But I bargained
for my holiday," he says, "and was told I might name
a substitute during my absence, and I have got
Mr. Butler to undertake it."

It was not unnatural for him to make this arrangement under the circumstances. Two days later he
reports, "To-morrow will be a busy day. There is a
meeting at eleven with Lord Edward Howard and the
sub-committee on his prisons motion; at twelve the
Parliamentary Committee, where I want to say a few
words as supplementary to my evidence; at 4.30,
i.e., as soon as we get away from the House of
Commons, St. Anselm's Society meets; and in the
evening I shall have Benediction at the convent, and a
school festivity." The next day he mentions again
that various employments have "made to-day's work
a hard one." The strain must have been severe, before
a man with his love of work would have alluded to it
so frequently as he did at the time.

It is a satisfaction to be able to add that these
labours were followed by adequate results. Those who
consult Lilly and Wallis's excellent *Manual of law
specially affecting Catholics*, will see that the chief measures
whereby the very substantial liberties which the Catholic
poor and Catholic prisoners now enjoy, were for the
most part obtained in the years immediately following
the labours of the Catholic Committees. It was in 1862
that the Poor Law Amendment (Certified Schools) Act
was passed, with further amendments in 1866 and
1868; the Prisons Ministers Act became law in 1863,
the Prisons Act in 1865, and in 1866 a Reformatory
and Industrial Schools Act. By these measures the
chief safeguards to the faith of the Catholic poor,

which were contended for by Canon Morris, are secured. Our poor children may be educated in Catholic schools, an accessible creed-register is kept in workhouses, the inmates of which may go to their own places of worship, where no religious service is provided for them within the house. Catholic priests are paid on a fixed scale to attend the various prisons.

From the above description of one of Canon Morris's occupations we may deduce a fair general idea of the course of his life at this time. Being in frequent contact with many sorts of men, as well with those who held public positions or had attained literary distinction, as with those who lived in religious retirement, his experiences would have enabled him to write a most interesting series of recollections. On the other hand, this very variety of his occupations makes it difficult for us to follow him with regularity and precision, while the part he played in each undertaking, though often toilsome, was rarely an important one. In general terms it may be said that his work was primarily secretarial. Upon him, as Secretary to the Vicariate, devolved the preparation of documents for the meetings and deliberations of the Bishops and other functionaries, as well as the drawing out of statements as to the Resolutions they had passed. These it was his duty to forward to Rome and to communicate the answers of the Congregations addressed to the persons concerned. There was work of a similar nature in connection with the Westminster Synods, and as Penitentiary to the diocese cases of conscience of many sorts were referred to him for solution. He had a part in the responsibility of keeping the finances in order, and the care of providing subjects for discussion at various conferences of the clergy, in which Cardinal Wiseman took special interest. Then there were confraternities of the faithful to be erected canonically, and too often the informalities of previous erections to be set right. Preaching he was always fond of, and having therein a considerable power and facility, he was frequently called upon for his services. Add to all this the routine work of a chaplain and a confessor, and it will be evident that in this position, as in others, he well merited his reputation of being a diligent labourer in his Lord's vineyard.[1]

It is further worth while remarking that he was then living on an income which was barely sufficient for a decent maintenance. When he came to London in 1859 he had agreed to undertake chaplain's duty at two convents of nuns, one of which had previously remunerated its chaplain at the rate of £60 a year. For the same amount of work Canon Morris now accepted £30 on condition that his income for all services should be made up to £100 a year. Not long after a re-division of districts was made, and attendance at the convent, with the £30 salary, was assigned to another priest. While Canon Morris's income was thus reduced to £70 a year, the other began to think himself illiberally treated, seeing that a predecessor had received twice as much as he, for the same services rendered.

When Canon Morris heard this, and the circumstance of the previous salary, of which he had been till then ignorant, he wrote very frankly to Cardinal Wiseman, submitting the case to his judgment.

"45, Devonshire Street, W., January 31, 1862.

" My dear Lord Cardinal,—I want to ask your Eminence's advice on a matter that has but just

---

[1] In proof of the number and variety of the calls on his time the following may be quoted. Writing on October 24, 1864, to Mr. Scott Murray, he says, "It is a bore for me that just at my busiest time, I have had to dawdle to-day, and shall have to attend to-morrow at the Old Bailey, as a witness against that O.J.C. man, who wanted to convert the Jews by a Puseyite Religious Order, and who turns out to be a swindler."

come before me, and which embarrasses me not a little. [After describing the circumstances we have just referred to, he continues:]

"With the information of Mr. ——'s salary comes the conviction that if Mr. —— has any ground of complaint on the manner of the division, it is against me, and not against the nuns that it lies. It is in this, therefore, that I ask your Eminence's kind guidance. What portion of the £70 I receive from the nuns shall I make over to Mr. ——?

"I cannot say that it is a matter of indifference to me because I am now living on *prospects*, which of course do not make it easy to make present ends meet. The Prisons Committee promised me £100 a year, but I do not suppose it is yet the possessor of £20 of its own, nor have I dared for six months past to take anything more from the Workhouse Committee, in dread of the lawyer's bill which this Committee must some day receive and meet. So that with the exception of Blundell, £1 12s. 9d., and an acceptable £7 4s. for an article in the *Dublin*, my last two quarters' receipts have been £17 10s., *i.e.*, £35 from the nuns for the half year. For the future, I have £40 coming in May from the *Ordo and Directory*, and a brilliant but precarious prospect from the prisons.

"My natural shyness makes it easier for me to write this to your Eminence, though I am coming out to Leyton to-morrow.

"Begging your Eminence's blessing on myself and all my occupations, I remain, my dear Lord Cardinal,
"Your very faithful servant,
"JOHN CAN. MORRIS.
"His Eminence Cardinal Wiseman."

How this incident ended, there is no present means of knowing. Incomplete as the account in itself is, it was sufficiently important to be mentioned here. Not long after, he received a small bequest which raised him above such petty anxieties for the future.

We may now, however, pass to a more important subject, the influence, namely, exerted by Cardinals Wiseman and Manning on the life which we are studying. Father Morris was during this and a subsequent period naturally brought into close relationship with their Eminences, and such intercourse could not fail to exercise a very considerable influence on his career and personal character.

He had become acquainted with Cardinal Wiseman not long after his conversion, and intimate relations had begun before he returned the second time to England in 1856, from which date he ever regarded the Cardinal as his special patron, referring constantly to him with singular confidence and openness. After finally joining the Westminster diocese, this confidence deepened into mutual affection and familiarity. They had many tastes in common. Both were scholars, though of different types. Cardinal Wiseman was the better linguist and theologian, Canon Morris a more accurate historian and lawyer. Wiseman's knowledge was extraordinarily comprehensive, Morris's remarkably precise. Both were of sanguine temperament and open character. Both were sincere well-wishers to the Gothic revival, but unswerving in their devotion to those Roman observances which custom had now fully sanctioned. Both, again, were enthusiasts for Canon Law and Rubrics. In Canon Morris's account of the Cardinal's final illness he tells us that one of the dying Prelate's last utterances was a whispered request to him respecting the ceremonies of the funeral. He said, with as much self-possessed calmness as though referring to some function he was himself about to perform, " I shall look to you and Patterson for the ceremonial. See that everything is done quite right. Do not let a rubric be broken." *Mutatis mutandis,* the expression of such a sentiment at such a moment would have suited Father Morris's character precisely.

A noble and noticeable feature characterizing each was an overwhelming love of the Church in all her Catholic breadth and dignity. Wiseman had this gift in a very marked degree. " I have never cared for anything but the Church," he exclaimed to Morris on his death-bed " My sole delight has been in everything connected with her. As people in the world would go to a ball for their recreation, so have I enjoyed a great function."

In Father Morris, too, this detailed yet all comprehensive devotion burnt with a like ardour. His enthusiasm for any particular branch of her work never hindered nor diminished his greater love for the Church as a whole. No doubt this excellent quality was much deepened and strengthened in him by his contact with Cardinal Wiseman. A firm friendship, however, as every one knows, needs other foundation to rest upon than simply similarity of character and tastes. It requires a certain dissimilarity also, a mutual giving and taking of what the one has to bestow and the other lacks. Such an exchange as this likewise found place between the two friends. Wiseman's decision of character, his wide aims, and reliance on his authority counterbalanced a tendency to changeableness and attraction for novelty which might have been observed at this time in his subordinate. While the latter could, on the other hand, supply what was wanting in his chief's power of attention to work and its details by his keen zest for formalities precise to the last particular, and an unfailing appetite for energetic work. If the Cardinal's nervous irritability as his bodily infirmities increased made him a difficult man to live with, the

Canon, on the other hand, was one who took a real satisfaction in overcoming such difficulties. Wiseman, again, leant somewhat to display, while his secretary affected severe simplicity; yet in their love for ecclesiastical ceremony they met on common ground, because it pleased the one by its grandeur and the other by its order and regularity.

We give here some of Father Morris's own avowals of the difficulties on his side, and of the way in which he overcame them. "When I was Cardinal Wiseman's secretary," he once remarked to another,[1] "I used often to notice that he seemed huffed with me from time to time. Sometimes I could make a shrewd guess at the cause of offence, and sometimes I was utterly puzzled as to what it could be. At first when I found him in this humour, I used to keep away from him, but I learned from experience that this rendered matters worse. So I made up my mind to pursue a different policy. Whenever I thought he was offended with me, I used to make a point of going to his room on some pretext or other, and talking to him on a general topic, altogether apart from the supposed subject of offence, and from any question that might prove a delicate one. Very often I would select some incident from the papers, and retail it to him; sometimes I even descended to the weather. It did not matter much what the subject of conversation was. I always found the result to be that the friendly relations which had been slightly interrupted were at once renewed, and he seemed to be as much relieved as I was. I have often tried the same plan with others since, and I have always found it successful."

Father Morris was engaged in carrying out what might have been a splendid memorial to his old chief,

[1] See "Some further Recollections of Father John Morris" published in *The Month* for December, 1893.

when his work was cut short by his death. He had been commissioned to write the Life of Cardinal Wiseman; the first chapter of which was already completed, together with some draught sketches of other episodes in the life, and he was arranging documents for the prosecution of the work when the end came to his own earthly career. No one could have possessed more exceptional advantages for carrying out such a work, and doubtless he would have shown in its execution the same genuine loyalty that he displayed, as we have just seen, in his personal intercourse with the Cardinal.

One scene in the Cardinal's life Canon Morris wrote long ago, with a master hand. His account of the last illness of Cardinal Wiseman is one of the best examples of his literary style. Almost photographic in its accuracy, nothing is carried to excess in the marshalling of details, while the picture and the pathos of the death scene are set before us with a simplicity, affection, and completeness which greatly help to awaken in the reader a new and irresistible sympathy with the character of the dying man. In proof of this the reader is so carried along with the interest of the story that he does not pause to notice the part which Canon Morris himself played in the scene.

At first we see him attending upon the Cardinal as a son might look after the failing years of his father. He accompanies him in his drives, and chats with him at his meals. With him the Cardinal rehearses the little speeches and short sermons he proposes to make at such ceremonies as he was able to attend. Their conversation wanders along over all manner of subjects, from the days and doings of boyhood even to the symptoms of death; but it turns most readily to the earlier times. Suddenly, on January 15, 1865, the Cardinal's vital strength seemed to fail him absolutely. He lost all consciousness, and it was with the greatest difficulty that the doctors could save him from immediate death. Then ensued a whole month of agony. Twice he received Extreme Unction, and five times the Holy Viaticum. Canon Morris was in constant attendance in the sick-room, with the exception of a fortnight, when to try the effects of entire rest the doctors would not allow their patient even to go to Holy Communion, a deprivation which drew from him the words, "They know not what they are depriving me of. A little fasting would tire me much less than this longing."

During the last ten days Canon Morris never left the bed-side, sleeping at its foot and saying Mass in an ante-room in presence of the sick man. When the Chapter was summoned to receive the Cardinal's dying commendations, it was Canon Morris who knelt close to him beside the bed and was commissioned by the dying Prelate to repeat to those around the words which he was himself too weak to utter aloud.[1]

One night, not long before the end, as the Cardinal lay wearied with his protracted agony, he begged the Mother Superior to bid him die out of pure obedience. As her courage broke down in trying to do this, Canon Morris was summoned. "I was sleeping," he narrates, "on the sofa at his feet, when Reverend Mother called me. He said to me, 'I wish to die out of pure obedience, *Cupio dissolvi et esse cum Christo.* Could you tell me to die?' I answered, 'You must wish to die when God wills, and to live as long as God wills.' 'Yes,' he said, that is what I wish; but *melius est*

---

[1] A scrap of note-paper from the Sister, the Mother Superior of the hospital at Great Ormond Street, who was engaged in nursing the Cardinal, intimates that Canon Morris has rather under than over stated the extent to which the Cardinal leant upon him at this supreme moment. He had, indeed, more trusted friends present, but from their advanced age they could not bear the honours of the bed-side so well as the young Canon.

mori et esse cum Christo;' and I shall never forget the plaintive, touching tone in which the last words were uttered. I rejoined, 'You will get all the merit of obedience, if I tell you to wish to live as long as God chooses, and to die when He chooses.' He said, 'Yes.' ' Then I bid you wish to live as long as God wills, and to die when He wills.' After a pause I added, 'Will you say, Give me here my Purgatory; in this sense that you wish to be with Christ and yet have to wait ? ' He answered, 'I will, I do. I say it from my whole heart. That is just what I mean.' .

" I suggested to him that he should use his present clearness of mind to make Acts of Faith, Hope, Charity, and Contrition. He replied, ' I will, do you make them for me out loud, slowly and distinctly.'

" I did so in the fewest possible words. He then said, ' I charge you, dear Canon Morris, as a Notary of the Roman Catholic Church, to record what I have just done in a solemn document, and to sign it in my name, to be kept always in the archives of the Church of Westminster; and say that I die in the faith and communion of the Roman Catholic Church; adding that I have never doubted nor wavered, and have always had those Acts in my heart which I have now made with my dying lips. Add also that more solemn Act which I made '—referring to his profession of faith before the Chapter. ' Do you accept my commission, and do you remember all I have said ? ' I answered, ' I remember every line of it, and will do all you have told me.' "

And so until the end, which came with extreme slowness, did Canon Morris continue his devoted and affectionate attendance upon the dying man. Of this sufficient has been said to show how close a bond of sympathy, confidence, and intimacy subsisted between them. Such relations are not unworthy of notice as illustrations of character, but here they are equally important as indicating how well disposed Canon Morris had been for profiting by the opportunities of the last few years, and how well he had learnt their lesson. He was but thirty when he came directly under Wiseman's influence, an age better fitted perhaps than any for gaining all the advantages of ecclesiastical training which circumstances then offered. It was one· of the most important periods of his life, and his firm hold on the esteem and affection of his chief proves that he had fully availed himself of his opportunity. A short period of apprenticeship to another Prelate of note alone remained to complete his ecclesiastical education before he entered upon the religious life in which he was to close his days.

" After Cardinal Wiseman's death I went," he writes, " to Brittany for change and rest. I had said Mass in the Cathedral at Quimper on a certain morning, and had gone into a *café* for my breakfast, when my eyes caught the words in a little French newspaper : *Monseigneur Manning a reçu ses bulles de Rome.* ' Our tour is over,' I said to my fellow-traveller, ' I shall have to go back now.' I telegraphed from Brest, 'If this news is true, send me your blessing,' and the answer, as I expected, was, ' Return at once. It is true, though I cannot understand it.' When I saw him, he said it had not been in his heart to desire that high station, if it were not for the good it would enable him to do."[1]

---

[1] When Father Morris, in 1875, wrote to offer the Archbishop his congratulations on his rumoured promotion to the Cardinalate, the answer was : "As to Rome I have no certain knowledge ; but they know that both personally, and for my life here, I had rather remain as I am." The paragraph quoted in the text is taken from Father Morris's article in *The Month* for February, 1892.

The term of secretaryship[1] which now ensued was in most respects similar to the last. There was the same participation in many important matters, a like proof of good workmanship, the same absence of any peculiarities distinctive of the workman. He stood, however, somewhat closer to his new chief in years, learning, and experience, than he had done to his former one. Both were converts, though there was of course no parity between their careers as Anglicans. Even before his conversion Father Morris refers to Dr. Manning in his letters with admiration, and the same spirit is constantly discernible in his subsequent correspondence. The most remarkable point in their various relations, and therefore the best for us to dwell on, was the very great affection and regard which each cherished for the other. Father Morris, like Pius IX., looked on the Archbishop as the providential man of his day. "Nicholas Cardinal Wiseman," he said, "was the man given us by Providence for his time: his successor, Henry Edward Cardinal Manning, was the providential man of the time that followed. All England might have been searched through and through, and no rival found for either." This thought he developed at length in two very felicitous articles in *The Month*,[2] the one written at the time of the Cardinal's Jubilee, the other at his death. For affectionate appreciation and truthful portraiture these short memoirs can well bear comparison with any of the notices which have been written about the Cardinal. Highly significant again is the compliment there paid by Father Morris to his old

---

[1] Archbishop Manning made a change in the titles of his *curia*. Mgr. Searle, who had been Secretary to the late Cardinal, now became Vicar-General. Canon Morris succeeded him as Secretary to the Archbishop ; and the secretaryship to the Vicariate lapsed.

[2] *The Month*, August, 1890, and February, 1892.

Superior by drawing out the points of similarity between him and St. Thomas of Canterbury, for Father Morris had deeply studied that Saint's character, and admired him as "one of the greatest Saints venerated by the Church."

Though not in the habit of preserving the letters sent to him, he had kept several written by Cardinal Manning, the character of which sufficiently shows that their intercourse was not dependent on letters for its continuance or true life and spirit. For they usually wrote to one another, as in the manner of friends, in a laconic off-hand style which, while it tells us little or nothing directly, serves indirectly to indicate the closeness of their intimacy.

The following letters may be quoted as a further illustration of the mutual relations we have been describing.

"Salford, August 18, 1877.

"My dear Father Morris,—I heard on Monday that you are going to Malta. Whatever you do in obedience is good; but that does not forbid me to say that I am sorry to lose you. Though I have written seldom I have never failed to cherish our old affection and confidence. And I have always thought of you as one who is seeking God's will and not your own.

"I do not know how soon you go, and fear that I may not see you. If I knew your time of going I would try to see you and bid you farewell. Let me have a line at the Bishop's House in Liverpool. May God be with you always.

"Yours affectionately in Jesus Christ,

"H. E. Cardinal Archbishop."

The next letter gives a list of places the Cardinal is to visit in the north of England.

" I say all this with little hope of your coming so far. If you could, it would give me great pleasure, and had it been a week later I should have been at Leeds.

" I believe that we have both retained the union which we had of old. I trust every blessing may be with you. As you say, the future is not with us, and in my seventieth year I feel the time to be short. May God bless and keep you.

" Believe me always,
" H. E. CARDINAL ARCHBISHOP."

" Archbishop's House, May 17, 1883

" My dear Father Morris,—I asked Father Whitty to-day to give you my love and to say that I had again and again wished to write to you. Canon Johnson told me of your kind inquiries. But I have only been able to keep up to the inevitable correspondence.

" I am, thank God, much better; but I have had more than four months of illness, with two *ricadute* which have pulled me down. The doctors say that there is nothing organically wrong, but I have been galloping for fifty years and I am wearing out. And I am thankful, and have no wishes or desires for anything but to make a good end.

" I hope you are well, and all your work prospering.

" The world has run fast down hill since you and I last talked about it. France is going a *rompicello*. We seem to be strangely restrained and in a manner self-controlled, thanks to the steady expansion of our political system. But will it last?

" Believe me always, yours affectionately,
" H. E. C. ARCHBISHOP."

" Archbishop's House, August 8, 1886.

" My dear Father Morris,—On St. Ignatius' day, at Farm Street, I heard with regret that you were obliged to rest; but I did not know that you were gone so far off. I am glad of it, for there is little rest near home, and Scotland is a fresh and, I hope, a bracing air to you. It is time that we should begin to crack a little, for we have had a good thirty years of work, a generation of men. But I hope you will soon come back with fresh force.

"I will write to the Holy Father and do all I can to speed our Martyrs. It would be a signal act for his Jubilee, and it would be a great joy for my last days to invoke publicly another St. Thomas. For privately I have long invoked him day by day.

"Thus far we have, I think, prospered in our cause.

"I hope you do not suffer so as to lose your rest.

"Believe me always, yours affectionately,

"Henry E. C. Archbishop."

Canon Morris remained in office as Archbishop Manning's secretary a little more than a year, and left at the end of 1866 to enter the Society of Jesus. The Archbishop's consent was given, unwillingly, it is true, but still freely and finally, as we shall afterwards see.

Later on, when Father Morris came to live in London, their intercourse was naturally resumed and became more constant, continuing to be this to the end. In a letter of Father Morris's, July 4, 1889, the following passage occurs:

"July 4, 1889.

"I have just come home from the Cardinal's. I had a long talk with His Eminence, who looks wonderfully well, and chatted with his usual friendliness. He said I had left him when his work was only beginning. I told him I had never been able to feel sorry for doing so."

CHAPTER VII.

WHEN Father Morris became a Jesuit he had already passed through a very complete course of training in ecclesiastical affairs. He had, as we have seen, made his theological studies at Rome, where the spirit, teaching, and method of government of the Church can be most readily learnt and appreciated. He there also acquired something of the practice of canon law by attending the ecclesiastical courts and undertaking several commissions in them. As a priest in England he had lived sometimes in quiet retirement as a tutor or chaplain, at other times he had undertaken charge of a country parish or laboured in a populous but poor mission close to London. He had acted as Secretary to a Bishop, and to a Cardinal, and had filled the office of Penitentiary to a diocese. And now towards the close of his fortieth year he entered the Society of Jesus, having contemplated this step for half his life-time, that is from his first conviction of the truth of the Catholic faith. This we gather from the account which has been already given on the authority of Bishop Virtue, that whilst Morris's father was, in 1846, revolving plans for sending him to China, he himself felt confident all the time, that if Providence *wanted him to be a Jesuit,* it would be able to accomplish its designs as easily in Asia as in Europe.

To follow out the course of an interior grace like that of vocation, is at once a difficult and delicate task. In the present case, however, we are fortunately in possession of documents, which set the main points in the clearest light, though it is impossible to determine every detail. It will be found to be a story of very peculiar and perplexing interest.

While, on the one hand, Father Morris had so early conceived the idea of joining the Society of Jesus, on the other hand, his taking the mission oath only six months later, proves that his ideas on the subject were at least exceedingly vague and indefinite. His letters during his stay at the English College, Rome, show much admiration for the Order and its members, but they give us no reason for suspecting that he then took any practical steps in consequence. The first actual move appears to have been made at the time of his ordination, when he spoke to the Holy Father on the subject, and the Pope's answer, though its exact terms are not recorded, were at least in favour of not neglecting the supposed call to the religious life.[1]

In consequence, probably, of Pio Nono's advice, Father Morris on his return to England in 1850 arranged to go to the Jesuit Novitiate at Hodder, and make a retreat under the well-known Master of Novices, Father Thomas Tracy Clarke, S.J. The latter's verdict on the case as set before him, left nothing to be desired in point of clearness. "You may say," was his final answer, "that I have doubted respecting the vocation to the Society of a great many people, but I have no doubt of yours." Such a decision left no room for

---

[1] The Nuns of the Good Shepherd at Hammersmith, in whose convent Father Morris served as chaplain before he entered the Society, state that, "on bidding farewell, he told them that, 'had he followed the advice given him by Pope Pius at the time of his ordination, he would have been a Jesuit long ago.'"

misinterpretation, and Father Morris was not only willing, but eager to act upon it. He therefore applied for a dispensation from his mission oath, with the result that his request was not granted, the reason alleged for its refusal being the scarcity of priests, and the consequent difficulty the Bishop would have found in filling his place. " The Pope has said," writes Father Morris in September, 1851, " that it is natural for the English Bishops to wish to have as many priests as possible, but yet that to interfere with the freedom of vocations was against the sacred canons and the prescriptions of his Apostolic predecessors, as well as against the Bishop's own interests."

The refusal, however, was far from inducing him to abandon all thoughts of his having a vocation. That the Pope should have based his refusal on the exigences of the times sheds, he declares, " a ray of hope " over his chances. Mr. B. Smith's testimony as to the continuance of his aspirations is very strong. " I met him frequently," he says, " and he nearly always expressed to me his yearning to become a Jesuit. . . The desire to belong to that great Order had taken possession of him." This desire, we may be sure, must have been greatly confirmed by the example of Mr. George Harper, a convert, who had been reading with him at Great Marlow, and who left him to join the Society, October 1, 1851.[1] Erelong an opportunity came of taking one step at least in the wished for direction. " As long as I remained at Great Marlow," he wrote to Cardinal Wiseman, in 1856, " I felt that the Bishop might always say with truth that he could not spare me," so " when the Vice-Rectorship of the English College was offered me, I did not hesitate to accept it." The English College then was deliberately

---

[1] Father George Harper, ordained in 1856, died in 1864, a martyr to his charity in attending a case of typhus fever. Foley, viii. p. 334.

chosen as a half-way house to the Society; and this appears still more clearly from a previous letter written to Mrs. Scott Murray.

" Another priest has asked leave to be a Jesuit, and though he had his Bishop's consent in writing, he has been refused by the Propaganda. So that I see the will of God for the present at least clearly enough, my *casa professa* is to be the English College, but for how long I do not know. Difficulties may give way even in a day, and that any day. Meanwhile I am contented and very happy.

" I made a retreat at the end of last month at S. Eusebio. It was given expressly to priests, of whom there were more than thirty present, and then there was the Greek College, blue boys with red girdles, and looking very pretty in their cotta besides. It was so funny saying Mass in the church, and eight other priests saying Mass at the same time at the other altars. The retreat was most edifying, on the part both of the givers and receivers. The Jesuits certainly know what they are about. One of the Fathers came to visit me every day, and he seemed really to have a fire within his wan and wasted body.

" Everything at S. Eusebio is admirably managed. You find the subject of your meditation on your table when you come back from the chapel, and the next time you go it is taken away and a new one substituted. We beginners in spiritual things can certainly make a better retreat when we have the points preached to us, and Father Zuliani gives them very well.

" I had a very fervent old priest in the room next to me with nothing but a door between us, so that I could hear all his ejaculations, *O povertà ! O'fuoco !* as well as the crack, crack, of his discipline, when the meditations did not keep moving to his satisfaction. Even an idle predecessor of mine in that room had recorded on the window in four languages a sentence that took this form in English, "How qik these eigh days are passed." Another had thus recorded in the table drawer his desire for prayers, partly in Latin and partly in Italian: "So-and-so, *pregate pro eo, molto indigno!*"

"You will certainly think that I am going to imitate Sir Francis Head and tell you the size and height of every room, and indeed I could not help noticing some details, such as the young Frenchman who rushed about without a biretta and took two turns round the garden to any one else's one; or the fat man, the General of the Chierici Minori I believe, who recited the Office in a very high tone note while every one else was very low; or the funny things in the refectory, and still more at breakfast, where I caught an Englishman dissatisfied with his *pagnotto* and pilfering his neighbour's, and then laughed when he caught my eye, and many other statistics, but I spare you.

"In spite of all this inattention and curiosity on my part, it was the best retreat I ever made, and has, I hope and trust, though I begin to doubt this already, done me permanent good. I do feel so immensely happy at having once more a Jesuit confessor, and my old Father, too, P. Mislei."

The tone and contents of this letter equally warrant the statement which it contains that he was " contented and very happy." There was still, it is true, something further to wish for, the realization, namely, of what we shall afterwards hear him call " the hopes and fears of six years." Still, these did not oppress him. Nor, indeed, need they have done so, because he foresaw that they might "disappear any day." One thing, however, he does not seem to have been prepared for, and that was the proximity of the hour of freedom.

When the Hierarchy was established in 1850, the number of priests increased greatly, and it became more and more difficult to maintain that no substitute could be found for him. " I thought," to use his own words,[1] " that if the time should ever come, which in fact has now come, when I could truly say that there were young men perfectly fitted for my post of Vice-Rector—then, if ever, the Holy Father would allow me to be a Religious."

Accordingly, in the beginning of January, 1856, Father Morris sought and obtained an audience of the Pope, and begged leave to repeat his petition. " The Holy Father," he says, " received me with his own kindness, and after hearing all that I had to say, he promised me an answer through the Secretary of Propaganda. From Mgr. Barnabo I since learn that the Pope has postponed his decision until my Bishop and my Rector have been written to on the subject. I must say that I hardly expect an affirmative answer, but I am deeply thankful to the Holy Father for the kindness and condescension with which he has received, and the consideration which he has bestowed on, my petition. I do not see also how it would be proper to regard the decision when he is pleased to give it, as other than final. If it shall please His Holiness to grant my petition, I shall be deeply thankful. If it shall please him to refuse it, though of course the thoughts and hopes of six years cannot be put away without pain, I will accept the decision simply and gratefully."

Somewhat to his surprise, the leave was granted with but little delay. In May he was back in England, and erelong had settled the day on which he was to enter the Novitiate. Then came a change of mind, the

---

[1] Written to Cardinal Wiseman, on February 9, 1856, and quoted, in part, on page 133.

project was suddenly given up, and as the reader has been previously informed, he was, before the close of the year, in charge of the mission of St. Thomas's, Fulham

The following letter, which is the only one to be found on the subject, gives the facts of the case with perfect distinctness, but does not throw any further light on the motives of this new decision.

" Danesfield, Great Marlow, August 28, 1856.

" My Lord Cardinal,—On consideration and con-sultation I think that I cannot do better than renew my request that your Eminence would have the good-ness to receive me into your diocese and give me London work, if it be practicable. Only one difficulty seems to me to stand in the way of my request. . . .

" The Holy Father might consider that I was treating him disrespectfully in not making any use of the leave he has given me. Of course that leave did not give me a vocation to the religious state, if I had not one before; the only question which arises with regard to it is whether I ought to give it up without previously entering the Novitiate, if it be only to leave it again. My own feeling and that of more than one person whom I have consulted is that I have no right to enter a novitiate in my present mind. My feelings have changed, and I ought not to continue to act as if they had not changed. I think that, if I write to Mgr. Talbot, representing to him the simple state of the case, the Holy Father, should the Monsignore think fit to mention it to him, having expressed himself so strongly about the secular life, and having given his leave so reluctantly, can hardly be displeased with me even if I do not enter a novitiate at all. Any way I am doubtless open to the charge of changeableness, and I doubt whether I should do myself any good, if in order to diminish such a charge, I should place myself in a state, where I did not feel a hope of permanence; indeed, I doubt whether any one would receive me into a novitiate with such feelings. Thus far, then, I think I see my way pretty clearly. . . .

"Begging ten thousand pardons for the liberty I am taking and the trouble I am giving, I have the honour to remain, my Lord Cardinal,

"Your Eminence's most obedient servant,
"JOHN CAN. MORRIS."

Those who have known Father Morris chiefly or only in his later years and firmer moods, might easily suspect that the persons whom he had consulted helped to involve him in this reproach of "changeableness." It may have been so, but Father Morris's own words when he afterwards alluded to the subject do not suggest such a supposition. He attributes the blame to himself alone, for he thus writes in one of his letters, "God has twice called me to the Society, though through my own fault, I threw away the first call."[1] And again, he makes this note, "I entered religion, as I might have done and ought to have done, eleven years sooner. Our Lord gave me that which I deserve to have forfeited, may His Name be praised and blessed for it."[2]

For the time being his vocation seems to have been completely laid aside. He settled down to very useful work, and, as we have already seen, thoroughly identified himself with all its interests. During eleven entire years his early aspirations slept what appeared to be the sleep of death, and their reawakening he always attributed to some providential and very especial favour from God. His own account of this is as follows:[3]

---

[1] Letter to Mother Stanislaus (Liefmans), October 28, 1887.

[2] *Journals of Retreat,* p. 336.

[3] See Father Morris's article on "The Cardinal Archbishop" in *The Month* of February, 1892, p. 164.

"One day [in the summer of 1866] I stated to Archbishop Manning that the physical labour of all the writing I had to do as his secretary was too much for me. He acknowledged this at once, and remarked that as two priests were coming that day to receive their destinations, I might have either of them to help me. He suggested one of these to me at first, and I acquiesced; but a little while afterwards I went to him, saying, ' My Lord, that choice just now was a mistake. Let me have Dr. Johnson instead. I am sure that he will do.' Dr. Johnson came, and it was soon clear that he could do my work far better than I could do it. Literally, before long I was without an office, and Archbishop Manning had a diocesan secretary immeasurably better than me.

" While the Archbishop was debating with himself what he would do with me next, he went out of town, and I seized the opportunity of going to Roehampton to make a retreat. Father Fitzsimon accepted me only on the condition that I did not trouble him then, as he was busy with the long retreat of the novices. I did not need him, for I had no sooner set foot within the chapel where the novices were making their meditation, than I saw clearly and, thank God, the light has never faded away, that the time had come, and that it was God's will I should enter the Noviceship. In Cardinal Wiseman's time, and in the early days of Archbishop Manning, the step would not have been possible. There was no one to take my place in an office that must necessarily be filled, and that no one coveted. I held a number of strings in my hands, and until some one else would take charge of them, I could not move. Such a person had now been found, and I have always regarded his coming as a special favour granted by God in His goodness towards me.

" In consequence of Dr. Johnson's perfect fitness for

my duties, Archbishop Manning *could* let me go; but *would* he? I asked Father Weld, who was then Provincial, whether he would receive me, and he said that if I came with the full consent of the Archbishop he would, but he 'would not fight for me.' He would take me if I were free to come; and on that supposition I asked him how long he supposed it would be before I could hope to enter the Novitiate. His answer was that if I was out of the Archbishop's house in six months, I might consider myself fortunate. I was out of the house with the Cardinal's full leave in less than a month. I asked him on the vigil of St. Andrew, 1866, and before Christmas he had let me go.

"That vigil of St. Andrew I am not likely ever to forget. It was against his Grace's wish that I should leave him, and against his judgment too, for he did not believe that I had a vocation to the religious life; but this only makes his speedy acquiescence all the more generous."

That the Cardinal's doubt as to Canon Morris's vocation was not so unreasonable as we, who regard it in the light of subsequent events, might consider it, appears from a reminiscence related by Father Gallwey. On the occasion of a difference of opinion between himself and the Canon Penitentiary about some dispensation, the discussion of the point became rather a warm affair. To his surprise the Canon appeared not long afterwards, and begged for advice respecting his intention of becoming a Jesuit [1] Father Gallwey answered that this was a matter requiring careful consideration, the good he was able to do in his present position being so evident, and changes made at his time of life so often turning out unfortunate.

[1] His chief adviser at this period was, I have been told, Father R. A. Coffin, C.SS.R., afterwards Bishop of Southwark.

It did not prove so in Father Morris's case. With him there was from this time forward no looking back, no halting, but a steady development of the whole mind and character. His powers began to find full scope, his zeal and energies entered upon the peculiar field best suited to them, and he advanced steadily along his spiritual course, destined to close so abruptly, yet with such thrilling effect, in the discharge of one of the highest duties of his ministry.

He left the Cardinal's house, he has told us, before the end of 1866, and betook himself for a few days to the chaplain's house at the Convent of the Good Shepherd, Hammersmith, where he had been acting as confessor for some time past. He joined the Noviceship at Manresa on the last day of February, 1867, although he did not receive till a week later the deed which embodied the Archbishop's acceptation of the resigned canonry, bearing date, March 8, 1867.

On the details of Father Morris's life as a Jesuit novice we need scarcely dwell here. There were but few external points in it calling for narration. It was, however, strongly marked by that internal and spiritual development which was to render him an able and experienced director of souls in the ways of sanctity. The volume of his *Journals kept in Times of Retreat* may be consulted for some of the lights and graces by which his steps were guided along the path of his spiritual training.

In the March of the following year, 1868, he was sent to the Belgian Novitiate at Tronchiennes, where Father Adolphe Petit was the Master of Novices, and he himself afterwards fully acknowledged how greatly he had been influenced by Père Petit's spiritual counsels. He took such pains in writing out his notes of the lectures given, that his fellow-novices used to joke him on the point, telling him that he was sure to be Master of Novices himself some day. In September he went to Louvain to read up his theology again before standing the examination for the degree of Doctor, which is requisite for profession in the Society. After passing this examination on the 30th of July, 1869, he returned to Tronchiennes for his annual retreat, according to his custom in after-years, and then went back to England.

This stay in Belgium, occurring so early in his religious life, helped much to train and form his spiritual character. He had to become thoroughly acquainted with the habits of the country, he learnt to write and speak its language with considerable fluency, and made many friends, especially among the Bollandists and other historians of the Belgian Province, who afterwards gave him material help in his antiquarian researches.

On his return to England he was variously employed until his destination for the following year was settled. "I have been much on the move," he wrote from Glasgow to Mr. Scott Murray on September the 29th, "since I returned from Belgium. After spending a week in London, and a week in Edinburgh supplying for an absent Father, I gave a retreat to a convent at Richmond, in Yorkshire, was a fortnight at Galashiels, and now am giving a retreat to the Sisters of the Good Shepherd here. I suppose the end of the week will find me beginning a year at St. Beuno's, where I hear I am to teach Canon Law. This will be a funny experience for me, as I have never yet taught anything in my life."

The idea of employing him as professor was not carried out at that time, but after a short stay at Stonyhurst, to examine manuscripts, he was appointed to the office of " Father Minister " at Manresa. This post would have given him the charge of temporals, of the discipline and domestic management of the house.

Early in 1871, Father Robert Whitty became Provincial, and chose Father Morris as his Socius, having been his Vicar-General years before when they were both in the Westminster diocese. Father Morris's new duties were almost altogether those of a private secretary, though they included also that of accompanying the Provincial in his annual visitation of the different houses and colleges of the Province, during which some special points come under his own inspection.

After eighteen months of this work, he was sent to Oxford, where his post was in some ways a difficult one. It had been expected that Father Newman would open a house and college there, but after much negotiation the mission was finally entrusted once more to the Society, which had started it in the last century. It was decided that a new church should be built, and the care of this undertaking was entrusted to Father Morris. A commencement was made in 1873, and the first stone was laid in the May of that year. We subjoin his account of the proceedings.

" On Tuesday, May 20th, the first stone of the new church at Oxford," he writes, " was blest and laid by the Lord Bishop of Birmingham. The secular clergy of the neighbourhood and the Fathers of the Province were well represented, and the ceremony was quiet and impressive. The weather, on which an outdoor function is so entirely dependent, was magnificent, and the attendance on the occasion was large. Admission was by ticket, and publicity had been as far as possible avoided; but seven hundred tickets were distributed, and there were some hundred applicants besides. This may be looked upon as a sign that the progress of the Catholic religion in Oxford excites considerable interest in the city. The majority of those present were Protestants, and it was remarked that many of them united with the Catholics in making their offerings on the stone at the close of the ceremony.

" A lithographed drawing of the proposed church was shown on the occasion, but as the contract has not yet been signed, it will be better perhaps to postpone for the present all description of what is to be done."

There were many delays before the plans and specifications could be decided. The building meanwhile was stopped and all progress was at an end, a state of affairs which, as may be imagined, caused Father Morris much anxiety. On the 17th of September he writes to Mr. Scott Murray : " No news whatever about the church ; it is a pain to see the place."

Shortly after this he left Oxford, and so was spared a still further vexation. When accurate specifications were sent in, it was found that the scale on which the church had been begun was far more costly than would admit of its being completed with the means at disposal for this purpose. Eventually the first foundations had to be removed, and the present church was built on less pretentious lines.

Orders of change of residence reached him just as he was commencing his edition of Sir Amias Poulet's Letter Books, and he thus announces the move to Mr. Scott Murray :

" September 27, 1873.

" I have just received marching orders to go to St. Beuno's immediately as Professor.

> Obedient Yamen
> Answered " Amen "
> And did
> As he was bid.

So Southey says in the *Rejected Addresses*, and I will be like Yamen.

"For health's sake I am very glad, as I have never felt well in Oxford, and was in dread of the coming winter. Community life too is far the happiest.

"I hope I may have time to finish what I am doing about Mary Queen of Scots, but most certainly I have no time to spare, and for a good while to come, must give my undivided attention to my new professorship."

He began his course of lectures during the ensuing month of October, and in the main followed the lines laid down by Father de Smedt, whose lectures he had attended when at Louvain. After lecturing for two years on History he turned to the subject of Canon Law. One of those who heard these lectures thus describes him in his capacity of Professor:

"He read his lectures for half an hour in the evening in English. He would not allow us to take notes during them; so you had simply to give yourself up to listen, and a very pleasant half hour it was, an interval of sunshine in a day otherwise neither stormy nor gloomy, but certainly trying, the school-day, namely, of the theologian.

"In private Father Morris was a delightful man to go to with a difficulty. 'Sit down,' I remember him saying, 'and I will tell you a story about that.' It was an education to come in contact with a mind so clear, precise, and well informed. He had a happy, humorous way of saying things which took off any edge of sharpness from his corrections. Thus he would come into the sacristy after Benediction and point out how the thurible had been mismanaged, how the acolytes knelt with fingers interlocked and the two forefingers extended, and with one foot over the other; 'not a good attitude,' he said, 'when you have a congregation behind you.'

M

With all this it was a comfort to hear how the two Fathers engaged in the more solemn part of the rite had done what they ought not, and had left undone what they ought to have done. In a word, Father Morris's presence in the house meant accuracy.

" But there was kindness too. He was fond of the society of his students, and glad to go out walking with them. He was very courteous and deferential in his behaviour even to the newest comer, he took you into his confidence, and valued your opinion."

Though this writer represents very truly the usual attitude of his auditors towards him, it is not to be supposed that his views were regarded by all alike. This could hardly be expected in the case of one who expressed himself so freely and forcibly. Some Britishers there were, we may be sure, who thought the above-mentioned points of observance rather trivial. There were others too who found his lectures when written and read over somewhat cut-and-dry, despite, or even in consequence of, their wealth of facts, figures, quotations, and references.

His free time was not spent in taking rest, but in giving missions and retreats, or examining papers at the Record Office, and in other manuscript repositories. In 1874 a considerable interruption of his usual work was occasioned by the hearing of the cause of the English Martyrs, of which more shall be told in the next chapter. Another break took place in the following year while he was making researches among the Belgian Archives, and in the Municipal and Episcopal records of the city of York.

The vacation of 1876 was especially laborious for him, as the following letters show :

" *June* 12.—My course of lectures in the College is over for the year, and on Friday I am going for a short visit to York, to search manuscripts in preparation for my next volume; after which I have three convent retreats to give, one after the other, at Holywell, Blackburn, and Chester, and then comes the clergy retreat of this diocese here in the College. This carries my work to the middle of August, and that is far enough to see one's way before one at a time."

On July 4 he wrote: "Your letter reached me at Stonyhurst, where I had not a minute to steal from the precious manuscripts for which I had gone there, and now I have begun a series of retreats at convents, in the course of which I shall not have much free time."

Again, on September 6: "Since I wrote to you last I have either been giving retreats, or suffering from a state of collapse after them, and all the while I have let my letters get grievously into arrears. I have given six retreats—four of them being full eight day retreats at convents, a clergy retreat, and a triduum to one hundred and twenty scholars training at Mount Pleasant, Liverpool, which is the work of a retreat crushed into three days. You know how absorbing and engrossing a retreat is while it lasts, leaving one neither strength nor attention for anything else, so you must not be astonished that I have not written."

On August 11, 1876, he wrote: "When I shall have finished with other people, I hope to see to myself. I am looking forward to the thirty days' retreat which has been promised me, a privilege that only comes twice in our lives, and I shall be very thankful to you for prayers then. It will commence in October, at Tronchiennes, in Belgium. Meantime I shall have the month of September in which to work away at my book. Though I have not yet passed a single page for press, I have corrected the proofs of, I suppose, sixty or seventy pages."

In accordance with the above plans Father Morris crossed over to Tronchiennes for his tertianship on the 13th of October, having refreshed himself after the fatigues of the summer by preparing a whole volume for publication within a month.

He wrote to a friend the following account of his long retreat on the very day in which he came out of it :

" We have got through the long retreat with very little fatigue. I found the midnight meditations (of which we had sixteen) not at all tiring, and they did not unfit one for the meditations of the day, as I rather expected. Of course I felt tired from time to time, but the day's repose when it came freshened one up again for a new beginning. We had three such repose days. Four of us are from England, two of whom I knew at St. Beuno's, and the other is Father Butler,[1] who was my fellow-novice at Roehampton—once Captain Butler, of the 87th—who has come from Jamaica on purpose, where he has been leading a hard missionary life for the last few years.

" Two of the thirty-nine are going away now the retreat is over, a Frenchman and a Belgian. An Englishman was to have left too, myself to wit, but I am happy to say that I am to stay on. I came here expecting one grace, and I have found two. I came for the long retreat, and in addition Father General has been so good as to give me the tertianship. It is one of St. Ignatius' finest strokes, a *coup de maître*, and I am very thankful to be allowed to pass through it. By rights I ought not to get it, for I have not made my

---

[1] Now the Right Rev. Dr. Butler, Bishop of Melipotamus and Vicar Apostolic of British Guiana.

studies in the Society, but it has been granted to me as a favour. It lasts up to the feast of St. Ignatius ; Lent, however, is usually spent in England in giving missions and retreats.

" The long retreat has gone by very fast, and it is now bygone. I look on it as the greatest grace of my life. I suppose that it is the most powerful instrument for good in existence, and as the Society is very chary of employing it, I shall probably never have it again. I asked for it once before, but could not get it. Having the tertianship, however, makes a great difference. It is really a third year's noviceship, and following straight on the retreat, at least doubles its value.

" I am much moved at the sight of all these young Fathers—not young in years, at least very few of them, for Ours are seldom ordained before they are thirty-three or thirty-four, but most of them have been ordained not much more than a year. They have their life before them, and the majority of them will be working for the glory of God after I am in my grave.

" In the house we are altogether one hundred and forty, of whom about fifty are priests. We keep fourteen altars well employed, but imagine what it will be on Christmas Day! The house in which we live is immense—an old Premonstratensian abbey—not old in our sense of the word, having no doubt been built in the last century. It is exactly suited for our purpose, and we have in it three different communities under one Rector—the novices, scholastics, and Tertian Fathers. I know it well and am quite at home, for I spent five months of my noviceship here.

" Have you read Père de Ravignan's Life by Père de Ponlevoy? If you have not, pray do. We are reading it in refectory, and it contains some very interesting and edifying things."

The exercises of the tertianship are too similar to those of the novitiate to require any further description. The Tertian Fathers are, however, tried during their year in giving various missions, and Father Morris, in compliance with this rule, was sent to Deptford. Returning to Tronchiennes after Easter, he remained there till the following June. On the 2nd of that month he expresses his sorrow that his tertianship is coming to a premature end. " I am to give," he writes, " a retreat to the clergy of Newport and Menevia in the first week of July, and I have no hope of returning to make the retreat at the end of this month with which the tertianship closes. Of course I am very sorry, but I am very grateful to have had as much as I have had, the whole of which has been a boon and a particular favour."

As regards Father Adolphe Petit, who had been his " Instructor " during the last scholastic year, he has already expressed, in connection with the second year of his noviceship, the very high opinion which he had formed of him. He now writes : " I have the greatest possible sympathy with all that he says, and look upon it as a singular piece of good fortune that I have again come under his direction and influence." Then ten years later he repeats, " It is one of the kind orderings of God's providence that I should have come across Père Petit, whose instructions many people did not value. They suited me exactly."

Father Morris's movements during the next few months, will be best traced out in his own letters :

While at Holywell he describes himself on June 22, 1877, as fairly tired, " but I do not," he says, " begin to rest till to-morrow, when I go to St. Beuno's to stay till Saturday. Ninety Sisters in retreat are, as you may imagine, occupation enough for a Father single-handed, and it was not till the last day that I got the help of a Father for the confessions. The good Sisters went through with such spirit that that took off half the fatigue. I am now supplying here for Father Baron for a few days, and am giving a tiny convent here just the first launch of their retreat, but I am sorry that I must leave them to finish it alone. It is, however, *Ad Majorem* that I should do so, for I must not go to Oscott in a state of collapse. . . .

"You should have seen how this letter has been interrupted—amongst other things I have baptized a baby, and given Benediction, along with an instruction on five of the Mysteries of the Rosary. I have not finished my day's work yet by any means, so I had better finish my letter. .

"This place attracts me very much. It is a real place of pilgrimage, the only one in England. People come here with all imaginable things the matter, and they get cured body and soul. This very place where I am writing has been the Jesuit missioner's house from the seventeenth century and probably from early in that century. A secular mission was next door for a hundred years, showing how the faithful have always flocked to St. Winefride. It is a little convent now. It used to be called the ' Cross Keys ' in the days of persecution, and this house was I think, the ' Star.' "

Another letter is dated, Stonyhurst, July 25, 1877. In it he remarks: "We cannot foresee our lives, and if that is true of a Jesuit always, more especially it is true of one just out of the tertianship and *en disponibilité*. Well, I have just received my destination, and I am to go out to Malta to open a new College there. How happy our lot is to be bound to the holy will of God. If it were possible to be tied to it more tightly, I would beg for those closer bonds. Now I must throw myself heart and soul into this very new life. It involves many and grave difficulties, my inexperience in that kind of work, the necessarily great poverty of a first beginning, and plenty more whose shadows I see—but success and failure are in the hands of God, and I hope that I may never be so foolish and wicked as not to trust Him. The College is to be called St. Ignatius', and our holy Father loved to send his men out without human resources and with none but God to look to. The one thing that I care for in this life is to be a child of St. Ignatius, and I must not fear what is after his heart.

" I will not fear, but I cannot help feeling; and I have a sacrifice to make to God in leaving many people and many occupations. But I know that it will be for the best both for them and for me. I would not for a moment dare to interfere with souls unless I were sent by God. He will more than make good to them anything He takes away."

On the 15th of August he made his solemn profession, a blessing which caused him the most lively pleasure. " By God's grace, on our dear Mother's great feast, I have made my last vows and am a professed Father of the Society, my mother. How happy it makes me, I do not care to try to tell." And again : " Thanks be to God a thousand times. The great words are said and accepted, and I am professed of the four vows. What is there left to desire now before seeing the face of God ? "

He was soon on his way to his new destination, and the following letters give us information as to his movements. From Rome he writes:

" Rome, Via della Valle, 41, September 9, 1877.

" I have half an hour to spare, and I devote it to you. I am then going to the Vatican in hopes of seeing the Pope and of getting his blessing on my new College. I have some misgivings that I shall not see him, as there is a strong scirocco wind, which can hardly fail to affect him. However I will hope for the best. If I have an opportunity, be sure that I will get the blessing of the Holy Father for you: and if I cannot speak to him, I will take care to pray for you at the tomb of St. Peter. I am in Rome, and barring the pain I feel at the change which I try to shut out of my thoughts, I feel thoroughly at home after twenty-one years of absence. I have not gone out sight-seeing. The only place I have been to, besides calling on Cardinal Howard, is the English College, where, however, there was no one to be seen as they are all at the country house at Monte Porzio. I saw the new church and admire it much, but it is sad to see the work at a stand-still. The old porter happened to be there, and I was glad to see one face I knew in the old place. This was the day before yesterday when I arrived in Rome. This done, I went out to Mondragone by the Frascati railroad, and got there at night-fall. The next morning I tried to get over to Monte Porzio, the sight of which gladdened my eyes, as I should have been glad to call on Dr. Giles, but I could not manage it. I went to Mondragone to study an Italian College and to ascertain what books were in use, &c., and I had only that morning to do it in.

"Yesterday afternoon I went across from Mondragone to Castel Gandolfo to see Father Cardella, the Provincial, to whom I am indebted for three of my staff. I found him in the old country house of the Generals of the Society, which Prince Torlonia has bought and lent to him as a refuge for the aged and the sick Fathers and Brothers. If it were not for this charity, I do not know what would have become of these dear old souls, who have there a roof over their heads while they wait for death. There must be twenty-five lay-brothers there, some of them of a great age. I left Castello this morning at half-past four, and got in here in time to say Mass at seven in a private house where three or four of our Fathers live.

" My journey I made in four nights and a day ; one day I spent in Paris, and as I wanted to see a French College, and to make acquaintance with two of my future Italian Fathers, the day was a fatiguing one. I then 'ran on to Florence without stopping, and after saying Mass on arriving I went with Father Weld, who had kindly come to meet me, up to Fiesole, and there I remained till the evening of the following day, refreshed and rested by the sight of our dear old Father General. He is eighty-two, though he does not look it except in his stoop ; but his gentle manners and kindness of heart, as well as his clearness and patient prudence, have an air of perpetual youth. He gave me a long talk, which was to me one of the greatest and deepest pieces of happiness that I have ever enjoyed.

" It is now time for me to make my way to the Vatican, but perhaps I may have time this afternoon to add a few more words. I hope I shall get the Pope's blessing. Being with Father General gave me quite a new love for the Society, and the sight of the Holy Father has always given me a more sensible love for the Holy See, and for Christ's Vicar upon earth.

" Well, I have seen the Pope, and I cannot tell you how the change these twenty years have brought has impressed me.[1] I was able to kiss his hand as he

[1] The Pope was then not far from his end. On February 20, 1878, Father Morris wrote, " The death of Pius IX. was sudden at last. I had a letter written from Rome by Cardinal Howard the very day the Pope died, saying that he was much better and again able to sit up. I was received into the Church six days before the death of Gregory XVI., so that all my Catholic life is coextensive with the reign of Pius IX.—R.I.P. God will soon give us a strong feeling of personal loyalty to the new Pope, who is the channel of that Divine jurisdiction, which affects our daily lives in every way that is good."

passed, and to ask his blessing for everybody—*per tutti quanti*—a phrase that amused him. I had to be quick, for an impatient Frenchman with a message from the Comte de Chambord cut me short. I followed the Holy Father through two or three rooms, but I was behind him when he made a little address in French. I could not catch it. It seemed to be on the Sunday's Gospel.

" The weather is exceedingly stormy, and I have three days before me on the Mediterranean. It is no slight mortification to start with. I have just been fortifying myself by a visit to St. Stanislaus, his tomb, and then the room where he died—one of the tenderest and most touching places in Rome. To-morrow morning I run down to Naples, and go on board straight, and I hope to be in Malta on the 13th.

" If I send you the Pope's blessing and Father General's, I must keep my tiny contribution to the next time, and yet for habit's sake I cannot help saying, God bless you.

" Yours always, very faithfully in Jesus Christ,
" JOHN MORRIS, S.J."

We have another letter from St. Giuliana's, Malta, dated September 17, 1877:

" You may report that Father Morris has arrived at Malta. Everybody is asleep while I write this afternoon and the mail goes out in an hour. Two mails a week—rather a change from our eleven posts a day in London! It gives the impression of being further away than we really are, for after all we get letters in four days.

" It is exceedingly hot, and I am very squeamish and all but utterly prostrate: but Father Sidgreaves tells me it is nothing to what it was when he came. It laid him up for a few days, but he is about again now. He and I and one lay-brother are all who have yet arrived, but on Wednesday I expect five, and then there will be only one more of Ours yet to come. I shall have four English who speak no Italian, and two Italians who speak no English: and a Maltese Father and myself to bridge over the gulf.

"The people here are impatient in the extreme to send their boys to us, and I am in the curious position of having to hold back lest I should get a greater number than will be manageable. I shall be obliged to take more than I wish, and indeed I should not mind how few I had to begin with. The fewer they were, the better I should hope their spirit would become, and the safer the future of the College would be. I cannot bear beginning in a showy way, and this unfortunately is what our friends here have set their hearts upon. I shall have a curious and wearisome time for the next week or two, seeing parents and boys and accepting some and rejecting others, I heartily beg our Lord to guide me to do what will be the best for the future of the College and the most to His glory, without offending anybody.

"Our house, thank God, is a very good one, though small for more than forty. The situation is excellent, in a suburb or village called San Giuliano, and our garden is separated from a bay of the sea by nothing more than a road. But, ah me! it is hot! And if it is hot now, what will it be in the summer? However, we have the winter coming, which is in the main, they tell me, like an English summer. This will serve to acclimatize us."

"*October* 31.—Thank God, we have got the College open at last. We were delayed nearly a month by the delay in transit of the beds we had sent for to England. However, they have come, and are occupied, too—that is, thirty-three of them, for that is the full number that our present house will accommodate. The first night after I had got them here I went round the dormitories after they had got to sleep, and I felt greatly touched and moved at the sight of all the little things God has given us to take care of. They vary from eight and a half to fourteen. Most of them are nice children, but they are indescribably backward, and I have had to tell the parents of big boys of fourteen that they know nothing at all. It is terribly hard on our poor scholastics, who can hardly leave them to themselves. The worst of all is the case of those who know neither English nor Italian, nothing but Maltese, which is a dialect of Arabic, and who consequently do not understand a word their master says to them. The masters are facing it in a famous spirit, and of course the difficulty will get less as the time goes on.

"I am very glad that for the beginning we have not a larger number, but by-and-bye I suppose that we must build. When that is done, we shall have boys from Sicily and all parts of the Mediterranean, I suppose. Now there are none but Maltese (barring Kenneth Mackenzie), and many of them are now leaving their mother's homes for the first time. They look tractable—and some of them look as if they could be impudent. Volatile one must expect them to be, born in this latitude, but take them all in all, I think they promise very well.

"I see that you are under the impression that we are still very hot. You cannot imagine what a change has come over us. The weather is now like the best English early summer weather. We have rain from time to time, and when it rains it pours. For the rest it is mainly bright and fine this month, and not too cold, though we often have gales of wind for two or three days at a time. Yet still there is something that we all find trying in the climate, but I dare

say it is nothing more than that we are not yet used
to it."

On February 20, 1878, he tells us: "The little
College goes on quietly. We had the week's holiday
at Christmas you inquire about, and we of the community spent it at Notabile, the ancient capital of the
island, where the Cathedral is. We have felt the cold
during the wet and stormy time we have passed through
more than in England. We are close to the sea, which
will be a consolation when the hot weather comes.
Pray for me and for all of us."

Then on February 27: . . . "We are in a tantaliz-
ing position in this island. Our communications with
the world outside the broad blue band that hems us
in are so few that in interesting times we get quite
impatient to know what is going on. We take the
Tablet and the *Weekly Times*, and they reach us on
Thursdays, and this is our one link with the busy world.

"Our weather is becoming magnificent. I expect
that up to the end of April the climate will be very
enjoyable. After that we shall find it by a great deal
too hot for five months. The scirocco in September is
the most trying thing here, and it comes when all the
strength has been taken out of you by the previous
heat.

"We had a splendid function in St. John's for the
repose of Pope Pius IX., everybody present, lay and
clerical—the Archbishop, Governor, &c.—and a sermon
of an hour and a half in the midst of it!

"I remember speaking to our new Holy Father in
1854, asking him about the wonderful relics of Blessed
Clare of Montefalco which were in his diocese. I hope
that whenever I am sent to England I may be able to
pass through Rome to get his blessing. As I came
here I received that of Pius IX. for the last time; and

then I was greatly shocked to see how changed he was. How glad he must have been to die. *Si, proficiscere.*[1]

As Father Morris gradually settled down in his new surroundings, he began to return to his literary hobbies, so far as circumstances would permit. In December he sends to Father Coleridge an article for *The Month* on SS. Callistus, Hippolytus, and the Philosophoumena, and then set to work preparing a second edition of Father Gerard's autobiography. As may be imagined, however, the work made no practical progress, and such time as he was not overcome with the heat, was sufficiently occupied with his duties as head of the new College.

The commencement of such an institution is usually attended with difficulty, and in the present case there were superadded the discomforts of a somewhat trying climate, and the confusions arising from ignorance of Maltese customs, which were sometimes as unlike what English people were used to as the climate itself. Hence ensued several funny incidents, which Father Morris would recount with great gusto afterwards. I recollect how he used to laugh over his first experiences in Maltese banking. His cheques were dishonoured as soon as he had made his deposit, and it was only after some inquiry that he found that the bankers kept separate gold and silver accounts, and that in spite of credit for gold, they refused it for silver.

Such adventures were amusing enough when past, but the difficulty of climate was permanent, and appeared to be irreconcilable with Father Morris's health. He was, moreover, wanted in England, and

---

[1] As nearly twenty years have passed since Pio Nono's death, some readers may not be familiar with this allusion. The prelate who was reading the prayers for the dying hesitated over the words, *Proficiscere, anima Christiana,*" etc.—"Go forth, Christian soul." Then the Pope said aloud, *Si—*"Yes"—*Proficiscere.*

was therefore recalled at midsummer, 1878, and reached home in August.

After his summer series of retreats had been given, he returned to St. Beuno's and there took up again his course of lectures on Canon Law. The years passed quietly, and few events worthy of mention are referred to in his correspondence. A short retreat given to the boys of the Oratory School, Edgbaston, at the beginning of Lent, 1879, gave him special pleasure, because of the opportunity of meeting Cardinal Newman. In June he made his retreat at Tronchiennes, and acquired, ere ' he left Belgium, some interesting relics of the English Martyrs. All these, with the rest of his valuable collection, through the generosity of a friend, were afterwards enshrined, and now stand, in a large and handsome oak case in the sacristy of St. Joseph's Chapel, Roehampton.

His health at this time showed some rather alarming signs of weakness, which are only lightly alluded to in the following letters, with which we conclude this chapter.

"*August* 28, 1879.—You want to know what the doctor said. Well, he said there was nothing organically wrong about the heart, but that the intermittent action, which was very irregular, showed that things must be attended to. He prescribed rest and change. Now as to rest, it can hardly be work that caused it, for it began to come on in my own retreat before I began to give any; and I am sure I have had enough change to satisfy the most intermittent heart. However, I acknowledge I am very low, and must try to get up again."

"*September* 14, 1879.—I am nothing like right yet, but there is no place like St. Beuno's, and this beautiful air will set me right soon, I have no doubt."

In that "beautiful air," however, he was not destined to remain any length of time, and a day or two later he found himself under orders to proceed to Manresa, where he was about to commence one of the most important periods of his life.

CHAPTER VIII.

THE ENGLISH MARTYRS.

As Father Morris's conversion and religious vocation were the most important events, of which we are cognizant in his interior life, so the chief external work of his life is connected with his efforts in behalf of the English Martyrs. In this cause he was engaged for forty years, not continuously indeed, but with interruptions due to the delays of others or to the pressure of conflicting occupations, not to any want of perseverance on his part. Fifty years ago the names and the fame of the splendid line of witnesses to England's lost Faith were in danger of falling into hopeless oblivion. They had already faded away into mere distant, indistinct memories, the long but inevitable silence of ecclesiastical authority concerning them having given rise to a feeling of uncertainty in the minds of Catholics. If the sufferers had really died for the Faith, why did they not receive the honour due to martyrs? Could it possibly be that there was something more than false accusation in the treason with which they had been charged by their persecutors? Hence had arisen timidity in speaking and writing of them, a timidity which was natural in those who had so long languished under a cruel proscription, and were now looking for fairer treatment from their former oppressors.

All this doubtfulness has passed away. The Martyrs are now honoured publicly and with all confidence; and considering the number and variety of their separate histories, great progress has been made in bringing to light the records of their lives and sufferings.

So happy a result has been achieved only by the prolonged and united labours of many persons. Our Episcopate has ever been most ready to forward the good work. On an occasion when devoted support was most necessary, the Fathers of the London Oratory made the freest sacrifice of their time and energies to ensure its success, while others by patient study and careful writing prepared men's minds for what was to follow. Father Morris's part was throughout a leading one. From the beginning he saw what means were requisite for the accomplishment of the end in view, and advised their adoption. He became in fact the apostle of the cause, and his reputation for fairness and learning, joined to the vigour with which he pleaded his case, probably did more than anything else to induce others to give it a patient hearing, to place trust in it, and to assist him in furthering it. Such service is probably the most effective that any one could have rendered.

Before narrating in particular what Father Morris did in behalf of the Martyrs, it may be well to explain briefly what canonization really is, and to give the meaning of some of the technical terms which we cannot avoid using in this chapter. Catholics look to ecclesiastical authority to give formal sanction to the honour or *cultus*, which they pay to the faithful departed. That sanction has various degrees, the highest of which is conveyed by a decree of canonization, wherein it is understood that the Church, in her office of teacher of religion and morality, proposes to her children such and such a servant of God as a model of heroic virtue. According to present custom this decree is not issued for many years after the decease of the person canonized, nor until searching examination has been made into his virtues and into the miracles which God works to show that He wishes His servant to receive honour before men. These preliminaries, which are rarely concluded in one century, and are often protracted over several, may be divided into three stages, corresponding to the titles of "Venerable," "Blessed," and "Saint," which are successively conferred during the process of canonization.

The first step is made when the Bishops of the country, where the servant of God is honoured, satisfy the Holy See that the cause in question is deserving of the attention of the Pope's own Court, and that it is likely to end in beatification and canonization, that the faithful already venerate him in private, and beg for miraculous favours through his intercession. To do this they collect the necessary evidence by an "Informative Process," also called an "Ordinary Process," because the jurisdiction by force of which the court calls and examines witnesses, is derived from the Bishop of the diocese, the holder of "Ordinary" jurisdiction therein. So when the Pope sends to collect information for Beatifications, or Canonizations, the process is called "Apostolic," because held by Papal authority. If the Ordinary Process is found satisfactory, the Pope then issues a decree ordering the cause of the "venerable servant of God" to be brought before his own tribunal, the Congregation of Rites. This decree is therefore called the "Introduction of the Cause" of Beatification, and with its publication ends the first stage of the process, and the servant of God, having been so described by the Vicar of Christ, may now be invoked (but in private only) as Venerable.

Before the decree of Beatification, which closes the second stage, a most stringent examination of the virtues of the deceased is required, with convincing proofs that God works miracles through his intercession. Canonization, which closes the third stage, is however withheld until clear marks of Divine approval are vouchsafed by the working of fresh miracles subsequent to the publication of the decree of Beatification.

What precise cause first drew Father Morris to interest himself in the English Martyrs, cannot be now discovered.

Happily devotion to the Martyrs has ever been preserved at the English College, and his Lordship the Bishop of Portsmouth perfectly remembers the fact that Father Morris within a year or two of his conversion used to talk of the canonization as an object devoutly to be hoped for.

The first clear indication of his taking up active measures occurs early in the year 1855, when he reports to Cardinal Wiseman that he has " searched Rome," as far as the great restrictions on visiting the various archives permitted, in order to find documents that might serve for his purpose, and in May he lays before the Cardinal a complete report on the probable steps that would have to be taken. As this document is the earliest complete statement on the subject, it may well find a place here, even though subsequently in the history of the case it took a slightly different and more satisfactory direction than had been foreseen.

" English College, Rome, May 12, 1855.

" My Lord Cardinal,—The following is a statement of the case of the English Martyrs.

" Fisher, More, and the Carthusians might perhaps be treated as *casus excepti*, though the latter might not be admitted as such, since they suffered in the year after the notable 1534, which is the year named by Urban.

"All who come after that time must be taken, either by the *via non cultus*, or by the *casus exceptus*. The *via non cultus* is the regular full formal Process, and the only one that I imagine has any chance by that method is. Father Arrowsmith.[1]   If the Ordinary were to construct a process on the *fama martyrii et miraculorum* he might become Venerable without any great expense, and this would probably arouse devotion to him, and so the cause might afterwards progress.

"The Martyrs posterior to the decree of Urban can only become approved by the *via casus excepti* in virtue of Papal indults.   Under this head we have: (1) Gregory XIII.'s leave to use the relics of the Martyrs in consecrating altars, in 1582.   Of this the sole witness is Yepez, Bishop of Tarraçona in 1599.   (2) Paul V. gave leave to the College at Rheims to sing a Mass of Thanksgiving on their deaths, granting a Plenary Indulgence to those who assisted at it.   Of this the sole witness is Bishop Challoner.   (3) The pictures of the martyrdoms of Campion and others (in 1581), which were painted in this College under the eyes of Pope Gregory XIII.   Also paintings of the Carthusian martyrdoms in the Certose of Trisulti and Florence. (4) In the Gesù are documents legally authenticated showing that Venerable Pope Innocent XI. called five Martyrs in his time, *Beati*, *Santi*, and *Martiri*.   The account of their martyrdom, saying that the faithful honoured them as Saints, was published by the Pope's order in the Roman Journals, and when the Inquisitor at Ancona refused to allow the same account to appear there, Cardinal Cybo, by the Pope's order, wrote to bid him permit it.   It was also published at Macerata,

---

[1] He evidently thought that for Father Arrowsmith alone a sufficient number of miracles were attested, to satisfy the rules of Pope Urban. Father Morris did not then know that miracles *on the joint invocation* would be reckoned in favour of *all* definitely included under the invocation.

Fano, &c. (5) Ribadeneyra says that an image of Campion was honoured by the Indians who invoked him as a holy Martyr. (6) Popes Gregory XIII. and Sixtus V., and authors without number, Cardinals Gotti, Baronius, and Bellarmine, Bozius, Ross, Bonanni, Meze, Yepez, Sanders, Ciappus, Allegambe, Rayssius, Louis of Grenada, Ribadeneyra, Andreas Endæmoniohannes, Bombinus, Bernardinus de Mendoza, Persons, Gerard, Genebrand, Miræus, Tanner, Father Suarez, Bartoli, &c. Most of these speak of Campion.

" Now as all these arguments, except (4), tell in favour of Campion, I am inclined to think that the wisest course would be to petition for the approbation of his *cultus*. I am very much afraid that in any application for a general Office, the Congregation will carefully exclude everything that is in the least specific.

" But some more documents and proofs may yet be found, though I have searched everywhere in Rome for them without success. The following dates are given by the Benedictine Ross as decrees or briefs relating to them : (1) and (2) St. Pius V., Feb. 21, 1567, and Feb. 20, 1570; (3) Gregory XIII., 12 cal. Feb. 1582; (4) Clement VIII., Aug. 7, 1601 ; (5) Paul V., 10 cal. Oct. 1606; (6) and (7) Urban VIII., Maii. 9, 1631, and Feb. 23, 1633; (8) Decr. S.R.C. Mart. 22, 1642 ; (9) Decr. S.R. et Univ. Inquis. Dec. 2, 1642.

" Doubtless (3) and (5) are the two most important decrees above mentioned. Urban VIII.'s must be valuable, and it is impossible that amongst so many, some of importance should not be found. Is it not possible that amongst Episcopal or College papers some of them may yet be found ? I hope your Eminence will not think that I am pressing if I venture to suggest that a series of queries might be widely circulated previous to the Synod, requesting every one to bring thither any information respecting the Martyrs. The questions would naturally be, whether any documents are known to exist, whether any altar has been consecrated with their relics; whether any picture with nimbus, rays, &c., is to be found, in old families for example; whether there are any relics and how kept, whether any miracles are recorded; whether any invocations have been practised, and whether there arc any local traditions on the subject: or anything else which may be counted an instance of ecclesiastical *cultus* towards them.

" I have forgotten to say that I know nothing of respect shown to them by the saints, except St. Philip's *Salvete flores martyrum*, but I think I have heard your Eminence give some other instances, and Mr. Estcourt has some materials for an article on that branch of the subject, which he never published. I have written to your Eminence a long letter about these holy Martyrs, for I hope we may give the saints in Heaven something to remember the Second Synod of Westminster by. . . .

" Your Eminence's devoted faithful servant,

" JOHN CAN. MORRIS."

If anything was done in the matter at that Synod, which was held in the following July, it was not of sufficient importance to find a place in the printed transactions. The next event I have to chronicle is that before Canon Morris returned to England in 1856, he had consulted Father Boero, the Roman Postulator in the causes of Beatification for the Society of Jesus, and had shown him his list of Papal Indults in favour of the English Martyrs.[1]

[1] In *The Month* of January, 1887, Father Morris calls this list, " Father Boero's paper," and " his note on the relevancy," and says that afterwards "many additions were made to it." Bishop Grant, writing to Father Morris, calls it ''your paper," and a copy of it is extant, with additions and corrections, *all* in Father Morris's own hand. The respective shares of Fathers Boero and Morris are therefore probably now no longer distinguishable.

But the Third Synod of Westminster, at which it may be remembered Canon Morris was Secretary, took up the matter in earnest.

"On July 16, 1859, the Fathers of the Third Provincial Council of Westminster, as we learn from the published *Acta*, decreed that 'as there is a question of the honour which the Holy See is believed to have permitted to be paid to those who, after the overthrow of the ancient religion in England, shed their blood for the Catholic faith and the primacy of the Holy See, the Bishops of Salford and Liverpool, in whose territory most of the missionaries of those times were born, should make an accurate examination of the question.' In writing this paragraph of the *Acta* Bishop Grant showed his usual quickness, but not his usual accuracy. It was a simple guess, drawn from a knowledge of modern rather than of ancient England, that most of the Martyrs were born in Lancashire. At any rate, of the 186 Martyrs of the reign of Elizabeth, given in Challoner's first volume, only 14 were natives of that county.

"But this is a trifle. A more important matter is the turn of the phrase, 'the honour which the Holy See is believed to have permitted to be paid' to the English Martyrs. This was the one view that in those days was taken of the Cause of the Martyrs. The Ordinary Process was regarded as hopelessly difficult and expensive, and the only hope that the friends of the Martyrs entertained was that in some way this Cause might be introduced in virtue of some privilege or concession of the Holy See. To this we will return when we come to describe the course that was taken by the Cardinal Archbishop in 1874.

"To the Third Provincial Synod a collection of extracts from authors of the highest name respecting the English Martyrs is added in the Appendix. A

curious fate befel this paper. As it is printed, it was
drawn up by Father Boero, and consists of twenty
quotations, having at the end an account of a reliquary
older than 1621, belonging to the Cholmeley family, and
in it some English Martyrs were associated with Saints
and Blessed. The copy which Cardinal Wiseman took
to Rome is very much fuller than that printed with the
Acts of the Council. Father Boero's paper had been
brought to England some years before, and numerous
additions had been made to it, chiefly from Papal
Briefs, this fuller copy being that which was sent to
the Holy See along with the Acts of the Provincial
Council. While Cardinal Wiseman was in Rome
on that occasion, Father Boero took the paper to
him, and it was brought to England and printed
with the Acts, none of those concerned being aware
that the copy actually presented to the Sacred Congregation of Rites was far fuller than the one thus
printed.

"To this document was attached, when it came to
be presented to the Sacred Congregation, a petition in
the name of the Provincial Council that the Holy See
would be pleased to grant to England a feast of All
the Martyrs of England—*Omnium Angliæ Martyrum*—
with a proper Mass and Office. As there are many
canonized English Martyrs, there would have been
probably little difficulty in obtaining such a feast, if
it had not been for the last lesson of the second
nocturn. The two preceding lessons had spoken of
St. Alban, St. Elphege, SS. Ursula and her companions, of St. Thomas of Canterbury, and other
Saints; but then came, 'Nec defuere alii utriusque
sexus et omnis cœtus qui pro S. Sedis honore san-
guinem suum fundere non dubitarunt'—or words to
that effect, with something more of an account of the
persecution and the numbers of the Martyrs. It is

not to be wondered at that the Congregation of Rites met the petition with a simple *Negative.*"[1]

After the above-mentioned refusal nothing seems to have been done in the Martyrs' cause for some time, the revival of efforts apparently coinciding with Father Morris's entrance into the Society of Jesus. Here he found in his Master of Novices one who had interested himself in the Martyrs for some time past, and with his co-operation inquiries were re-opened in .Rome as to the best way of proceeding, and the new plan then formed was laid before Bishop Grant, in whose diocese the Novitiate was situated. In order to avoid the rock which had wrecked the first petition, no dispensation from the usual procedure of commencing with the ordinary Bishop's inquiry was directly asked for. It was nevertheless hoped that the seemingly insuperable difficulties of a regular Process would be avoided if the Holy See could accept in lieu thereof the inquiries which Bishops Smith and Challoner had already made into the subject.

The drawing up of the form of the proposed petition took some time; and before it could be formulated Father Morris was sent to Belgium, where he was too much occupied with his novice duties and the study of his theology to do much for the Cause of the Martyrs. Then came the Vatican Council, and the invasion of Rome by the Piedmontese. And so, though Father Boero urged action and averred that the Pope and the Roman Courts were exceedingly favourable to the Cause, three years slipped past before the petition could be forwarded. It was signed by Archbishop Manning and his suffragans in Low Week, 1871, according to the form which Father Morris had drawn up in the previous year. In December the translation of Challoner was completed, and in February next the

[1] *The Month*, ut supra.

petition was formally laid before the Holy Father by Father Boero, accompanied by a supplement from himself as Postulator of the Cause in Rome. The drift of this subsidiary paper was to urge the parity of the case in hand with that of the Corean Martyrs, for whom the Pope had permitted a mode of procedure very much like the one now desired.

The Pope received the *supplica* with evident favour, and Father Boero reported that the commission from the Congregation of Rites, which had been appointed on March 7th to examine it, seemed inclined to give it the fairest hearing. By the 10th of June the *Promotor Fidei* had reported on the documents, and proposed three questions about them. First, whether, all things considered, it was well to discuss the question at all; if so, whether the privilege asked for should be granted; and finally, if this was not granted, what other mode of procedure should be advised.

The first question, or *Dubium*, as it is called, was not intended to cast any doubt on the truth or importance of the martyrdoms, but was put forward in order to ascertain whether the English Government and people would take umbrage if the petition of honours for the Martyrs were sanctioned. The Cardinals decided to wait and consult the opinion of the English Bishops on the point, and on the 14th, Cardinal Patrizi wrote to Archbishop Manning, asking him to make fresh inquiries and report accordingly. Ere this inquiry had been made, and its results notified to the Roman Congregation, the year was already far spent. In the meanwhile something worse than delay had occurred to try Father Morris's perseverance. The Congregation had refused in any case to allow the report of Bishop Challoner to be accepted in lieu of a formal Process, and when the answer to the Archbishop's letter came on the 24th of April, 1873, it was found to consist of advice that he should take informations in the usual laborious manner, in technical language—*informativos et compulsoriales Processus propria Ordinaria auctoritate ad formam juris construere.*

The crisis in the history of the beatification of the Martyrs had arrived. It was now plain that if ecclesiastical sanction for their *cultus* was ever to be obtained, it would have to be won by proving their claims in full legal form. The difficulties in the way were considerable. With our small number of priests it is no easy matter to find a sufficient number to start a new mission, whence then were to be found persons free enough to fulfil the many offices requisite to constitute a full and dignified court of inquiry? Then, even if such a court were constituted, the chances against success were by no means slight. Unless all the legal formalities were strictly observed, its labours would be wasted, and its deliberations would be considered valueless by the Roman lawyers. But no one in the country had any practical knowledge what form the proceedings of such a court should take, and the only means of obtaining information on the subject was by long and heavy correspondence with Rome. No wonder then that, after so many efforts made in vain, and such difficulties lying in the way of success, most of those to whom Father Morris appealed for assistance met him at first with apologies, excuses and refusals—refusals, however, which he declined to accept. A year was spent in studying the legal forms to be observed. For this purpose he procured handbooks from Rome, and after mastering their intricacies as best he could under the circumstances, he proposed such doubts as remained to Father Boero for solution.

By the next spring he was ready to take action, and in May, 1874, the Fathers of the Oratory, in response to an invitation worded by Father Morris, and signed by the Archbishop, agreed to undertake some of the most onerous work in the cause. This news, a happy foretaste of success to come, reached Father Morris by a good omen, on the 4th of May, on which day we now keep the feast of the English Martyrs. In Father F. F. Knox, D.D., Father Morris found a coadjutor for whose assistance he never thought himself sufficiently grateful. Dr. Knox undertook the laborious duties of notary, and the successful issue of the whole Process was in great measure ensured by his painstaking care to secure exact compliance with all the prescriptions of the Canon Law. At first the Archbishop had thought of holding the sessions in the Seminary at Hammer-smith. So great, however, was the readiness of the Fathers of the Oratory to assist, that they placed their " Little Oratory," as well as several members of their community, at his service for the purposes of the Cause.

Here perhaps we cannot do better than revert to Father Morris's account of the proceedings already quoted :[1]

" It was indeed a tremendous undertaking, and it may be said here at the outset, that if the Fathers of the London Oratory had not lent themselves to it heart and soul, it could hardly have been carried out, however imperfectly. As it was, the work was so well and completely done that the Promoter of the Faith, the Roman official whose business it was to find fault with it, says that ' in everything relating to the examination of the sixteen witnesses who gave evidence, not only all was observed that the Common Law requires, but all that the more minute and exact laws of our tribunal require.' Let any one carefully examine what Benedict XIV. lays down, or let him look through one of the hand-books that have been written for the guidance of

[1] *The Month,* ut supra.

Church Courts in these circumstances, and he will see at once that a very remarkable degree of diligence and care was wanted to earn such praise. That diligence and that care were bestowed, and that praise was earned, chiefly by the late Father Francis Knox, of the London Oratory, himself a good theologian, a good canonist, and a good historian, to whom the great labour that fell upon him in the Martyrs' behalf was a labour of love.

" The Church's manner of investigating the virtues of a Confessor or of establishing the fact of a martyrdom is a judicial process, just as if she were examining the validity of a marriage or trying an accused person for a canonical offence. For this a Court must be formed, the essential parts of which are, first a judge or judges, secondly the notary, and thirdly the promoter. If the Bishop himself sits as judge, he needs no assessor ; his Vicar-General has one delegated judge to assist him ; and if neither the Bishop nor his Vicar-General sits as judge, then three ecclesiastics are deputed by the Bishop for that purpose. In our case the judges were Father Stanton, of the London Oratory, Father Bagshawe, then also of the London Oratory, now Bishop of Nottingham, and the Rev. Edmund Surmont, D.D., of St. Thomas's Seminary. The Promotor in all suits is the official whose business it is to see that the law of the Church is heard and respected. In matrimonial cases he is the *Promotor matrimoniorum*, to defend the validity of the marriage : in criminal cases he is the Promoter Fiscal ; in the causes of the Saints he represents the great Roman official, who is vulgarly called the Devil's Advocate, rightly the Promotor of the Faith. In the Episcopal Court the work is done by a Subpromoter of the Faith, who in our case was the Rev. Joseph Redman, D.D., then of Harrow, since of Brentford. Father Knox was the

Notary of the Court, upon whom the brunt of the labour fell. Every word that each witness said was written down by him, and every occurrence however slight was recorded. There has to be besides an inferior official of the Court, called the Cursor, whose business it is to summon each witness in due form, and to certify the Court that he has been duly summoned.

" The witnesses are in the main selected by the Postulator, but it is usual that when the witnesses proposed by the Postulator have been heard, the Court should itself call two or three, who are called *ex officio* witnesses. In our Martyrs' case I was the Postulator. Sixteen witnesses were examined, amongst whom I remember were the Duke of Norfolk, the late Lord Petre, Lord Arundell of Wardour, Bishop Hedley, Canon O'Toole, Father Stevenson, Brother Foley, Mr. David Lewis; and, if I remember rightly, the *ex officio* witnesses were Bishop Weathers and Provost Hunt—altogether, as the Promoter of the Faith said of them, they were *testes omni exceptione majores.*

" I remember being greatly amused with the case of one witness who did not appear. The late Sir George Bowyer had been summoned, and, as I knew, he wished to give evidence respecting the Knights of Malta who were martyred under Henry VIII. When his name was called as the next witness, I had to read to the Court a note he had written to me to say that the time did not suit him. The Court decreed that he be discharged of his attendance and the next witness be called; and, much to his chagrin, Sir George was not examined, as he had hoped to have been. The old civil lawyer had forgotten that he was dealing with a Court that was not going to allow itself to be trifled with, and that had the power of punishing contumacy with excommunication.

" The Process was opened in the Domestic Chapel

of the Cardinal Archbishop on June 19, 1874. Frequent sessions were held in the Little Oratory between that day and the 15th of August; then they were suspended for the copying of the Depositions, and resumed and completed in September. The last session, like the first, was held in the Archbishop's Chapel, and the late Lord Henry Kerr was sworn to convey to the Sacred Congregation of Rites the duly collated copy of the original acts, which latter were deposited in the Archives of the see of Westminster. They constituted two thick folio volumes of manuscript."

A few words must be added as to the particular part taken by Father Morris, for it will have been noticed that he mentions nothing about himself except the bare fact that he was the Postulator in the Cause. The legal theory which accounts for that name, and briefly explains its functions, is this. He is supposed to be the friend of the Cause. The proceedings commence by his appearing before the Ordinary, *i.e.*, in this case the Archbishop, and *suing* (*postulare*) for proceedings to be instituted. When any new stage is to be begun, or witness ·introduced, he has to appear anew in court, and again *request* that the step be taken, or the witness be heard. Theoretically then he is supposed to have the Cause warmly at heart, the case at his fingers' ends, the necessary documents in his bag, and sufficient witnesses at his back. As it is easy to see, great exertions were necessary to effect all that this theory required. Witnesses had to be found, and, when found, encouraged to appear, an ordeal from which many naturally shrank at first. Even the language of the court had its difficulties. Latin is obligatory for all the formal proceedings, the evidence of witnesses may be taken down in the vernacular, but must afterwards be translated into Latin or Italian. Documents, often of great length, had to be copied, and all concerned

o

looked to him for encouragement and direction in their arduous undertaking.

The following translation of a graceful little Latin speech, in which Father Morris returned thanks to the Archbishop at the close of the last session, gives a summary of the amount of work which had been done:

" This session, which I apologize for prolonging, in my importunity, is, Most Reverend Lord, our thirty-seventh. Of these twenty have been occupied in taking the testimony of witnesses, seven in the collation of the whole Process, while the other ten have been passed, partly in receiving the oaths of the witnesses, partly in the trial and acceptance of documentary evidence. In all, the witnesses number sixteen; the days occupied, thirty-one; the pages of the original Process, written from first to last by the notary's hand, nigh on seven hundred. Your Grace will see what pains they, to whom you entrusted the execution of this work, have expended on their task.

" The work is yours, Most Reverend Lord Arch-bishop, begun under your patronage, confirmed by your authority. God grant that among the glories of your episcopate may be reckoned this one—that this Cause may be not only commenced, but also happily con-cluded, and that our Martyrs may be raised to the honours of the altars by that same authority of the Roman Pontiff, in the defence of which they gladly died."

" This Process, then, the result of some months of hard work, was duly carried to Rome by Lord Henry Kerr and deposited with the Sacred Congregation of Rites. It was there opened with the requisite formalities. Our hope was that, at no great interval of time, the case might be ready for hearing; and a petition was presented to the Pope, and was granted by him, that we might be dispensed from the law requiring ten years to elapse between the presentation of the Ordinary Process to the Congregation of Rites and the proposal in the Congregation of the Introduction of the Cause. But Rome moves slowly, and we could make no use of this Rescript. Twelve years have passed, and the law was more than kept.

"The first thing that happened to our Process was that the translation of the English evidence, which we had sent with it, was rejected, and an entirely new translation of the whole was made in Rome. The Process was, when this was completed, put into the hands of our lawyers, the Avvocati Alibrandi and Lugari, whose business it was to arrange all the matter contained in the depositions of the witnesses and in the documents, in the shape in which it should be put before the Sacred Congregation. The great number of the Martyrs and the mass of the matter to be handled, made this a long proceeding. This had all to be printed, and there was a fresh cause of delay even in the manner of the printing, for His Holiness had established a private printing-press for his own use in the Vatican Palace, and in order to lessen the weight of its expenses, he ordered that all documents in the Causes of Beatification and Canonization should be printed at that press only. It is needless to say that they were taken in hand only when the press wanted 'copy.' At length two large folio volumes were ready, and constituted our statement of the case. These were now placed in the hands of Mgr. Caprara, the Promoter of the Faith, and they seemed to our longing eyes to disappear. We waited long, but it must be acknowledged that we did not wait in vain. If Roman officials seem to do their work leisurely, no one can blame them for not doing it effectually. The Promoter's printed *Disquisitio* contains a careful examination, not only of the Process and the documents in general, but of each particular case proposed. The result of it was that of the 353 names in the list attached to the Process, he assented to the introduction of 277. There were thus 76 to whom he made objections. His objections were answered by our lawyers, and with such success that in his rejoinder—called *Additio ad Disquisitionem*—the Promoter of the Faith withdrew his objections to 32, raising the number of unopposed names to 309. There remain 43 cases to which he continued to object, and the single case of Father Henry Garnet in which he held himself neutral. The 43 names still officially objected to, are those of Martyrs who died in prison, and the ground of the objection is generally that, though they died *in* prison, it had not been proved that their death was caused *by* the hardships of the prison. To this the Advocates of the Martyrs have no official right of reply, but an answer was printed by them, called *Memoriale ex gratia legendum.*"

This was not at all unsatisfactory, but a still greater consolation was in store. Some months previously the following extract from a letter, written by Mgr. (now Archbishop) O'Callaghan, who is joint Postulator with Father Armellini, S.J., had been sent on to Father Morris by Cardinal Manning's secretary, to whom it was addressed :

"*Rome, June* 5, 1886.—Please tell the Cardinal with my respectful regards that I have had the consolation of helping on very materially the Cause of the English Martyrs, by submitting for more attentive examination, the book of engravings published in Rome in 1584, representing the paintings in our church. Yesterday I had a long interview with Mgr. Caprara, who spoke of the book as *un Documento grave*, as it was published *cum privilegio Gregorii XIII*. He therefore said that he must reconsider his course, and see whether it would not be advisable to propose at once some for Beatification," &c.

Mgr. Promotore was as good as his word. In his *Additio ad Disquisitionem* he expressed his conviction that these engravings were proofs of an ecclesiastical *cultus* accorded to the earlier Martyrs by Pope Gregory XIII., and thus these earlier Martyrs were accepted by the Congregation as worthy of "equipollent" or "equivalent" Beatification. This it did at its sitting of December 4th, 1886, when the cases were throughout decided in accordance with the views of the Promoter of the Faith. The two decrees of the Sacred Congregation were confirmed by the Pope on the 9th and 29th of the same month. On the former day he signed the Introduction of the Cause of 255 English Martyrs, who were henceforth honoured as *Venerable;* and on the feast of St. Thomas of Canterbury he confirmed the decree which admitted 53 of our Martyrs to the honour of Beatification.

This decision gave the keenest pleasure to all those who were interested and earnest in the cause, and Father Morris received warm congratulations from many of his friends. Cardinal Manning sent to him the following note ·

"Archbishop's House, Dec. 9, 1886.

"My dear Father Morris,—Many thanks for your letter. I heartily thank God. My share has been but small, but yours from the beginning has been great and constant, and we owe much to you. . . . I thank God with you to have lived to see this *in diebus nostris*. It is like the resurrection of the witnesses, whose bodies

have lain so long in Babylon, and the world sending
gifts over their bodies. They seem to be coming out
of their sepulchres to appear amongst us. It will give
a great impulse to the faithful to aspire to a higher
life, I hope. I have long invoked St. Thomas More
in secret, and now write him so for the first time.

" Believe me always,
    " Yours affectionately in J. C.,
        " HENRY E. CARD. ARCHBISHOP."

The good news was especially seasonable, because
at the time Father Morris was slowly recovering from
a serious breakdown of his nervous system. Even
then, in spite of failing powers, his first thought was
to do what he could to improve the present occasion.

It was now necessary that Offices of the Martyrs
should be composed and approved, both for the Church
in England at large, and for such dioceses and Religious
Orders as desired special Offices wherein to commemo-
rate the Martyrs with whom they were more closely
connected. The lion's share, both in the compilation
of these Offices, and in the more laborious process of
getting them approved in Rome, fell upon Father
Morris. His also was the task of drawing up litanies
and other devotions in their honour; and he exerted
himself to the full measure of his limited strength in
making them better known by lectures and sermons.

The future progress of the Cause had next to be
considered, and a choice made between two courses
of action. Either the Cause might be proceeded with
promptly, and pushed on in the form in which it had
already been cast; or its list of names might be made
out afresh and might receive many additions. In
favour of the first alternative—that of working at once
for the canonization of some at least of our Martyrs,
and leaving the rest alone—it was obvious that much

could be said. To have had even one or two officially declared *Saints*, would have been wonderfully consoling and satisfactory. But there were also obvious disadvantages, of which the chief was that, had the canonization of one or two been successfully accomplished, there would be, humanly speaking, little chance of the courts subsequently going back to reconsider the claims of other Martyrs whose names were, for a variety of reasons, omitted from the list of those for whom the honours due to martyrdom had been in the first instance claimed from the Holy See. Thus the names of a considerable number of Martyrs were actually unknown when the Cause began, and had been discovered since then. Fresh documents had been found, which showed that the cases of some originally passed over as hopelessly weak, were in reality very strong.[1] The second alternative therefore commended itself to Father Morris's mind, and he now proposed to request the Roman authorities to pronounce on all the names which had ever been honoured among Catholics as those of English Martyrs. This of course involved a new Process on behalf of the *prætermissi* from the first Process, and this he suggested to Cardinal Manning, who took up the matter with alacrity.

In September, 1888, therefore, the new Process of the *prætermissi*, who numbered about 200, was formally instituted. With respect to many of these, as might easily be expected, no very great amount of information could now be obtained, still it would have been very unfair and inconsistent to have left that little untold. The sessions were held at the Archbishop's House, and with the experience of the previous Process as a guide, this one worked easily and smoothly. The late Bishop

[1] It was not at first known how far the Martyrs would be judged of *in globo*, and whether the breakdown of one case might not affect all the rest.

Weathers was the Deputy Judge; Dr. Redman, as before, the Promotor Fiscalis; and Father Guiron at first, but for the greater part of the time Father Robert F. Clarke, of Great Ormond Street, discharged the onerous duties of Notary. The witnesses were the Archbishop of Edinburgh, and Father Stanton, of the London Oratory, *ex officio*, while the late Father Joseph Stevenson, S.J., Dom Aidan Gasquet, O.S.B., Dom Gilbert Dolan, O.S.B., Father Thaddeus, O.S.F., Joseph Gillow, Esq., and the present writer were the ordinary witnesses.

The first session of this Process was held on the 24th August, 1888, the sixtieth and last on the 13th August, 1889; the transcript of its proceedings was then carried to Rome by Dr. Giles. So far no judgment has been passed upon it; but it has been there as yet only half the time that elapsed between the conclusion of the previous Process and delivery of judgment. The officials have moreover been occupied in examining the claims to Beatification of the martyred Abbots of the three great Benedictine monasteries of Glastonbury, Reading, and Colchester, and their companions. The judgment on their case, delivered on May 13th, 1895, is all that Father Morris could have desired. The three Abbots and their companions, with Sir Adrian Fortescue, and Thomas Percy, Earl of Northumberland, are *Beati.*

Such in outline has been the course of events which have led up to the present extension of devotion to the English Martyrs. The chief cause for that extension is no doubt the decision given in their favour by the Holy See. But Father Morris's part in preparing the way for that decision was in many respects a leading one. He claims therefore a large share in the credit for the good done, though something still remains to be told about the assistance which his literary labours contributed towards the accomplishment of the same result, and much might have been added about memorials, petitions, papers, lectures, and sermons, had this biography been written on a larger scale. Enough, however, has been said to enable the reader to form an idea of the amount of labour expended in this work of a lifetime. We may now pass on to a new phase of Father Morris's career.

CHAPTER IX.

ALL Father Morris's books are conspicuous for scholar-like precision. This was in part due to his accurate mind and retentive memory, and was perhaps assisted by his long training in the post of secretary. He was naturally quick at assimilating details, and became a good historian, rubrician, and antiquarian, having also at his command abundance of sound information on architecture, moral theology, and Canon Law.

He possessed one special advantage for the acquisition of positive knowledge in his aptitude for rapidly taking down well selected and well arranged notes. Even his most hasty jottings were clear and intelligible, and the facility with which he reduced a complex subject to a series of heads was remarkable. He wrote a beautiful hand, and his papers, finished without erasure or correction, were models of distinctness and order. " How I envy you your sober, graceful, disciplined, weighty, and characteristic handwriting," wrote Dr. Jessop to him, in a letter of January, 1877. Another letter from the same writer dated July 14, 1879, opens with the words: " I envy you as one of the happy men who seem quite independent of *pens!* Whatever your instrument, you always seem to me to write precisely the same hand. We weaker vessels are what pens make us, dominated by them, inspired by them, convinced and mastered by them. Sometimes stirred by them to a certain *pruritus scribendi*, sometimes paralyzed by them into hopeless helpless lassitude."

Though honesty and precision were the most conspicuous features of Father Morris's literary character, they represent but half what he was, and perhaps the less attractive half. The mind that worked with such regularity and accuracy, was deeply stirred by affections of singular strength and warmth. In truth had these not been restrained by the hand of discipline, they might easily have been excessive in their manifestation. As it was, the presence of force in reserve was ever perceptible, and when he spoke in public with the intention of awakening the emotions of others, his own emotion often outran theirs and seemed to carry them along with itself. As soon, however, as he had set himself to write calmly at his desk, his passion for facts and figures and details outweighed every other consideration. Indeed readers of Father Morris's books have its results continually, and perhaps unduly, obtruded upon them. He is perpetually amassing names, dates, references, and quotations, and he had a positive aversion for summarizing a document, when he could possibly insert the original passage *in extenso*.

The first work in which the literary qualities, which we have been describing, were displayed, was his *Life of St. Thomas Becket*, whom Father Morris considered one of the greatest characters in history. He must also have been drawn to study the Saint's life by finding himself placed under his patronage, first at the English College in Rome, and again, both at Marlow and at Northampton, where he was associated with places which would vividly bring Becket's life before him. He was deep in the work as early as 1853, at the time of his second stay in Rome: and it will be remembered how the brief sketch of his life at that period, speaks of his "scream of delight" when reading aloud certain passages in which he thought he had been happy in catching some trait of the blessed Martyr's character. The enthusiasm and fire of Father Morris's character are perhaps seen to greater advantage in this than in most of his subsequent works. The varied materials at his command are here so grouped together as to form one connected drama, wherein the great Saint lives and moves, so that we can read his high purpose, and admire the courage with which he fought out the long struggle that ended but with his heroic death.

Shortly after the publication of this Life in 1859, another book appeared treating the same subject from an exactly opposite point of view; and critics had the pleasure of contrasting the work of the Canon of Northampton with that of James Craigie Robertson, Canon of Canterbury. The objection raised against the former was a curious one. Reviewers were, as may be supposed, as little or less acquainted ·with hagiography then- than they are now, and they gravely lectured him on the impropriety and incongruity of professing to write history, while venerating as a canonized saint the man whose story he was recounting. Still the book at once made its mark, and was soon out of print.

When writing this first edition of the Saint's Life, Canon Morris had been obliged to collect his materials as best he could out of the veritable chaos in which they had been left before they came into his hands. The second edition was long deferred, and did not appear till the year 1885, when it was found to have been recast and greatly enlarged by the introduction of fresh matter drawn from sources of information now first brought to light, and chiefly from the recent publications, issued under the authority of the Master of the Rolls. The desire to benefit by these new opportunities of studying Becket's life and character had in fact been the motive for the delay.

It is curious that the longest break in his career as a man of letters should come immediately after his first success. This was due, not to any abandonment of his studious pursuits, but to the full occupation of his time with the duties of his post as secretary to Cardinal Wiseman. We have seen that his taste for literature was not effaced by his various employments, though they only left him sufficient leisure to write a few articles in the *Dublin Review*, and to prepare year by year for the publication of the *Ordo* and *Directory*.

After six years he resigned his position under the Archbishop of Westminster in order to enter the Society of Jesus. This step, we have said, was shortly followed by a great increase in his efforts to obtain the beatification of the English Martyrs. These efforts led in turn to a corresponding increase in literary activity. If the Cause of the Martyrs was ever to prosper, they must be known. Hence · his constant endeavours from this time forward to bring their history before the public. During the period of his novitiate he had of course nothing to do with actual publication. But he had time for reading and for the study of ascetical theology; while his year for repeating dogmatic theology at Louvain gave an opportunity of further educating his mind. His stay in Belgium also introduced him to the Bollandist Fathers, who were able to show him in the Belgian Archives much that proved afterwards of very great service.

Returning to England in 1869, he introduced to the public a book which had been privately printed at Manresa while he was a novice. This was the excellent translation by Father G. Kingdon of the *Autobiography of Father John Gerard*, one of the early Jesuit missioners in England. Rich in stories of hairbreadth escapes and heroic endurance, the book sets before the reader a vivid picture of the times in which its writer lived, and possesses surpassing interest for all who are attracted to the history of that period. Father Gerard was one of the few men who succeeded in escaping from the dungeons of the Tower, and his account of the bold adventure is excellently written. He was, moreover, in dangers often—in the city, in the country, in journeys, and from false brethren. Even when he falls into the hands of the men of the law, they fail to gain the advantage over him. In one most amusing scene an Anglican dean meets him dressed in secular attire, begins by unsuspectingly reading him a serious homily, but ends in discomfiture and retreat, to the enormous delight of his Catholic hosts. He sets forth admirably the aims of the missioners, and describes their methods of action, he refers not unfrequently to persons of importance in the kingdom, and makes us acquainted with the details of some events of historical moment. We can well understand, therefore, how powerfully the book appealed to Father Morris's historic sympathies, more especially in his distinctive vocation as the message-bearer of our Martyrs; and how diligently he applied to its editing all such moments as could legitimately be spared from the discharge of other duties.

Its need of able preparation for the press was one of its peculiar features. Though Father Gerard wrote in 1609, after he had finally retired from England, it was still impossible for him to name directly either the persons with whom he had dealt, or the places where he had lived. If he had done this any spy who might gain possession of a copy of the book, would have had the means of betraying many of the noblest Catholics in England. He therefore indicated persons by long and disguised descriptions; and even so the work, despite its general interest, was never allowed to be published. These circumlocutions naturally weaken the force of the narrative, and an editor able to supply the missing names correctly would considerably enhance the value of the story. This Father Morris set himself to do, and found it to be no easy task.

So difficult indeed was the solution of its innumerable riddles, that it was morally impossible to provide an answer to them all in the first edition. The greater portion of the volume was therefore given up to Father Gerard's *History of the Gunpowder Plot*, and only so much of the Autobiography itself was published as sufficed to place beyond doubt the character and reliability of its author. In the second edition the tangled skein was all unravelled, save in a few comparatively unimportant particulars.[1] The task of finding illustrative matter also required great diligence on the part of the editor. Father Gerard, like the rest of his brethren, was pursued by the Government as if he had been a criminal, and secret agents were active in forwarding to the officials such information as could be obtained regarding his personal appearance, places of abode, and the like. It was therefore necessary to search among the Public Records for these documents, and to incorporate in the book such of them as would throw light on the main story.

Both these difficulties were grappled with successfully, and by overcoming them this further advantage

---

[1] An idea of the difficulties which Father Morris experienced owing to the want of adequate catalogues may be gathered from the fact that after inquiring for a whole year as to the whereabouts of Father Greenway's Italian translation of Gerard's *History of the Powder Plot*, he could not learn where it was until too late to make any use of the information. By aid of the Historical MSS. Commission's publications, such a question would now be solved in a few minutes. The cataloguing of private muniments has also greatly advanced since then.

was gained, that the reliability of the story even in its minutest points was clearly proved. We never trust a writer's accuracy more entirely than when we have found him correct in numerous small details, in which he would least of all expect to have his trust-worthiness tested. Father Morris, in his editorial comments, applied this test to Gerard's Autobiography, and therefore brought home with great force that lesson in our history, which he seemed raised up to teach—that the story of Catholicism under Elizabeth deserved not only the sympathy, but the respectful admiration of Englishmen. For if Gerard's story were believed, that was its irresistible moral.

Though the Life of Gerard has probably done more towards effecting this than any of Father Morris's other volumes, the series entitled *Troubles of our Catholic Fore-fathers,* which he next published, did much to strengthen and deepen the impression already made. The three numbers of the series contain contemporary accounts of the sufferings of our Catholic ancestors in the defence of their faith. The first volume includes nine such narratives, the most interesting of which are the story of Margaret Clement and the Carthusian Monks, the imprisonment of Francis Tregian, and the adventures of Father Blount.

This volume was very well received, but the next, though exceedingly erudite, failed to defray the expenses of publication. It was an edition of the *Letter-Book of Sir Amias Poulet, Keeper of Mary Queen of Scots.* The manuscript of this book, I can remember hearing Father Morris say, was brought to him in a parcel, while he was at Oxford, by Dr. Blackett, who asked him to look at it and give him an opinion as to its value. Being in the midst of other work, Father Morris laid the parcel on one side, and had forgotten all about it, when he spied one corner peeping out from under some papers. He opened it, began to read, and soon felt assured that the hitherto neglected parcel contained papers of no small value. They were duplicates of the letters sent by Queen Mary's keeper to Elizabeth's Ministers. The existence of many parts of this correspondence was known from other sources, but the recovery of the whole threw fresh light on a large number of incidents in poor Mary's captivity.

At the time Father Morris wrote, Mr. J. A. Froude's *History* had but lately been published, and these letters disclosed how astonishing a liberty he had taken with the records of facts before him in order to paint those striking pictures with which he never fails to entertain his readers. Nothing can be more judicious than the combination of moderation and power with which Father Morris kills these vivid creations of Mr. Froude's fancy.

Mr. Swinburne's estimate of this book is noteworthy. Though he differed widely in his sympathies and historical methods from Father Morris, he describes[1] the Letter-Books as "a volume nothing less than invaluable, as well as indispensable to all serious students of the subjects in hand." Yet its failure to obtain a sale or interest many showed that the book was unfortunately above the heads of the general public. When writing to Miss Lambert, on June 18, 1875, Father Morris says:

"I am very much pleased to hear that Mrs. Lambert was interested in *Poulet*. The book has been such a failure that it is an encouragement. My new book I am less afraid of. *Poulet* was not the book to interest Catholics, though I think literary people would have liked it, if it were possible to get them to know of the existence of anything Catholic. It fell between two stools. But I think Catholics will read *Weston* and

[1] *Miscellanies by A. C. Swinburne,* 1886, p. 381.

P

Tyrrell.   I am selfish in wishing to interest you in those times, for I have not done with them yet."

In March, 1874, he returned to his *Troubles,* and began to arrange for press the interesting autobiography of that admirable old confessor of the Faith, Father William Weston, S.J., with which he unwisely coupled the discordant and repulsive confessions of Anthony Tyrrell, a man who played a despicable part in the history of that period.   Not having the courage to bear imprisonment for the Faith with patience, he came to terms with the enemies of his Church and his brethren, and became a participator in many of the worst practices of Elizabeth's Government, all which villanies he afterwards admitted in his confessions. The study of such a career throws valuable light on the history of the time, but it is far from pleasant reading. The volume therefore never became very popular, though his more literary critics praised it even more than the first of the series.

Not long after the publication of this volume, Father Morris was allowed some leisure to prosecute in the Belgian Archives the researches he had begun there a few years previously.   As is well known, the English Jesuits, with all other Religious Orders, were obliged by intolerance at home to set up Houses and Colleges abroad, in which they had perforce to keep all their muniments, as well as their literary and historical papers.   At the time of the Suppression of the Society in 1773, the Austrian Government laid hands on nearly all these papers, and they were long lost to the view of the English members of the Society.   In 1857, Father Cobb made a tentative search through the Archives of Paris, Arras, St. Omer, Brussels, and Bruges, but had little success in finding anything of moment, as the Archives had not then been put into order, or sufficiently catalogued.   Later on, some of our Belgian

Fathers, in searching the Government Archives, came upon various traces of the confiscated papers, and at their suggestion Mr. Simpson and Mr. Charles Weld made a little tour in Belgium, and copied not a few documents of value.

In 1869, Father Morris made the acquaintance of Father Charles Waldack, S.J., whose researches in connection with the history of his own Province had given him a very extensive knowledge of the manuscript repositories of Belgium, and he received from him the clue to the places where in time the long lost documents, or at least what remained of them, were discovered. After that Father Morris made several short visits to Belgium, and did some useful work during the years 1871 and 1875. As he was obliged in these brief expeditions to rely upon his own pen for copying, the transcripts that he brought back with him were not very numerous, but their value for the history of English Jesuits was considerable, and they opened the way to further investigation. It so happened, however, that he was never able to publish much of what he had collected in Belgium. His materials were more largely used by Brother Foley and Father Hogan than by himself.

A few weeks after this trip to Belgium, he again broke what was practically new ground. He had long desired to trace the papers left by the " Council of the North," which in Elizabeth's time had so unmercifully harassed the Catholics of Yorkshire and the neighbourhood, and he suspected that many of these papers might yet be found among the voluminous records of the Castle and Cathedral at York. Thither he accordingly went with an introduction to the Archbishop, who in turn recommended him to Canon Raine, than whom no better guide could have been found. With his assistance very satisfactory results were obtained.

Though the particular papers which Father Morris was in quest of appeared to be no longer extant, much new matter came to light in the Corporation House-Books. Copying here was facilitated by the good offices of the nuns of the Convent at Micklegate Bar, whose acquaintance Father Morris had made in 1863. They have supplied some recollections of his visit, from which a few passages may be quoted.

"The treasures which the House-Books contained exceeded his expectations, so that, finding more work before him than he could get through alone, he asked the Rev. Mother for 'the loan of some of her nuns.' Three of us were told off to help him, and a delightful three weeks we had of it. Interesting in itself, the work was rendered more so by the information it called forth from him. He would sometimes stop proceedings to draw attention to some point of special interest, and the quiet humour in his face showed how thoroughly he enjoyed handing over certain passages for transcription, such for example as referred to 'Jesuites and other such wicked persons.' His dry decided way of giving directions afforded us some amusement, and among ourselves he was playfully styled 'Father Master,' a title of affectionate reverence which touched while it amused him. The love of the antiquarian for the 'dear old books' showed itself many a time in characteristically simple fashion. He handled them all tenderly, but a special favourite would get an affectionate pat, or be held aloft for a parting look from the scribes before being returned to the Municipal Archives."

Owing to the diligence of those who thus assisted him, the materials for the next volume of *Troubles* were soon ready, and laying aside the idea of incorporating with them the reminiscences of another renegade called Wadsworth, the editing of whose memoirs he had begun, he filled the whole of this book with papers relating to the Catholics of the North. The volume was an interesting one, though it suffered somewhat in popularity from the disconnected character of its contents.

Though he little thought so at the time, this volume, the Preface of which bears date November 30, 1876, was to be his last. Never again would he have leisure to write, until he was so broken in health that he could not face the labour of producing a large work. He did indeed manage to steal sufficient time from his other occupations to bring out another edition of Father Gerard's Autobiography in 1881, and of the *Life of St. Thomas of Canterbury* in 1885; and during his latter years he contributed to magazines a goodly number of short studies on the various subjects of which he was master. But his days of initiation had practically closed. Active duties henceforth left him no spare time for that prolonged preparation which all thorough work must cost its author.

It is indeed wonderful how he managed to write as much as he did, seeing that he was seldom wholly free for literary work save during the short periods usually set aside for vacation. The labours connected with such posts of authority as Father Minister to a community of fifty or sixty persons, or as Socius and Secretary to the Provincial, seem altogether incompatible with the publication of the five volumes which, as will be seen in the Appendix, were brought out during the three years he held those offices. Nor was his period of Professorship at St. Beuno's in itself a favourable time for the publication of historical works. His primary duty there was not writing, but teaching. Proof of his conscientiousness in discharging it are three fat volumes, containing in all about two thousand pages, in which all his lectures are written out in full.

The penmanship is faultless throughout, and they are full of references and extracts copied *in extenso :* in fact they are ready for printing as they stand. The following extract from a letter to Canon Estcourt, November 19, 1875, illustrates his method of work.

" I have Canon Law to teach this year and I am giving my whole time to it, putting Queen Elizabeth and all her persecution away for the present. I am thinking of publishing an English handbook of Canon Law. I think it would be useful, but it is not easy to make up one's mind at what length to enter into subjects or to discuss difficulties. Besides it is rather a thorny subject, as practice and law do not always coincide, and I am not sure that it would be free from the appearance of teaching my betters. At any rate I will prepare my lectures with a view to publication."

Father Morris was also generous of his time in assisting others. Dr. Jessop, while engaged from the years 1873 to 1878 on his admirable study of the Walpoles, was in frequent communication with him by letter, and in his Preface to Father Walpole's letters, he says : [1]

"Father Morris, the learned editor of *Troubles of our Catholic Forefathers*, and of Father Gerard's Autobio-graphy, and Account of the Gunpowder Plot, has again and again come to my assistance. In the midst of studies, which, one would have thought, might well have excused him from turning aside to hunt up references and the like for a stranger, he has never once failed me, and I have rarely applied to him for infor-mation without receiving more than I had hoped to gain."

When Father Morris's name became known as an authority to be relied on, a constantly increasing number of inquiries were sent to him concerning

[1] P. vi.

obscure, doubtful, or little-studied points of the subjects with which he had made himself familiar. Not only was he ready to answer such questions fully, but also to encourage others to enter his own field of study and research, and undertake what, it might have been supposed, he would have preferred to retain for himself. Thus he sent Lady Georgiana Fullerton, June 20, 1871, a letter, too long for insertion here, in which he urges her to undertake a book on the lives of the Martyrs, as she contemplated doing, and gives her a short but clear account of the sources whence the necessary information could be drawn. Yet similarly, in the letter which follows, he is willing to entrust to another a work which, as he was wont to say, his hand itched to write.

"111, Mount Street, July 29, 1874.

"My dear Father Stanton,—P.C.,—The Martyrs cannot be in better hands than Mrs. Hope's, and I resign them to her with the satisfaction of feeling that they will be gainers. It would be some little time before I could do anything for them, as I am going to give my intervals of time in the first instance to Father Weston's narrative. I love them well enough to know how to give them up. . . . By all means encourage her to undertake the book, and make them popular.

"Yours very faithfully in Jesus Christ,

"JOHN MORRIS, S.J."

In one sense it is true to say that Father Morris's literary career, viewed as a means to a definite end, did not reach its intended term. He never completed the work which he most of all wished to achieve, and with regard to which he considered such books as he did publish to be preliminaries. When presenting Father Stanton with a copy of his second series of *Troubles*, he says:

"Louvain, June 10, 1875.

" In the book you have just received I have adhered to my original plan of editing unpublished papers of the time of persecution, instead of undertaking as yet what I should have been far more glad to do, the lives of the Martyrs. I am thus acquiring and perhaps diffusing some general information respecting the times of persecution, which will be more or less useful when we come to the Martyrs. For this latter work, however, it would be necessary to be free from other engagements, and if I had the time to devote to it, I would place it first and do it at once. . . . I may have more time to give to the Martyrs by-and-bye "

These lives remain, alas! still unwritten; and in this sense the great literary work Father Morris aimed at accomplishing was never finished. From another point of view, however, it is true to say that his success was complete, as the following criticisms show.

Dr. Jessop, in the *Academy* for July 9, 1881, states:

" Mr. Morris is one of the few living writers who have succeeded in greatly modifying certain views of English History, which had been long accepted as the only tenable ones."

In the *Athenæum* for January 27, 1877, a more detailed testimony is borne to the same effect:

" We have to congratulate Mr. Morris on having left his mark on Elizabethan history; the historian of the future can never afford to pass him by without a tribute of gratitude, and the homage always due to conscientious toil and original research. . . . Although possessing an eye for the picturesque, he yet never appears before us in any other character than as a scholarly and painstaking critic. He gives us his facts, produces his evidence, and leaves us to ourselves to make the best or the worst of the case. He does not even aim at being an advocate, much less a judge in the cause. Whether that cause be good or bad, at any rate he has no misgivings; he is always profusely candid. His notes and comments are always strictly explanatory, and become more and more so with each succeeding volume. . . . Indeed it is surprising how, with the very strong temptation that must be upon him at times, Mr. Morris should never allow himself to appear as a controversialist. The theological and polemical element is absolutely eliminated, the historical is not only in the ascendant, it is paramount."

Again, two months later on, Canon Raine writes in the *Academy*, March 24, 1877: "Nothing can exceed the fairness with which he discusses matters on which he must feel most deeply, and the moderation which he shows towards the agents in a persecution of exceptional severity and duration."

Such encomiums quoted simply by themselves, and without other criticism, might arouse suspicion. We are now, however, in a position to discuss them without fear of misunderstanding. We have here an acknowledgment by no party organ and in no exaggerated terms that he had made known the message, which it was his mission, as a writer and as a historian, to deliver, that he had introduced to the knowledge of the many a history which had till then been a tradition, known only to a few. This is not to be understood as implying that he was the only historian who has ever told this story, or that as its teacher he will never be surpassed. Before his time Mr. Simpson had written on the same subject, perhaps with even greater erudition; and he was shortly followed by Brother Foley, whose publications were incomparably more extensive. Dr. Jessop, Father Gibson, Canon Estcourt, Father Knox, and others among his contemporaries, helped to make the same historical period better known; and since their time there has arisen a new generation of writers, headed by Fathers Gasquet and Bridgett, who have extended the limits of known history in many directions. Yet we are sure that these would be the first to acknowledge the importance of the good service done to his cause by Father Morris as a writer.

It is not necessary to maintain that his views found equal favour with all readers. The Protestant public, as far as it interested itself in the facts at all, seemed not averse to accept his negative conclusions, and to admit the want of moderation and humanity in the Protestant Reformers. That Father Morris should have carried his co-religionists further was indeed to be expected, but the success is not on that account to be underrated.

We are a hard race to move, and when he began his crusade we were almost giving up the belief that our Martyrs were worth fighting for. That their *cultus* should be restored and confirmed, and that the confirmation should be welcomed with intelligent acclamation, was made possible by Father Morris's painstaking writing, not less than by his persevering action.

CHAPTER X.

THE MASTER OF NOVICES.

WE left Father Morris, three chapters ago, under orders to proceed to Manresa. Father George Porter, then Rector and Master of Novices, and afterwards Archbishop of Bombay, had been summoned to Rome, and some one was wanted to give the novices their long retreat. Father Morris was chosen for the work, and thus announced his change of occupation to Mrs. Scott Murray:

"*September* 26, 1877.—A line to tell you—in case you have not yet left Danesfield—that I have been sent to take Father Porter's place for three months, including the month's retreat. I enjoy the prospect of the last, as I bewailed that I should never make the long retreat again, and giving it is next best. The retreat will be from November 25th to December 25th. This is a big place to have charge of. I suppose there are one hundred of Ours here, and no less than fifty-one scholastic novices. Thank God for their number, but the responsibility is heavy. . . . I say no more, for I have plenty to do.

"*December* 1.—Our long retreat is now fairly launched. This is the seventh day, and the day after to-morrow is our first repose day. There are thirty-three making it, of whom six are priests. Pray for us all, and pray especially that no one's health and strength may fail.

It is surprising how much weaker people are than they used to be.

" I return to St. Beuno's when Father Porter comes back, but when that will be I do not yet know. He will stay on at Rome when the Provincial leaves, and the pace things will go in Rome no one can estimate.

" The work with the novices is delightful, but I do not relish the rectorship of this big place. Pray for me, and I will pray for you."

Father Porter did not return from Rome for two or three years, and in 1878 Father Morris received his patent as Rector and Master of Novices. He had some valuable qualifications for his new post, though, as so often happens, they were accompanied by one or two defects, which we cannot altogether pass over. From reminiscences set down by some who were novices under him at the time, it may be gathered that his chief characteristics were his precision and exactness (or, as it is called, " logicality ") of mind, and a wonderfully warm heart. He was logical in carrying out the principles by which he guided himself, and logical almost to a fault in the manner in which he taught them to others. He was precise in seeing that all rules, whether they regarded the ceremonies of the Church or the customs of the community, were carried out to the letter. But the depth and warmth of his affection formed his most remarkable gift. Personal love of our Lord amounted in him almost to a passion.[1] His generosity, the spirit of our

[1] A few sentences from one of his journals of retreat show this very beautifully . "Oh, then, for the love of Him ! I said Mass as devoutly as I could, with that touching Passion to read, that I and all who are dear to me may love Him *sensibly* better than we love anything whatever, and that this sensible love for Him may bring all its consequences—longing to be with Him, to speak with Him, to tell Him I love Him, to hide not a thought from Him, not to have a thought in which the love of Him is not

Seventeenth Rule, was most striking. The influence he exercised was due far more to his character than to any speech or action that can be described on paper.

His "exhortations"—short discourses to the novices on the rules and method of life in the Society—showed him to advantage. The familiar style of the discourse, which yet leaves room for much elevation of thought and language, suited his tone and manner. It allowed his earnestness of mind and readiness of expression to have full effect, and was not 'injured by certain defects of delivery, which, though slight, prevented his rising to high rank as a preacher.

The ideal which he was trying to realize may be inferred with tolerable certainty from the following extract of a letter to a nun who had just been appointed Mistress of Novices. "Your charge is a very interesting but, at the same time, a very anxious one, as I know from experience. You speak to me of your difficulty in the discernment of character. No greater difficulty can be proposed, for God alone can read hearts. The great thing is for you to forget yourself, and to try always to be God's instrument and nothing else. Pray steadily for light, especially in anxious cases, and take care when human nature is touched, never to speak on the spur of the moment. Wait until you have prayed over it. Another general rule is not to be severe except in very rare cases, when you are convinced that it is best, and even then with extreme care not to go too far. By

felt. There is nothing in life that would not be safe, if only we loved Him so! He will not refuse it, for He wants to be loved. . . . I begged our Lord to give me such a love for Him, that I may think of Him at once, and that the thought of Him may engross my thoughts. All that I have loved shall be loved a thousand times better, and Jesus and Mary shall be loved above all. With love the heart expands and grows larger. What will it not be when filled with the love of Jesus and Mary." (*Journals,* pp. 122, 130.)

kindness you can win them best, and by imitating the sweetness of our Blessed Saviour's Heart."

It cost him no little struggle to act up to his own ideal. There was, for one thing, his quickness of temper, to which he once thus alludes while asking for prayers. "Fatigue and tension always tell on the temper with me. Quick enough by nature, it gets sharpened most unpleasantly. I saw the colour in a man's face yesterday at something I said in a *motus primo-primus*, but he bore it beautifully. It won't do though. Will you help me to conquer it?"[1]

His sallow complexion and cold exterior also told somewhat against him, and even his extreme love for logical precision, which has been not inaptly described an "almost aggressive common sense." Illogical persons and actions were almost beyond his ken. Hence his advice, though sure to be based on the highest principles, was not always so well adapted to human weaknesses. Experience, learning, and great affection, however, did much to supply for this failing.

Father Morris was not only Master and spiritual guide to fifty or sixty novices, he was also Rector of the whole house, which generally contained a community of which the novices formed less than half.

His government as Rector of Manresa reflected the qualities of the man—vigour, decision, and largeness of mind. In his idea, a Rector should make himself felt, otherwise he was unfaithful to his duty, he was put into his office in order to give a unity and personality to the administration, and his powers were granted to him in order to be used, he was meant not only to reign but to govern. Further, as he always had very definite views on the points which presented themselves to his mind, disliking vagueness and uncertainty in any form, he always knew his own mind and

[1] See also *Journals*, p. 128.

made it up quickly, and he followed definite lines in his government, so that it was possible to foretell how he would act under given circumstances.

If he had anything to complain of, he told the person in question without delay, so that the matter might be settled at once. This directness and high-mindedness gave a sense of security to those who worked under him. They felt that they could not lightly forfeit his esteem, while he endeared himself to them by his generosity and unselfishness.

These reminiscences are very much in keeping with the even more interesting picture which he has uncon-sciously drawn of himself in his "Journals kept during times of Retreat." We may there discover as much as can be made known of his strong faith, his love for our Lord, his struggles against his own impatience and other failings, his tender affection for his fellow-Religious, his novices, his friends, and penitents. It would be affectation to try to describe these things again, and even his own words, if quoted apart from their context, would hardly reproduce the effect which they give in his journals.

The year after his arrival at Manresa, the number of his community was greatly increased by the reception of the French Jesuit novices, exiled by the M. Ferry's Bill. The following letters give some particulars as to his work, and the spirit in which he undertook it.

"*October* 16, 1880.—. . . No! I am not director of a hundred and fifty novices, because the number of our novices is sixty. We have besides in the house nearly forty juniors, almost all of whom were my novices last year. There are eleven Fathers in the house, and the rest are lay-brothers, making one hundred and thirty in all."

"*January* 13, 1880.—If the thoughts of the brain photographed themselves legibly, you would have a long answer with plenty of details, but as it is, and until Edison turns his attention to this little matter, you must be content to know from me, with all that is kind, that I am not ill—barring an obstinate cold—but that I am utterly destitute of time. To write a long proof that I have no time to write, touches my penchant for the logical—so you are spared the list of my occupations, and so am I. But I am spared the list only, not the occupations, and my letters have suffered to an extent that simply pains me. But so it is. There they lie in heaps, clamouring for answers long due, and harm I fear coming in some cases—but what can I do? I thought of sitting up last night, when the Office was said, to let you know that I was not ill; but I thought it too absurd to make myself ill, or at least to spoil to-day, in order to show that I am well. I have cut off a bit of each end of the night, and can spare no more, for I need sleep, and shall need it till I get clear of the thing that has eyes and eyelids.

"The pull is heavy, but I enjoy it thoroughly, all but the temporal charge—but it *is* a pull, and two or three times I have found myself at leisure but too tired to use it. Hand and brain both struck work, but they go on again when compulsion returns; and unluckily you are just out of the pale of compulsion. Are you though?

"I had written thus far with my morning letters lying unopened before me, when the bell rang for me to go to the novices for their repetition of yesterday's exhortation. It is a serious part of the work, three exhortations a week in the house and two out of it. But, oh, these letters! There is a serious case of conscience referred to me. Then I have applications for forms of petitions for the Martyrs, and I ought to write to the Bishops and Chapters to petition. I have urgent letters, written to me during the long retreat, not yet attended to, to say nothing of heaps of later ones, some involving difficult points. But if I go on writing thus, I shall have tumbled into my illogical defence, like Dr. Gentili, when the bell rang by the Bishop's order to stop his long preaching, and he preached for half an hour after the bell rang on the merits of stopping preaching at the sound of the bell.''

Father Morris's work at Manresa was so close, that he rarely had time for anything outside its walls. The following letter, however, shows how he could enjoy a change, and season all with his interest in antiquity.

"St. Philip's Church, Arundel, March 2, 1880.

" I have been sent down here to give a little mission for a fortnight, which is running out fast. Next Monday, the 8th, I return to Roehampton. This church is such a consoling place. First it is such a splendid church, worthy of the prince of a Duke who has built it. And then it does fill so famously. A large number of Protestants have attended the mission, and I hope that something may come of it. The annual number of converts here is very large. The Duke's influence is just what it should be, without any ' bread and butter.' During the mission he has allowed all his workmen and labourers an hour after breakfast, and many men have made use of it to come to the church.

" I think that the legend of St. Clare carrying the Blessed Sacrament herself has arisen from the pictures. The painters have painted her with It in her own hand, just as they paint Archbishops carrying their archiepiscopal crosses in their hands, which in real life

Q

(excepting St. Thomas at Northampton) they never touch. And the legend springs out of the picture, just as St. Denys is said to have carried his head after death, because the painters paint him with his head in his arms. Originally they meant nothing more than that he had been beheaded."

"A singular accident.—November 26, 1884.—My novices are in their long retreat, and a singular accident gives me a morning to myself. Lest you should get an exaggerated version of it from anybody else, I think it better to tell you that I had yesterday some of the milder symptoms of strychnine poisoning from a very moderate dose that I was taking as a tonic to keep down neuralgia. Unfortunately it seized me at dinner, so that I had all the community witnesses of my mild form of tetanus. Till we knew what caused it, it was of course a little alarming, but as soon as the cause was known, it resolved itself into a singular experience that has done me no harm. I could quite well have begun the novices' retreat myself, but it was thought prudent that Father —— should take the first day for me, and certainly the novices will be no losers by that.

"Until I knew what was the matter, the extraordinary symptoms of course made me think it possible that something very serious was wrong, and naturally it brought the possibility of a speedy end of life before me pretty plainly. For that I am very thankful. It is a great benefit to have something of a test as to the reality of one's indifference, and it seemed to me that I was more indifferent to life and death than I expected, but I did not feel pious a bit, and the whole episode confirmed me in my impression that the coming of the end will not alter me very much. This attack did not seem to increase any good feelings I had. Thank God

I feel that God is my good Father, and that I am always in His hands. That feeling was not wanting then, and a wonderful amount of solid comfort there is in it. But instead of wanting to say prayers, I felt inclined to discuss what the matter was, &c. There, when I began to write about it, I did not mean to go into things quite as much as that."

In the record of his doings as Superior, mention must be made of the buildings he constructed at Manresa. Father Porter, his predecessor, had commenced the north-east wing of the house and St. Joseph's Church, but they were afterwards discontinued. Father Morris recommenced and completed both undertakings. He also built the south-east wing of the house, which, large as he found it, he left more than as large again. There was a great function for the consecration of St. Joseph's Church, July 24, 1883. "The consecration of our church and its two altars was delightful," he writes, four days later, with characteristic enthusiasm, "but I have not yet got over the sense of fatigue. Nothing could have been better than the ceremony. God be thanked for all His goodness."

For literary work his other manifold employments left but little leisure, yet he found time to write in 1882—83, a series of articles on English Relics, which displays his singularly full and varied knowledge of the subject. In 1881, he brought out a second and very much enlarged edition of the *Life of Father John Gerard*, at which he had been working for some time. In 1885, he similarly completed his second and enlarged edition of his *Life and Martyrdom of St. Thomas Becket.*

For archive work he had little opportunity, except that of visiting the records of St. Omer, where some MSS. belonging to the old English College had been discovered and arranged. With the aid of two copyists he was able to make good use of a short visit there in June, 1883.

In 1886, he subjected himself to a severe strain, which, supervening on previous unperceived trials to his strength, resulted in a break down, from which he never fully recovered.

He decided to make his annual retreat during Holy Week. In addition to the considerable mental labour, which any retreat conscientiously made entails, he resolved to observe rigorously the fasts of the Church, from which for health's sake he was generally dispensed. Then he himself celebrated in the long and fatiguing services, he extended his usual mortifications, and finally, in order to encourage all by his example, he undertook instead of his usual outdoor exercise the most laborious manual labours of the lay-brothers. Never did a retreat go better, never did holy thoughts suggest themselves faster, never did he feel more eager to do his best according to the high ideal which the retreat set before him. " I feel and know that I am at a crisis in my life, when God wants me to make a start forward in sanctity such as I have not known for years." All this the reader will find indicated in his notes, which form the tenth chapter of his *Journals of Retreat.*

Early in his retreat he had found himself drawn to make an offering to Almighty God, which he thus records.

" To make quite sure, I said Mass this morning that God would be pleased to take from me all that is dearest to me in the world, if it was in any way His will, if it would in the very least further His glory, or if thereby I and mine might advance one degree towards perfection or in union with Him. I included in this expressly the good opinion of me that so many

have, and my novices and my work here, if God shall
please to give it to some one worthier of it. If it is His
will, I am content to live unknown and useless, offering
Him for homage all the chafings of my impatient and
proud spirit. . . . I heartily pray God to take away
from me, in any way He chooses, all repugnance to His
holy will. I heartily beg Him to do His holy will in
me, in spite of any repugnance He may find in me.
I heartily pray that His will, not mine, may be done,
and I want to say it with all the sincerity and all the
simplicity of the Prayer in the Garden. But I cannot
find it in my heart to say unconditionally, ' Take away
from me all that I love.' I would say it if I knew it
was God's will. But it seems to me clear that it is not
His will, and St. Ignatius himself inserts, ' Provided
it be for the service and praise of His Divine Goodness.' If it is, then I say it too. But can it be for
the service and praise of God that all who love me
should turn against me? I cannot ask for that absolutely; but I will and do ask that His most holy will
be done in me and concerning me in all things, however
painful to me. That and such reputation as I have,
and the two seem to go together and to be practically
one and the same thing, are all that I can see of which
I could be stripped. I will not cling to them for their
own sakes—that would be natural; and when they
cease to serve God, may they go.''

Scarcely was the retreat over than God took him at
his word. The sacrifice which he was prepared to
make was called for. The step forward in sanctity
was to be made in a way eminently characteristic of a
Providence which mysteriously rules with the Cross,
and triumphs in defeat. Father Morris had specified
" *my* novices and *my* work," with " such reputation as
I have," as the most serious sacrifice that could be

demanded of him. God did not take the latter part of this offering, but the former he accepted at once, ere the week was out.

In the beginning of Easter-time his nervous system seemed suddenly to give way, and he became the prey to violent alternations of excitement and depression, and a painful loss of rest and sleep. He was practically a broken man, and never fully recovered his strength.

He had to leave the house, and gladly availed himself of the generosity of a friend, who franked him to Lourdes. The following letter gives an account of this visit.

"*Lourdes, May* 25, 1886.—Yes, I am at Lourdes, and I thank God that I am here. The spirit of faith and the spirit of prayer is around us everywhere, and it seems as if the outer world were completely shut out. I will tell you what I have just seen. I have been watching the arrival of the pilgrims from Lyons. Two trains have brought twelve hundred pilgrims of all classes, of whom one hundred and fifty are sick people come to ask for their cure. What these will get I do not know; but last year I am told that the Lyons pilgrims got forty cures out of about as many sick as this time. The worst cases were brought up on bath-chairs or litters, and of them there were sixteen or eighteen grouped in front of the Grot. A confraternity of gentlemen and ladies of Lourdes drew or carried the sick from the railway station, no inconsiderable distance, and gave them water from the fountain to drink; and while this last was being done, a priest belonging to the pilgrimage led a couple of decades, ' that all who needed it might have the proper dispositions for gaining a miracle or some signal favour.' It is the only time in my life I have ever prayed with that intention. They were then led away to their hospices, the sick to go to bed, the rest to return in procession to the parish church at 5.30 p.m., and I have come away here to write a line. How the sight carries one back to our Blessed Saviour's life, when the sick were brought to Him and He cured them all. All are not cured here, but forty out of one hundred and fifty shows that our Lord's hand is not shortened, and that He loves to work through His Mother as at Cana. I shall never read the words *in lectulis et grabatis* without thinking of the patient white faces I have seen to-day.

"The place is simply delightful. The weather is perfect, the scenery is perfect, but the eye of the soul is better satisfied than the eye of the body. You may pray elsewhere sometimes, but here you can hardly help praying always. It is a most refreshing oasis in the road through the desert of life, and it makes you long for the end of the journey, when we shall find ourselves at our Mother's feet, and she will take us to Jesus, and the trouble and anxiety will all be over.

"We are very fortunate on arriving here. The good Fathers of the Immaculate Conception, who have charge of the Sanctuary, have taken us into their house, the ways of which are very like the ways of our own houses. Thus we are close to the Basilica and the Grot, and we can go there in our birettas and gowns, and are launched into the devotions of the place in a most satisfactory way. . . .

"*May* 26.—I have just come up from the Grot, where I went after my Mass and breakfast. I was in time for the end of the Mass which the Lyons pilgrims heard there, and which ended by the whole body of them accompanying in procession the Blessed Sacrament, that had been consecrated for their Communions. They were all of course in the open air all the time. The sick were then led away to the Piscines, as they call the baths. Doubtless from the Pool, or Piscina, of Bethesda, and it looked very like it to see the sick all grouped about waiting their turn. All the people were praying, often with arms extended, and there was an absence of human respect, or rather there was the simple confidence that religion was the one business in life, with a faith and charity that touched me deeply. Fancy what a field for charity in one hundred and fifty sick in the trains for that long journey—the special trains for the pilgrims are very slow—and here too where a confraternity, called *l'Hospitalité de Notre Dame*, looks after the sick.

"You will want to know about myself, but I have not much to tell. I cannot say that I yet feel any stronger, and the nerves that are moved by touching words and sights have been in play ever since I came here.

"I was interrupted, and now must get my letter off. They tell me there have been four cures this morning of those good people from Lyons. The gentleman who told me, said that at half-past four there would be the usual medical inquiry, but that for his part he had seen four people carried to the fountain who had walked away. It brought the man in the Gospel before me, who said, 'Whereas I was blind, I now see.'

"I have felt bound to give up the Bruges retreat, and when I shall go back to Manresa, I do not the least know."

As his improvement was exceedingly slow, his Superiors gladly let him avail himself of the proferred hospitality of various old friends. Accordingly he spent some months in their houses, so as to obtain as complete a change as possible from his previous occupations. In the autumn he came to Stonyhurst, where he remained for somewhat more than a year. Though he was never again the man he had been before, he was able soon after his arrival to turn to literary work, and he delivered on All Saints' day an admirable lecture on " The English Martyrs, why they died, what they suffered, what sort of men they were." It was soon in demand throughout the kingdom, for a month later, all Catholics were rejoicing at the unexpected beatification of fifty-four of their number.

Father Morris, as might have been expected, was much cheered by the news, and felt that this was " something worth having lived to see."

At the beginning of 1887, he gives a more cheerful account of himself. " I have got my hands full, and, thank God, need no longer pose as an invalid. It is a blessed emancipation, and there are few physical things more enjoyable than the sense of returning power." In March he was put in charge of the preparatory school at Hodder for a few weeks, and afterwards gradually resumed his old work of giving retreats, though these efforts obliged him to confess at times that he was " *au bout de ses forces.*" His chief work was to transcribe the MSS. about the Martyrs at Stonyhurst. The present writer was sent in the autumn to assist him, and the work was finished with the close of the year. He then came to London in the beginning of 1888, and settled at Farm Street, where the department for writers was being put on a new footing. Father Coleridge was still its Director, but next year he was visited with a slight stroke, from which he never fully rallied, and Father Morris was appointed his successor, and continued in this post till the end.

His new position suited him admirably. Failing health prevented his undertaking larger literary enter-prises, but he had plenty of vigour left for less prolonged efforts, though he had to leave town several times to obtain rest and change of air. In February, 1888, he entered into the controversy in the *Times* on "The Bones of St. Thomas of Canterbury," and afterwards joined issue with Mr. Gladstone over the "Elizabethan Settlement of Religion." The legal and historical issues involved in the Lincoln Case also interested him deeply, and he wrote several articles about them in the pages of *The Month*. In 1889, he was elected Fellow of the Society of Antiquaries, in whose proceedings he took a constant interest, and often joined their discussions. A glance at the list of his contributions to magazines and periodicals will show how varied his occupations and interests were. His voluminous correspondence with persons of all conditions and classes, were it not too confidential for publication, would give ample proof of the amount of good he was able to do at this time. Several of his correspondents have kindly forwarded letters received from him, and have given permission that any characteristic passages deemed advisable should be made use of. The selection given in the next chapter will in some measure, though imperfectly, represent him to us as an adviser of others.

This account of Father Morris's later days and last labours should not, however, be closed without reference to his unimpaired capacity for enjoying a holiday, and for helping others to enjoy it along with him. The interest which he took in an excursion, especially if some relic of antiquity was its object, would have done credit to any vigorous boy, while the freshness and free flow of his conversation enhanced the pleasures of the occasion for all the party. The account which he wrote of his "Run into Bavaria," shows this plainly enough. The life he threw into the narration of his holidays in "Italy before the Railways," gives clearer proof of this still. If he could not manage to get abroad, and happened to be too tired for his favourite studies, he could make himself thoroughly happy over a good novel, a boy's story, or a lively magazine. An incident belonging to this period which much interested Father Morris, was his meeting Mr. Gladstone at Minley Manor, the seat of Mr. Bertram Currie, to whose wife Father Morris acted as chaplain. He has left in a letter dated May 21, 1893, very full particulars of the several conversations which they held together. A copy of this letter having been sent to Mr. Gladstone, he wrote from Dollis Hill on May 15, 1894, acknowledging its "extraordinary accuracy," and adding that, "although we have never met except on that single occasion, I was greatly pleased with him, as I think was unavoidable."

What chiefly impressed Father Morris was the excellence of Gladstone's conversational style, and the character of the subjects which he selected to talk about, as well as the earnestness he brought to bear upon them all, and the wonderful power of his memory. Father Morris had the advantage of hearing the veteran statesman's views upon the physical and moral status of the present generation, the character of Apollo as drawn by Homer, the disappointments of a statesman in those selected by him for ecclesiastical promotion, the purely negative theology of the disestablished Irish Church, the condition of Presbyterianism, the characteristic excellence of Newman's preaching and Cardinal Wiseman's power of argument, besides a variety of other matters. But he also availed himself of the opportunity of bringing to Mr. Gladstone's notice the grievances of Catholics in regard of the expense to the poor of registration for marriages, concerning which the latter declared that he did not know of it before, that he could not tell when he had been more surprised, and that he thought it a real hardship.

CHAPTER XI.

Having had occasion to refer to Father Morris's spiritual work as preacher, missioner, or Master of Novices, and more constantly perhaps as a director of souls and giver of retreats, it will not be amiss to say something of the manner in which he fulfilled these duties.

Father Morris's influence was primarily a personal one, and such, no doubt, is the characteristic of all efficient teachers. His high aims, the order and method of his life, the quickness of his perceptions, and his zeal and impulsiveness in action were soon recognized.[1] Yet it came even on his friends as a surprise, to find how strong were the passions, how warm the heart of one whose exterior seemed perhaps stiff and frigid.

"On the moral side of his nature," said Father Purbrick when preaching his funeral sermon, "two

---

[1] A little example of this, of which I was myself witness, may find place here. We had been looking over an old church in Kent, and as we left, our guide, the verger, lifted a mat in the passage, and pointed out an old altar-stone, with its five consecration crosses, placed there by the Reformers in order to be trodden under foot by all comers. "When I showed this to Dr. Pusey," said the verger, "he went down on his knees and kissed it." In a moment Father Morris had fallen on his knees and kissed it too. "Now you may say that some one else has kissed it," he remarked to the wondering rustic. Although he had dirtied his face in the process, the intense earnestness of his expression forbade all laughter at his absurd appearance.

things have struck me, both indicative of a force and strength which I have rarely seen equalled. He was liable occasionally to sudden and violent storms of anger passing over the surface of his soul. Those of you who knew him will have probably never suspected this, yet it is a fact, and only shows the energy of his disposition, and the power and the might of the will which so effectually controlled it and allowed it to exhibit itself so little externally. The second point worthy of notice is the depth and intensity of his feelings and affections, over which he held continual and sovereign control. Indeed, outwardly he appeared so stern and cold that many, until he came to be known, may possibly have taken him to be hard and unsympathizing. You all remember that face, with its abiding expression so sagacious, fearless, and firm. But those who knew him thoroughly found in him the staunchest of friends,[1] the most sagacious and trusty of counsellors, and one who could enter into the feelings and minds of men in all positions, and sympathize with them in all their trials. Within the last few days I have received letters from various quarters, from religious persons, from holy nuns, who reckoned him their truest friend and wisest adviser, and who were in a manner inconsolable at his death, as if there were no other heart so large and so quick of sympathy as his."

Keeping this aspect of Father Morris's character before us, it will not be difficult to see where his power lay. He formed to himself exalted ideals, which he loved ardently, spoke of with enthusiasm, and urged almost imperiously upon others. It often happened,

---

[1] To a lady who had complained of a friend, he sends an expostulation ending with these words: "There, I have done, or you will think me implacable, which I am not. I speak plainly, bear no malice, and am a warm friend, and you won't find it quiet work pitching into —— in my presence. I have put that into slang, lest it should look too serious."

indeed, that this very vehemence at first estranged the person it was meant to convert. In his younger days he was cleverly nicknamed the " Bashibazouk " by Father Faber. Even in riper years, when his manner became much gentler and more mature, he never acquired facility in adapting himself promptly to the various moods and characters of those with whom he had to deal. Here is his own confession of his weakness: " Of St. Ignatius it is said that the instant after a very severe reprimand, he was completely himself, speaking to the next person quite calmly. With me it is rather like turning from a deaf person to whom I have been speaking loud, and shouting to a person who is not deaf."

In the notes of his retreat for the year 1883, the following passage on the same subject occurs: " At Bruges I was surprised that each time I was asked to help some one, the request was accompanied with · ' Please be kind to her.' A lady who came to consult me when I was at Tronchiennes last year, told me that she went away *avec le cœur serré*. That cannot be right. Our Lord would not have sent her away so. Is it pride on my part, or slothfulness, or what? I say what I think is the right thing, and there I leave it. For those that understand it, it does very well. They get their answer in a pithy shape, and they go away with it. But in the majority of instances, trying to save time, I either have to spend a good deal more in putting the answer into more acceptable forms, or they go away disappointed."

The lady in question became afterwards one of Father Morris's great friends, nor is it improbable that many of his sincerest friends felt regarding him at first some dread or suspicion similar to hers.

It was while giving retreats, that he found his happiest opportunities of communicating to others the deep religious feelings with which he was himself animated. With the subjects treated in St. Ignatius's Spiritual Exercises he had made himself thoroughly familiar, and he was a master in the art of explaining them to others. He was constantly engaged in giving retreats to individuals and congregations, to colleges and religious communities, to the members of his own Order and of the secular clergy, and these always resulted in a great renewal of fervour and increase of zeal. Next to his success in the work of his own sanctification, which must in all reason be reckoned first among the achievements of his life, this work for the souls of the others must rank as the most important which he ever did.

It is not possible to draw out here a detailed account of one of these retreats.[1] Instead of trying to do this, some of his letters have been collected which treat on subjects suggested by them, and exhibit to us the character of his spiritual teaching.

He thus writes to one who instead of entering a convent, as she wished to do, remained at home in obedience to a clear call of duty:

" Your letter has interested me very much, for though there is little in it, that you have not told me before, yet somehow I hardly grasped it or appreciated the peculiar trials of your life.

" The main point of it is the sacrifice of the religious life. The sacrifice usually consists in leaving home for Religion ; with you it consists in leaving Religion for home. In either case God is Lord and Master, and His choice is our opportunity to show ourselves faithful.

---

[1] The *matter* given is very well set before us in *Notes of Spiritual Retreats and Instructions given by the late Rev. John Morris, S.J.*, 1894. (Art and Book Company.) Those who know his manner will recognize it again, though no notes could well explain this to those who have never heard him.

The difficulty does not so much lie in the commencement of a sacrifice as in its continuance. It is so in Religion, and all the years of one's life one goes on learning more and more of what is meant by the sacrifice we have made. So it is with you; but that means that God condescends still to ask, that He is interested in the details of that which He asked, that He constantly sends fresh graces, and that you accumulate new merits. This means fresh difficulties as time goes on, or at least that the old pains still hurt. Nature rebels sometimes, but do not be discouraged at that: if it were not so, there would be no fresh sacrifices to make for God, and no call for fresh graces from God.

"One word that may be useful. When I say, Why do they not think of *me?* I am myself giving a specimen of that of which I complain in them.

"I heartily beg our Lord to strengthen you, that your constant, steady generosity may please His Sacred Heart."

The next letter gives comfort and encouragement under desolation.

"Be brave, be brave, be brave. Remember that your state is ordained for you by your loving Father, that it is not only not bad for you, not only good for you, but the best for you, and that it will end when it is for your good that it should end. Be brave, and bear it thoroughly well. Do not lose a particle of the good it is meant to do you. It is really a Purgatory on earth, but think what Purgatory is meant to do. What is purgation? Think how the dear souls in Purgatory[1]

---

[1] Father Morris's sympathy with the holy souls in Purgatory was exceedingly strong and tender. He might very justly be called the Apostle in this country of that devotion, which bears the name of *The Heroic Act of Charity.*

welcome the cleansing fires in their love of cleanliness. *Blessed are the clean of heart, for they shall see God.* To see God is the end, and the purity of heart is obtained in the penal banishment and darkness and pain. Imitate their dispositions—especially their loving patience. They would not enter into Heaven if they could before the purity of heart has been attained. Yours is a meritorious Purgatory, which theirs is not. Yours gains for you, every moment that you are faithful, more and more of the only possession worth having—a larger heart and more to fill it eternally. So be brave in God's love and filial fear, and trust Him, " though He should kill you."[1]

" Your state is that of desolation. By its definition, desolation is that which makes heavenly things distasteful and difficult, and earthly things attractive. In it, look back to past consolation—the Apostles in the Garden should have looked back to Thabor. In it, look on to future consolation—whether in this world or not, I know not; but if it were God's will that it should continue so till you die, you would enter all the sooner into fuller joys in eternity.

" What is your desolation compared with our dear Mother's when she lost our Lord and knew not whether she would see Him again ? What is it to Mary's sorrow at the foot of the Cross ? Oh, that dark sky overhead, and Jesus in agony ! Where is the Eternal Father ? To hear her Son speak of the desolation of His Heart ! But think of Mary's brave, faithful Heart, that did not flinch while the sword pierced it. Invoke her, the Comfort of the afflicted.

" What is your desolation to that of Jesus in the Garden ? Yours was there, and He tried it by feeling it Himself, that He might test that it was not too much for you. If you bear it, it should be found by you in

[1] "Although He should kill me, I will trust in Him." (Job xiii. 15.)

R

the Compassionate Heart, where it then was with all its pain, where it now is, with His Divine compassion.

" I will say Mass for you to-morrow, and I will commend you to Him whom I then shall hold in my hand. Take Him to your heart. Do you not remember the story of the three Communions some saint saw—the first the Holy Infant went to tenderly and caressingly, and the last with every sign of repugnance, buffeting and striking—and the saint who saw it and thought that the first was a saint and the last sacrilegious, was told that the first was a beginner who needed encouragement, and the last the soul that was truly dear to Him, who condescended to buffet her with His blessed hand.

" Lovingly expostulate with Him if you will, and say to Him, *Usquequo Domine*—'Without the light of your countenance I cannot live'—but in your inmost heart let Him see written deeply a charity that many waters cannot drown, that come what may, you are His, that His will you would not change if you could, and that you would not hasten His good time. For ever His. What can the few years of life matter, or how they are spent, so that we are for ever His. Nay, they do matter, and the desolation is very precious, for by it we are more truly His. Shall He not do what He wills with His own ? "

The same subject is continued in a subsequent letter.

" I hope that some of the thoughts I suggested to you in my last letter may have been of some help to you in your desolation. But I am anxious that an end should be put to your trouble once for all. I do not mean that the desolation should come to an end. It comes from One too wise and too loving for me to wish to change His treatment of you. Besides, nothing can be more purifying, nothing so really elevating, nothing that can render your love of God more disinterested than this very painful state. Steadiness under it will do more for you that is deep and lasting than an essay to fly in time of consolation. Fidelity is required in both states, and the fruit of fidelity in desolation is grand. The effect of steadiness now, and as long as this trial shall last and whenever it shall recur, will be to become so firmly and solidly rooted in God that nothing shall be able to detach you from Him.

" I do not wish that the desolation should go from you till it has done the work it has been sent to do. The sooner that is done, and the sooner the Heavenly Physician is free to remove it, the better. It has to teach humility, self-distrust, self-abdication first, then hatred of sin and of all infidelity to grace. The person who is most tempted against purity should thereby become an angel; the one who is most vexed by pride, the most profoundly humble.

" Now remember—and I think that this thought is quite capable of putting all right with you, and of enabling you to look at desolation as it really is— remember that our Lord felt it all. All *your* desolations, your very temptations, He felt in you. The devil suggested to Him, ' Can you hope to make anything of —— ? Will all the pangs of your Heart, or all the drops of your Blood, prevent —— from being sensual or proud ? Can you save —— from falling as low and lower than the animals or devils ? Can your graces keep —— steady to you and your will all through life ?" Every temptation you have had, our Lord had about you, and He answered them all by persevering in His love for you. To you He turns to say, ' Rejoice that through Me your name is written in the Book of Life. Persevere, and I will give you a crown in My Kingdom. A little longer and I will come to fetch you to be with

Me. Heaven is not far off, and it shall be yours. I have bought it for you; I give it to you.'

" Is anything more wanted to put all straight with you, and to keep it straight for life? He met your very temptations, and answered them by more suffering and by more love. Think how He turned from them, rejecting them, refusing to believe them of you—*loving them down:* can you entertain them? Turn from them to Him with love, and you are the gainer by them, not the loser.

" . . . I am very hard pressed for time, so I say no more. But have I not said enough to put this matter right once and for all? . . .

" To put it in short. He is faithful, can you be unfaithful? His Heart is now what it always was, can you change towards Him? Read Dr. Newman's fourth Sermon to Mixed Congregations on the distinction between the love of St. John and St. Peter, the angelical and the penitential love. And see whether you cannot get hold of *what to do.* And then if you read his Sermon on the Sufferings of our Lord in His Soul, you have food for life."

To a sick nun he wrote these words of comfort :[1]

" With all my heart I wish you a happy Christmas, and all the more happy in spiritual graces in proportion to the weight of your temporal trials. I take blame to myself for not having written to you since my long

---

[1] Sister Gertrude Willis, of the Institute of Mary, was sent home from Calcutta invalided. Taken to a hospital abroad, in Belgium, she gradually sank and died there from the effects of a painful sore which spread over her face, consumed the flesh, and necessitated many operations. Her sad state appealed strongly to Father Morris's sympathy. He tried his best to cheer and strengthen her by his letters from England, and induced others to interest themselves also in her case.

retreat. I have often thought of doing so, and now your letter has come and leaves me without an excuse.

"I am sorry to hear of the necessity of your repeated operations—sorry, that is, in one sense, and from every human feeling of compassion; but there are higher and truer feelings than those which are simply human, and with eternity in view I cannot be sorry that you have so large a share of the Cross of our Lord.

"'I often despond' comes in your letter. Dear child, banish the thought from your heart. Why should you despond when our dear Lord Himself has charge of you? It is a great honour that He should take you from amongst your community, and condescend to act as your Religious Superior Himself. This is what He is doing; and He is allotting to you the degree of actual poverty in which He would have you to resemble Him. In our vow of poverty, *as far as we are concerned* we strip ourselves of all; and then our Lord Himself ordains for us what our actual poverty shall be. The more actual poverty we have, the more He is accepting of our offering, and the more He is drawing us to true poverty of spirit.

"You must make a community for yourself, so as never to feel yourself to be outside of community life. All the angels who throng around the Tabernacle that is so near you, and your own Guardian Angel and those of all the persons in the same house with you, are wondering why you do not join their community and become one of them. Are they not children of Mary as well as you? Your sense of banishment and loneliness would soon vanish if you became *at home* with them. Now you will try, will you not?

"Now courage, child; and love God and His holy will. Cortenberg is as near Heaven as Calcutta, and nearer when there is more of the Cross. Ask the Babe of Bethlehem to make His abode in your heart, and beg

Mary and Joseph for more and more of His spirit. Bethlehem was a long way from Nazareth, and Egypt further still.

"I beg our Lord to send you all His best blessings during this holy time, and the greatest of all that you may lose no particle of the great merit He offers to you. I thank you and your kind friends very heartily for the good prayers you have given me or obtained for me. I will not be ungrateful.

"I pray God bless you abundantly."

Respecting the Third Degree of Humility:[1]

"Make haste, and lose no time. Whatever you do, do not let this opportunity slip past of a real visit to the heights of the Third Degree of Humility. Make the most of your chance. God gives us few. Always keep your eyes open to avail yourself of one when it comes.

"This is a bigger one than usual, and therefore more precious. You had been going on so smoothly, and had had so much confidence reposed in you, that I was waiting to see what God would do to save you from the dangers that are inherent in such a state of things. The offer of the Third Degree of Humility at such a time is all the grander, because it is harder—as you feel a sudden change from hot weather to cold. The state to try to come to is, to take prosperity with your heart set on humility, and therefore taking kindly to humiliations when they come. This can only be brought about by forming a habit, and a habit will never be formed by mere aspirations and prayers. On your knees ask for the grace *and the occasion* to exercise

---

[1] The Third Degree of Humility, in the language of the Spiritual Exercises, denotes that *complexus* of virtues, which leads to accepting humiliations with joy for the love of Christ our Lord.

it: and jump at the occasion when God presents it to you. Keep your mind in that direction, so that you may *advert* to the occasion as soon as possible, may recognize it as the thing you have been praying about and offering to God, and turn the whole into reality by taking the right step interiorly without loss of time. The more promptly and the more intensely, the further will be the progress made in the formation of the habit. . . .

"Now I earnestly advise you to *face* this difficulty, and see what you can secure out of it in the way of humiliation towards the Third Degree. Be content there should be a misunderstanding: be glad of the pain and worry of it; and do not move to clear it up except distinctly and solely because God's service requires it. If you do not want crosses to rankle, hug them. If you do not want rebellious thoughts to crop up incessantly, make a thorough generous offer and resolution, if God wills, to lie under the misunderstanding all your life. I promise you a taste, on such terms, of how sweet the Lord is."

The same subject continued:

"'To be esteemed vain (*i.e.*, worthless, good for nothing) and a fool, 'without my giving any occasion for it, provided only it be without offending God's Divine Majesty.' There is the *medulla* of the Exercises and of the Constitutions of St. Ignatius, of whom the Church says: *Mirum est, quas ubique locorum ærumnas ac ludibria devoraverit.*[1] Look at that verb and see what it is to be a child of Ignatius. Do you care for anything except to be the product of the Exercises of Ignatius, and to be worthy of them? This is it: 'I desire and

---

[1] "Wonderful it is, what toils and taunts he everywhere devoured." (Lesson V. at Matins.)

choose rather poverty with Christ's poor than riches, reproaches with Christ, saturated with reproaches, than honours, and I had much rather be held worthless and foolish for Christ, who was held for such before me, than be accounted wise and prudent in this world.'

.'' Show of whose spirit you are. Look at Him who stood in white to be taunted and jeered at by Herod and his Jews; look at Him who sat with a crown of thorns and a purple rag, and a reed for a sceptre in the midst of those Romans—look at Him and do not philosophize about cause and effect, when you might be saying with Ignatius in the Kingdom of Christ, 'I wish and desire, and this is my deliberate determination (provided only it be to Thy greater service and praise), to imitate Thee in bearing all insults and all reproach, and all poverty, as well actual as spiritual.'

"Your condition—'if only'—is verified. Nothing can be clearer. 'It gives the greater service, the greater praise to God.' There is no 'displeasure of His Divine Majesty.' The only thing that could hold you back is gone. 'I wish and I desire, and I choose, and this is my deliberate determination'—and *I* let the time pass and lose my chance? God forbid.

"Make hay while the sun shines. These are the moments when God smiles on us. Be Ignatian now, and He will do what you like for you. Smash that pride up now. You can put a year's work into a week. It will rise and rise again, and the battle you think you have gained one minute will have to be re-fought the next. *Faut mieux*. It is not victory we want yet, but fighting. Something within me has to be taught how, and it cannot be taught by a victory won *hic et nunc*. Win *that* battle that has to be fought over these words; and the battle that must be fought at each renewal of the thought. The more battles, the more often the free soul deliberately chooses 'reproach with Christ saturated with reproach '—and, O my God, to think that I who struck Him in His scourging *may* sit down beside Him, and be mocked with Him now! Would I clear up a misunderstanding if I could, when that means less of the *cum Christo*. *Humbly* then, or it is not like Him, *gladly* for the love of Him, and *happily* rejoicing in Him. . . .

" God bless you. Are you a child of my father Ignatius? Angels are looking to see. *Spectaculum 'facti sumus.*"

The same subject still continued :

" God bless you. I *am* glad. You have sent me the most acceptable birthday greeting I could have had. For the rest do not alarm yourself, and do not be over subtle in your self-analysis. Your reason *illuminated by God's grace* is your true guide—reason lighted by faith. Be brave and steady about it. Make no attempt at explanation till it becomes a duty. If asked, tell the truth ; but volunteer nothing until you see that you ought (are bound) to do so. God bless you—and bless you He will, if you learn humility by humiliation."

And again, shortly after :

" Do not think me hard-hearted if I say that as far as you are concerned I have no wish that circumstances should change. It is a most splendid opportunity for you. One so good could hardly have been hoped for. It is in circumstances such as these that the work of years is done in months. Yes—the fruit of your retreat should be the spirit of our Blessed Father in the love and desire of contempt and humiliations. Remember that word *devoraverit* I quoted for you from the Breviary Lessons for his feast. *Mirum est, quas ubique locorum ærumnas ac ludibria devoraverit. Devorare ludibria* speaks of a good wholesome appetite to be like Christ our Lord."

To one whose brother was now safe in Heaven, he writes :

"I have been a great deal longer than I intended to be in thanking you for the consolation conveyed by your letter. The story of your brother's conversion and happy death is most edifying and consoling. The pain of the loss of an only brother, all the more dear for the anxieties he has caused you, was necessarily very acute; but God in His good Providence has ordained that time should take the sharpness from the pain that nature suffers, while the consolations brought by faith grow stronger as time goes on. To have one safe whom we love is ten thousand times better than to have him living. Life has its ever-recurring dangers, but death once safely passed through, and the safety is secure for ever. As we live we draw ever nearer to reunion in safety, for which any partings, those of Religion, those of death itself, are but a light price to pay. Thank God then for the hope that is in us. We sorrow not as those without hope, and it is among the blessed graces of this holy Easter-time to strengthen within us the hope of the Resurrection and to carry us forward to it in anticipation and in holy and earnest longing. Every one that goes before us makes us desire Heaven the more, and it is part of God's tender condescension to our weakness that thus earthly treasures are joined to the heavenly, where our heart is fixed.

"I need not tell you that I said Mass for the repose of your brother's soul when I received your telegram. I had not then received your first letter, but your previous requests for prayers enabled me to understand

what God had done for you, and what cause you had
to be grateful to Him.

"Courage now, and show all the gratitude that is
due to our good Lord and Master by giving yourself
without reserve to His loving service. *Bonum Dominum
habemus :* who can help loving Him ? "

On the subject of seeking the palpable he writes :

"I congratulate you very heartily on your coming
retreat, for I am quite sure that Almighty God will
help you greatly, so that you may make a fresh start
forward in the spiritual life by the graces of the retreat.
A private retreat is harder work and requires greater
effort, more courage and more fidelity than a preached
retreat, but it is proportionately more fruitful when
well made.

"Aim with all your heart and soul and strength at
loving God perfectly ; but let it be for God's own sake,
and do not yearn after sympathy. You feel it if you do
not meet with the encouragement and sympathy you
desire ; but what is this but looking for some self-
satisfaction after all, even in the holiest things. When
you are repelled and driven back upon yourself, take
this too, as coming from God, as indeed it does, for
His providence neglects nothing that concerns you.

"I say the same of 'I wish I could grasp at something very striking and palpable.' What would it be
worth if it were not the will of God ? Besides, I wonder
what your self-love would grow to then ! No, no ; we
cannot improve on God's ways with our soul, and if
there is anything that is entirely and unmistakably
His, it is most certainly the right to choose what He
will ask of us. Mind : His service, for which He made
us, is doing His will and nothing else—and therefore
not the attainment of high sanctity by means of our

own choosing. So you may take for granted that you will not be able to overleap all obstacles and to overcome yourself and leave the world behind, to live in peace and perpetual calm, with the work done once and for all. Why should you desire it if it is not God's will? There is much more of humiliation in slowly and laboriously climbing the heights of sanctity, and putting aside patiently and perseveringly one little stone after another. Have patience with yourself, and be sure that till that spiritual lesson is learnt, God will keep you learning it. Desire the highest sanctity ardently, never be satisfied with what you have attained, pray hard for more, but be patient to go by the way of humbling failures and incessant recourse to God, never losing courage or patience, and always beginning again.

"I say the same of prayer. You think God is good when you get a gushing feeling of love, but a tyrant when you have no sensible feelings even of faith, and when mortification seems a mockery. Depend upon it that then God is not less good to you—to the full as good. He measures the trial to your strength, He seems to withdraw, but He is really close by looking on, and the real substantial grace to do His will is there for you in abundance. Could anything be more fatherly? It is the Heavenly Physician curing your soul as no director or confessor could do; it is the Great Captain testing the bravery of a soldier; it is the loving Father wishful for a proof that He is loved for Himself and not for the sake of His gifts."

Father Morris thus counsels the generosity required for resting:

"A little sheet for a little word.

"You are greatly mistaken in supposing that there is no generosity required in being a burden to others.

Self-love can say, as well as charity, 'I want to save people trouble.' And not only charity, but self-love too, can be pained when we have to leave trouble to others. But true humility steps in and teaches us how to accept services; and then generosity takes nobly and cheerfully what humility teaches her.

" It is very generous to lie unrepiningly on the bed of sickness and leave others to do all their own work and take care of us besides. I do not know that the enclosed prayer is St. Ignatius', but it is very beautiful. There is a picture of a Belgian Father in our refectory in London with an inscription in Flemish—I think it is, ' Work without rest, death without honour, prayer without consolation.' [1]

" I suppose that you are out of the sick-room, though you do not say so. From your account I should judge that it has done you good and not harm. This has been because by God's mercy you were prepared for its dangers, and on the whole met them properly. Trials always leave us better or worse, and the little extra comforts ordered by the doctor are a trial, just like absence from Mass, loss of the sacraments, &c. So is that sort of incessant scrupulous trouble you used to have. It has benefited your soul, I do not doubt; but you need not feel trouble that nothing troubles you now. The present calm comes from God, as the old trial did. They are both in the order of His Providence for good, succeeding one another as sunshine comes after frost. But do not forget that winter comes after summer, just as summer comes after winter; and that if and when God sees it to be good for you, interior trials will come. ' In time of consolation look forward to desolation, in time of desolation look back on conso-

---

[1] The quotation runs: *Arbeyten sonder ruste; Leyden sonder trost, sterben sonder ehre*—" Work without rest, pain without relief, death without honour."

lation.' Such is St. Ignatius' rule, and you must act on it wisely, laying up, as Joseph did in Egypt, corn from the years of plenty to serve through the years of famine. And just as, by facing the trials of sickness, you have by God's help not only deprived them of their power to hurt, but by them you have gained strength, so interior trials when they return, must find you prepared to be a spiritual gainer from what God sends you only for your profit and out of love."

The miscellaneous letters which we have quoted may be taken as representing fairly Father Morris's ordinary style of spiritual teaching. Forcible as they are, they fail to reproduce the impressiveness of his spoken discourses. The following notes of meditation from his Journal of Retreat, written down while his mind was still fresh from prayer, exhibit the vigour of his thoughts with singular effect :

" *The woman with an issue of blood.*—The contrast is very great between the many physicians from whom during twelve years ' she had suffered many things, and had spent all that she had, and was nothing the better, but rather worse,' as St. Mark says ; and our Lord, to whom she said not a word, to whom she paid nothing except her love, from whom she suffered nothing by experimental and ignorant treatment, by whom she was cured when she touched His cloak, in an instant, completely, permanently. What a touch was that ! ' If I shall touch but His garment, I shall be healed.' Making her way through the thronging and pressing multitudes, she succeeds in deliberately and intentionally touching the hem of His garment; and though He submits to walk amidst this dense and eager crowd, where many are pressed up against Him and unintentionally touching Him, it is not till this woman's touch came that He asked, ' Who is it that touched Me ?

Somebody hath touched Me, for I know that virtue hath gone out from Me.' How much 'virtue,' creative power there is waiting to go out of Him, for the help of those who shall touch Him as this woman touched Him! It is to be had from the very hem of His garment, for He wills it always whenever the rightful dispositions come to claim it. In Holy Communion multitudes throng and press Him, but how many touch Him so as to obtain the Divine virtue, to benefit by His omnipotence, to awaken His love? Be my touch this morning like that of this holy woman, that I may be made whole.

" When our Lord stopped and turning to the multitude said, 'Who hath touched My garments?' the people fell back, all denying that they had purposely touched Him. They deny that the virtue that had gone out from Him had entered into them. How unhappy to have to deny it! Those who got nothing from our Lord are ready to say so; the one happy person to whom the virtue had passed from Him, wishes to go away unnoticed. But the people cease to throng and to press, when one amongst them had received an immense blessing from the thronging and pressing; and into that open space, surrounded by a crowd of witnesses, she comes, fearing and trembling, thinking that she had been presumptuous, that He was so holy that healing could not help coming even from the hem of His garment, but not knowing that it was the longing of His Heart to find faith like hers, and she casts herself down before His feet and kneeling there, looking up into His blessed face and seeing there no blame, she forgets the people about, and says, ' For twelve years I have had a flux of blood. I have suffered many things from many physicians. On them I have spent all I had, and yet I was nothing the better, but rather worse; but when I heard of Jesus of Nazareth, I said to myself: If I shall but touch His garment, I shall be whole. I touched the hem of that blessed garment, and I was immediately healed.'

"This story was one that was to live, and to be the means of life to multitudes, and hence our Lord would not let it be hidden. So the secret deed of faith on her part and of goodness on His, was ratified in public, and He said to her, 'Daughter, thy faith hath made thee whole; go thy way in peace, and be thou whole of thy disease.' 'Go thy way in peace,' fear not to be troubled for that which thou hast done. Thy boldness in taking a miracle instead of asking for it came from a grand faith that all men may well copy. The cure that thou hast taken, I freely give. 'Be thou whole of thy disease.' *O beata femina*, that took for granted that His power was for her, that she might take it without asking, and who had no fear till she had gained what she wanted. Jesus lives for me. Though others press about Him, in the throng there is room for me. I have but to hold out my hand and touch Him, reach between other people and from a distance succeed in touching the hem of His garment, and the virtue will come out of Him into me. He knows it, though no one sees it; but He will have it declared before men for His greater glory in my after life, whole from my disease."

"*A Meditation on Death.*—Thank God for the best meditation on death that I can remember to have made. The three points that suggested themselves to me were separation, completion, beginning. Separation from all that can come between the soul and God. Thank God for such a separation as that; would God it would come now. This is what it is to die to the world, to be crucified with Christ. Separation from all else, however good and dear, but for a little time, to make the reunion more happy; just as I might leave anything to make my retreat, and go back to it afterwards, to enjoy it in God twice as much as before. God does not mean death to be any loss to us.

" Death will be the completion of all I am to do for God with the glorious vóluntariness of the service of this life. After that, no more power of proving our love as here it can be proved. To prove it in absence, to prove it in darkness, to make it superior to repugnances, to make it command sacrifices, while sacrifices and repugnances are possible. All that I can now do, and when death comes, I can do it no more. Oh, that the tale may be full ! What when there is so much to undo ! What when so much time has been lost, when the end is not far off ! If Stanislaus could reach mature sanctity at eighteen, cannot I now redeem the time, work double tides, wórk as one does who loves ? Then death will be the completion of what God has done and is to do for me in the work of grace. His picture is finished, the last touches given before it is hung up to be looked at as His handiwork. Have I hindered or am I hindering its perfection ? Oh, that I may be the picture of Himself that He wishes me to be !

" Death will be the beginning of the better life. We cling to this because we know no other, but when we have seen the other we shall wonder what we found here to cling to. At my death I shall see Him, see His dear face, see His eyes, see His smile. Then I will tell Him that I love Him, and He will tell me that He loves me. How the love within me, half latent now, will spring into life and power. What force there is in a word, what force in a look. I shall leave Him, to go off to Purgatory to be made fit for His Presence, with a true love for Him that will make all easy. That look, that word, will have changed me for ever. All that is cold will have vanished before the sun, and at length I shall really love Him whom I have always wanted to love."

s

CHAPTER XII.

THE END.

THE month of February, 1892, completed Father Morris's twenty-fifth year in the Society, and it marked the period when both his thoughts and words began, as it would seem, to anticipate the approaching end with more than ordinary earnestness. His friends of course took the opportunity of congratulating him on the occasion, and towards the close of a graceful letter of thanks, in answer to one of these, he made this very characteristic remark: "I do not see how a man can deserve a reward for living twenty-five years anywhere."

Ever since his illness in 1886, his realization of the approach of death had become more distinct, but now he spoke of it so frequently that a good nun once asked him whether he had received any forewarning. "What made you ask such nonsense?" was the answer. "No, not I; God does not tell His secrets to the likes of me. Pray for me, for no one needs prayers more than I do. I am a sign-post on the road to Heaven. 'He that knoweth his Lord's will, and doeth it not'—you know the rest."

Though he had no such foreknowledge, his mind was evidently often occupied with the retrospect of the past, and such thoughts found characteristic expression in the intention to write some reminiscences of "the many interesting persons whom he had met, and

FATHER JOHN MORRIS, S J
1892

To face p. 274.

places which he had visited." This intention was but partially carried out, and what he did write has been already made use of in the course of the narrative.

The same tendency to look back appears also at this time in the Journals of his Retreats, but always with the purpose of dwelling on the points that would animate him to begin anew, as if nothing had been yet done. "Begin again at the very beginning," is the conclusion of his retreat in 1891. "If you look on the whole past as one large failure, you will not be far wrong. Begin again, like a little child, with the first elements of the spiritual life."

These are the words of a humble, eager man, who thinks nothing done, while further and fuller success remains attainable, but unattained.

His thoughts on this subject are set down with great fulness in his last retreat, and notes of daily meditations. We cannot refrain from quoting one passage at length, though it treats of that inner life, which this biography is not intended to describe in detail. It dwells upon the very signal grace conferred upon him of a strong and undisturbed faith, and explains the motive of the statement with which the last paragraph of our quotation begins.

"In all my life as a Catholic, now full forty-seven years, I cannot remember a single temptation against faith that seemed to me to have any force. The Church's teaching is before me as a glorious series of splendid certainties. My mind is absolutely satisfied. Faith is an unmixed pleasure to me, without any pain, any difficulty, any drawback. The gift of faith, as a virtue by which I believe, comes to me from God, and the material object of my faith, God's revelation, comes to me from God, and it consists of what God chooses to tell me about Himself and all things that are His.

I am the recipient of His truths, and it is an unmixed pleasure to receive them. I have no private judgment to overcome, and no desire to exercise my private judgment. It is a greater pleasure to receive and possess truth with certainty, than to go in search of it and to be in uncertainty whether it has been found. The teaching of the Church is perfectly worthy of God, and it makes me happy. A declaration or definition of the Holy See is a real joy to me. So much more of certain and safe possession of truth. So much more of God's teaching. So much more of God, the God of truth.

" My work in this retreat does not lie, then, in setting matters right there. God can and will give me more of that which He has already given to me most liberally. *Adauge fidem meam, Domine mi.* But I have no reproach of conscience here. God has done it all. He has not let me feel the temptations against faith and the difficulties that beset some people so sorely. He has planted it in me and made it part of myself. I can hardly feel that I have co-operated with the grace of faith, or made meritorious acts of faith. God has done it all. I have been acted upon, and do not feel as if I had acted. As far as the faith goes, I feel that there is something in me for which I can say, *Gratia Dei sum id quod sum.*

" And this is as true of confidence in God. I never experience a trouble respecting it. God has given it to me and there it is. I have had no more to do with producing it than with producing my eyesight or my hearing. It is a part, and a very happy part, of my condition, and I owe it entirely to God.

" Once more, it costs me no effort to see that all things come from God. I see it, as I see the trees or the earth or the sky. It is like eyesight, and I have no more created it as a habit by frequent acts than I have created my eyesight. God has given it to me, and it has cost me nothing. I do not always use it, but that is through inadvertence, not through difficulty. I simply know that it is so, and I have not to teach myself that it is so.

"God has done all this for me, in a way so independently of all effort of mine, and He has placed these things so in my possession, that I may have and enjoy them without conflict, because He knows how miserably I should fail if I had to fight for them, as many people have.

"With such a start as this, I ought to be far in advance. I have not to struggle for the great instruments by which sanctity is achieved. But instead of this I am frightfully in the rear. I am like the people in southern countries, who, having a fertile soil and splendid climate, content themselves with what the land produces of itself, with the very minimum of labour. Those who dwell on a rock, like Malta, care for every handful of soil, and take the utmost pains with it. The Belgians live on sand, and make it bring forth large crops by incessant labour. Would that I were like them. God has done everything for my soul, I have done nothing for His glory. Spiritual sloth can hardly go further. I accept God's will with a sort of inevitable acquiescence and content, but I do not exert myself in anything *to do* God's will."

The same feelings find expression in the following remarkable words, written on the last anniversary of his ordination : [1]

"Four-and-forty years a priest ! How fast the time has gone, and how soon the end of the little remnant will be here ! How many mistakes that might have

[1] *Journals,* pp. 335, 336.

been avoided, how much harm done to others, how many sins committed, what opportunities lost, what cowardice, what slothfulness, what neglect, what seeking of self! Will not Christ say to me : 'Amen, I say to you, you have had your reward.' In the midst of the forty-four years of priesthood I entered Religion, as I might have done and ought to have done eleven years sooner, and our Lord gave me what I had deserved to have forfeited—may His Name be blessed and praised for it. There at least I did well, though it was tardily done, and in entering Religion, and binding myself by the Vows, God gave me my second baptism. How lightly those Vows have sat upon me, how little I have lived as though I were living with such pledges given to God. . . . God may well please to put a speedy end to a life in which so little good is done, so little merit acquired, so little prepared for Heaven. My one feeling is that of profound trust in His mercy. I have nothing to show for my life but God's gracious intentions frustrated, unusually great graces and opportunities spoiled, lights innumerable wasted, life a failure and a shame— yet God still patient with me, and willing to recommence His work even now. I thank Him for His great goodness, and I will trust Him till I die and see His face. *Laudetur in æternum propter misericordiam suam.*"

One of the first cares of the present Cardinal Archbishop of Westminster was to ask Father Morris, May 15, 1892, to undertake the Life of Cardinal Wiseman. " No one else," he writes, " could do it so well as you, for many reasons, and it should be undertaken at once. I will not add more. . . . Only let me know that you are not unwilling, and I will then proceed to collect the materials."

Though no longer possessed of the strength to face lightly the labour which such a task must necessarily entail, and now often incapacitated from writing by rheumatism in his hand, Father Morris did not refuse, and when circumstances allowed, proceeded to Ushaw to examine the portions of Cardinal Wiseman's correspondence, which are preserved at the College. This, however, was by no means his only occupation, as is evident from the following account, which has been abbreviated from the *Ushaw Magazine*,[1] and will serve as an illustration of the way in which, wherever he was, he filled up his days with work.

" From the 2nd to the 13th of December, we were favoured with a visit from Father Morris, S.J. From His Lordship the President to the youngest among the students, that visit was a most delightful treat—or rather, a series of delightful treats—for it is amazing what an amount of edification, instruction, and entertainment Father Morris was able to crowd into the short ten days between his arrival and departure. His coming had been long looked forward to, and had had to be postponed once or twice owing to his ill-health and other engagements.

" His Lordship, desiring to promote devotion to the English Martyrs amongst us, had requested Father Morris to give us some lectures about them. He accordingly delivered four in the Hall, before the whole body of the students and professors, and some of the neighbouring clergy.[2] . . .

" Nothing could have been more soul-stirring than Father Morris's exhortations to us to imitate the zeal of the Martyrs, but his work amongst us did not stop here. On the feast of the Immaculate Conception of our Lady he acted as assistant priest at the Pontifical High Mass, and after the Gospel preached eloquently

---

[1] January, 1893.
[2] A brief summary of the lectures is here given.

on the feast. Again, on December 12th, he preached in the evening, before Benediction, to the boys of the Junior College, on ' Devotion to our Guardian Angels,' having previously, on the same day, delivered a Conference to the divines on the ecclesiastical spirit and their preparation for the work of the mission.

" On the evenings of December 10th and 11th, he delivered two most interesting and entertaining lectures in the Hall on ' Canterbury Cathedral,' the lectures being beautifully illustrated by magic-lantern slides, which he had brought with him from London. At the conclusion of the last lecture, his Lordship the President, in a short speech, thanked Father Morris most warmly on behalf of all. He mentioned that in the course of the past few days they had discovered that, before their conversion, they had been boys together at Harrow, and remarked upon the wonderful ways of Providence in bringing them together again in the one true fold of Christ, after a lapse of more than fifty years, to celebrate at God's altar the feast of His Immaculate Mother. This little speech was continually interrupted by the expression of the feeling of the audience in ringing Ushaw cheers, which told unmistably how grateful all were to Father Morris."

During the months that had by this time elapsed since his first undertaking the Life of Wiseman, a very large quantity of His Eminence's letters had accumulated. They proved, however, to be in some ways as much a hindrance as a help to the biographer. Cardinal Wiseman had the habit of preserving every letter received by him, with the result that letters of consequence were often lost beneath piles of communications which ought to have been destroyed as soon as answered. Hence it was thought better, when the work of .writing began, that Father Morris should obtain more space for sifting papers, as well as greater security against interruptions, than he had in his rooms at Farm Street. He therefore transferred himself and all his papers, in August, 1893, to the new College at Wimbledon, of which the Society had entered into possession but a few weeks before.

Father Morris had been connected with the Wimbledon mission since its foundation. As Superior at Manresa he had been the first to send priests thither to work it, and during the rapid progress of the undertaking few steps had been taken without his advice and co-operation.

Getting into steady work, he soon finished the first chapter, descriptive of the Cardinal's boyhood, and as a preliminary to further advance, he found it necessary to collect and arrange the correspondence of the ensuing years in proper order. This part of the labour, however, proved too heavy to be accomplished single-handed, and he asked that I should be allowed to go down to Wimbledon and assist him.

To the week thus spent in sorting papers, I shall always look back with pleasure. Innumerable were the stories and recollections which he told when I asked about the history or import of some document which to another might have been unmeaning. By Sunday morning the first stage in the arrangement was finished. I went to his room, and found him reading to Father Thurston the last pages of what has since been published as " Daily Meditations " · at the end of his *Journals*. He mentioned to us that he intended founding his sermon on the matter he had just read, and so saying left the room, and after exchanging a few words with the lay-brother in the kitchen, he went down to the church for the purpose of preaching. In less than half-an-hour a boy ran up from the church to say that Father Morris had fainted in the pulpit. I hurried down, and met at the church-door a lady wringing her hands and crying, "He's dying, he's dying, and no priest with him!" On entering the sacristy, I found twelve gentlemen kneeling round his body, the nearest of whom turned round to me, and said, "He is gone!"

The particulars of this most striking and sudden death were as follows. Taking as his text the question in St. Matt. xxii. 17, "Is it lawful to pay tribute to Cæsar, or not?" he had, during some twenty-five minutes, been expanding his subject with his usual clearness and force, when his words were suddenly arrested. There was a long pause, followed by a gasp, a deep cough. Grasping the edge of the pulpit with his left hand, he passed the right over his forehead, while an effort to smile lit up a face that otherwise betrayed signs of an awful struggle within. Making a supreme effort to conclude his sermon, he repeated the words, " Render therefore to Cæsar—the things that are—Cæsar's," the ever-increasing difficulty in pronouncing them made each one sound more and more emphatic as he completed the sentence, " and to God —the things—that—are God's."

They were his last words. For another moment he stood erect, and then fell backwards into the arms of a gentleman who had run up the pulpit-steps to assist him, and by him and others he was carried into the sacristy. Father Kerr, from the altar, had given him the last absolution as he was falling. There was evidently a failure of the heart's action, and it is impossible to say at what precise moment he died.

As the fact of his sudden death became more widely known, many and heartfelt were the expressions of esteem and regret to be heard on all sides. The grief of those who had looked to him for guidance can be more easily imagined than described; while men able to pronounce with greater authority were heard to speak of his loss as that of one of the chief men in the English Province of the Society, and a foremost champion of Catholicity in these countries. On the Wednesday following his death a Requiem Mass was sung in the church where he had so lately preached, and a large congregation came from London and other parts to assist in rendering to him this last act of their respect. The funeral sermon (since published) was preached by Father Purbrick, and was remarkable for its earnest sympathy with him who had been so suddenly summoned from their midst, and for its just and discriminating appreciation of his character. The absolutions were pronounced by their Lordships the Bishops of Southwark, Emmaus, and Amycla, and Father Morris's remains were then taken out for burial to the Catholic portion of the Wimbledon Cemetery.

APPENDIX.

BIBLIOGRAPHY.

1. *Ordo Recitandi divini Officii Sacrique peragendi*, etc. Canon Morris edited the issues from the year 1858 to 1867.

2. *The Life and Martyrdom of St. Thomas Becket, Archbishop of Canterbury and Legate of the Holy See.* By John Morris, Canon of Northampton. London: Longmans, 1859. viii. and 433 pp. 8vo.
—— Second and enlarged edition. By John Morris, Priest of the Society of Jesus. London: Burns and Oates, 1885. xxxvi. and 632 pp. 8vo.

3. *Formularium Sacerdotale*, seu diversarum benedictiones religionum, quas in unum collegit Joannes Morris, Can. Northantoniensis. Londini: apud Burns, 1859, pp. 60. 8vo.

4. *The Catholic Directory*, Ecclesiastical Register and Almanac. *Permissu Superiorum.* London, Burns, 8vo. Canon Morris edited the issues from 1861 to 1867.

5. *The Last Illness of His Eminence Cardinal Wiseman.* By John Morris, Canon Penitentiary of Westminster. London: Burns, 1865. 62 pp. 8vo. (Reprinted from the *Dublin Review* for April, 1865.)
In fide et lenitate ipsius sanctum fecit illum.
Translation.—Cardinal Wiseman in seiner letzten Krankheit, . . . übersetzt von einem Priester der deutschen Mission zu London. Münster, 1865. 8vo.

6. *The Condition of Catholics under James I.*
Father Gerard's Narrative of the Gunpowder Plot.
Edited, with his Life, by John Morris, Priest of the
Society of Jesus. London: Longmans, 1871. Second
Edition, 1872. cclxvi. and 344 pp. 8vo.

Father Gerard's narrative was written in Latin, and is
preserved in a contemporary transcript at Stonyhurst. This
was translated by Father G. R. Kingdon, S.J., and printed in
Letters and Notices, 1867, and re-issued separately with the
title, *Autobiographical Narrative of Missionary Life in England
during the Persecution, by Father John Gerard, S.J.* Roehampton, 1867. Father Kingdon also republished his translation
under the title, *During the Persecution*, The Autobiography of
Father John Gerard, of the Society of Jesus. London: Burns
and Oates, 1886. (Quarterly Series.)

Father Morris reprinted the Autobiography, with many
additions, under the title—

The Life of Father John Gerard, of the Society of Jesus.
By John Morris, of the same Society. Third Edition,
rewritten and enlarged. London: Burns and Oates,
1881. xiv. and 524 pp. 8vo.

Translations.—Memoiren eines Jesuiten (P. Gerard), nach
dem Englischen, von M. Hoffmann. Freiburg: Herder, 1872.
viii. and 190 pp. 8vo. Zweite neu durchgesehene Auflage. viii.
and 251 pp. 12mo.

*Un Missionnaire Catholique en Angleterre, sous le règne
d'Elizabeth*, Mémoires du R. P. Gérard, S.J. Traduits par le
R. P. James Forbes, de la C. de J. Paris: Vaton, 1872, 207 pp.
12mo.

Memorias del P. Juan Gerard, de la Campañia de Jesus,
misionero in Inglaterra durante la persecucion de Isabel,
traducido al idioma castellano para la propaganda de Nuestra
Señora de Lourdes. Madrid, G. del Amo, 1889. viii. 359 pp.
8vo.

Pamiatnik ojca Gerard wydany przez O. Morris (z. angielskiego) Warszawa, u druk. Czerwinskiego i Spolki, 1873.
242 pp. 8vo.

7. *A Remembrance for the Living to pray for the Dead, by James Mumford, of the Society of Jesus.* Reprinted from the Edition of 1661, with an Appendix on the *Heroic Act.* By John Morris, Priest of the same Society. London, Burns and Oates, 1871. xvi. and 114 pp. 8vo. (St. Joseph's Ascetical Library, No. II.)

—— Second Edition, 1872.

—— Third Edition, 1874.

The Heroic Act of Charity. (Published separately, Fourth Edition.) London: Catholic Truth Society, 1893. 32 pp. 32mo.

8. *The Devotions of Lady Lucy Herbert of Powis,* formerly Prioress of the Augustinian Nuns at Bruges. Edited by John Morris, Priest of the Society of Jesus. London: Burns and Oates, 1873. xv. 492 pp. 8vo. (St. Joseph's Ascetical Library.)

Translation.—Œuvres spirituelles de Lady Lucy Herbert de Powis, prieure de l'abbaye des Augustines de Bruges au dix-septième siècle. Ouvrage édité pour la première fois à Londres en 1873 by John Morris, S.J., traduction de l'Anglais revue par un prêtre de la même Compagnie. Paris, 1886. xvi. 584 pp. 12mo.

9. *A Hundred Meditations on the Love of God, by Robert Southwell, Priest of the Society of Jesus.* Edited, with a Preface, by John Morris, Priest of the same Society. London: Burns and Oates, 1873. xix. 534 pp. 8vo. (St. Joseph's Ascetical Library, No. VI.)

The only known copy of these Meditations, which is at Stonyhurst, contains a dedication to Lady Beauchamp.

10. *Troubles of our Catholic Forefathers, related by Themselves.* Edited by John Morris, Priest of the Society of Jesus.

First Series, London, Burns and Oates, 1872. xii. 434 pp. 8vo.

Second Series. London. Burns and Oates, 1875. xi. 512 pp. 8vo.

Third Series. London. Burns and Oates, 1877. xv. 482 pp. 8vo.

The last two volumes have been issued separately under the titles—

The Catholics of York under Elizabeth, 1891.

Two Missionaries under Elizabeth. A Confessor and an Apostate, 1891.

Translation.—P. J. Morris, S.J. *Die Bedrängnisse der Katholischen Kirche in England.* Beiträge zur Geschichte der Katholischen Kirche in England nach Documenten aus dem 16, 17, und 18 Jahrhundert. Aus dem Englischen. Autorisirte Uebersetzung. Mainz: Kirchheim, 1874. viii. 404 pp. 8vo.

11. *The Letter Books of Sir Amias Poulet, Keeper of Mary Queen of Scots.* Edited by John Morris, Priest of the Society of Jesus. London: Pickering, 1874. xliii. 401 pp. 8vo.

12. *Epistolæ et Monita* in usum P.P. Missionariorum Provinciæ Angliæ Societatis Jesu. Roehampton, ex Typographia Manresana, 1880. 72 pp. 16mo.

13. *The Text of the Spiritual Exercises of St. Ignatius.* Translated from the original Spanish. London: Burns and Oates, 1881. xii. 125 pp. 12mo.

—— Second Edition, 1893.

14. i. *Meditation.* An Instruction for Novices. Roehampton, 1885. 72 pp. 12mo.

—— Second Edition, 1890.

15. ii. *Vocation*, or Preparation for the Vows, with a further Instruction on Mental Prayer. Roehampton, 1889. 62 pp. 12mo.

16. iii. *Daily Duties.* An Instruction for Novices of the Society. Roehampton, 1889. 74 pp. 12mo.

17. *The Pictures of the English College at Rome, which have conferred the Title of Blessed on fifty-four of the English Martyrs.* Reproduced from the contemporary engravings, with a Preface by Father John Morris, S.J. Stonyhurst College, 1887. 35 pp. 4to.

18. *The English Martyrs.* Why they died, what they suffered, what sort of men they were. A Lecture given at Stonyhurst by Father Morris, S.J. Illustrated from contemporary prints. Stonyhurst College, 1887. 32 pp. 8vo. (Also issued without plates.)

Revised Edition. London : Catholic Truth Society, 1888.

Die Englischen Martyrer. Ein Bild aus der Reformationszeit nach einem englischen Vortrage, von J. Morris. Berlin, Germania, 1893. 50 pp. 16mo. (Katholische Flugschriften zur Wehr und Lehr. No. 70.)

19. *Blessed Edmund Campion at Douay.* By Father Morris, S.J. Roehampton: Manresa Press, 1887. 17 pp. 8vo. (From the *Month.*)

20. *The Venerable Sir Adrian Fortescue*, Knight of the Bath, Knight of St. John, Martyr. By Father John Morris, S.J. London : Burns and Oates, 1887. 40 pp. 8vo. (From the *Month.*)

21. *The Relics of St. Thomas of Canterbury.* Canterbury: Drury, 1888, 28 pp. 8vo. (Reprinted from the *Month,* cf. *Tablet,* 1891, pp. 852, 853.)

A controversy as to the relics began in the *Times,* Feb. 16, 1888. To this controversy Father Morris contributed several letters.

22. *Canterbury, our old Metropolis.* Canterbury: Crow, 1889. 23 pp. 8vo. (Reprinted from the *Month.*)

23. *The Tombs of the Archbishops in Canterbury Cathedral.* Canterbury: Crow, 1890. 31 pp. 8vo. (Reprinted from the *Month.*)

Father Morris contributed to a correspondence on this subject in the *Times* during March and April of the same year.

24. *Canterbury. A Guide for Catholics.* Canterbury: Crow, 1891. 32 pp. 12mo.

25. *Canterbury Cathedral.* A Lecture to accompany magic lantern slides. London: Catholic Truth Society. 32 pp. 12mo.

26. *Archiepiscopal Jurisdiction.* London: Catholic Truth Society, 1889. 28 pp. 8vo. (Reprinted from the *Month.*)

27. *The Kalendar and Rite used by the Catholics since the time of Elizabeth.* Communicated to the Society of Antiquaries by Father Morris, S.J. Westminster: Nichols and Son, 1890. 16 pp. 4to. (Reprinted from the *Archæologia*, vol. 52.)

28. *On a Wall Painting in St. Anselm's Chapel in Canterbury Cathedral Church.* Communicated to the Society of Antiquaries by Father Morris, S.J. Westminster: Nichols and Son, 1890. 4 pp. 4to. (Reprinted from the *Archæologia*, vol. 52.)

29. *Blessed Juvenal Ancina.* London: Catholic Truth Society, 1890. 16mo. (Reprinted from the *Month.*)

30. *In Devout and Loving Memory of Mary Sibylla Holland.* (A funeral sermon.) Canterbury: Crow, 1891. 12 pp. 8vo.

31. *Catholic England in Modern Times.* By the Rev. John Morris, S.J., F.S.A. London: Burns and Oates, 1892. 104 pp. 8vo. (Reprinted from the *Month.*)

To these may be added two volumes published after Father Morris's death.

32. *Notes of Spiritual Retreats and Instructions*, given by the late Rev. John Morris, Priest of the Society of Jesus. Leamington: Art and Book Co. xii. 353 pp. 8vo. 1894.

—— Second Edition, 1896.

33. *Journals kept during Times of Retreat by Father John Morris, S.J.* Selected and Edited by Father J. H. Pollen, S.J. Roehampton, 1895. xvi. 388 pp. 8vo.

CONTRIBUTIONS TO MAGAZINES.

To the *Rambler.*

" The Priest's Portfolio." A series of brief articles during the years 1850, 1851.

Workhouse Papers.

These papers appeared monthly, beginning in May, 1860. The Series appears to have been entirely written by Father Morris, and describes the cases and proceedings taken up by the Workhouse Committee. Only seven numbers seem to have appeared. London: Burns, 8vo.

To the *Dublin Review.*

(*a*) " The English Poor Law and the Catholic Poor Law." August, 1860.

(*b*) " St. Thomas and Battle Abbey." November, 1860.

(*c*) " The Last Illness of His Eminence, Cardinal Wiseman." April, 1865.

(*d*) " Mr. Gladstone and the Elizabethan Settlement of Religion." October, 1888.

Mr. Gladstone's article had appeared in the *Nineteenth Century* for July, 1888. He replied to Father Morris's answer by " The English Church under Henry VIII." in the *Nineteenth Century* for November, 1889. Father Morris answered this in the *Dublin Review* by—

(*e*) " Mr. Gladstone and Blessed John Fisher." January, 1890.

(*f*) "Jesuits and Seculars in the reign of Elizabeth." April, 1890.

A remarkably broad-minded review of Mr. T. G. Law's book bearing the above title.

(*g*) " Probability and Faith." October, 1892.

To the *Month*.

(*a*) "The Martyrdom of William Harrington." 1874, vol. 20, pp. 411—423.

(*b*) " The Tower of London." Vol. 22. pp. 441—457.

(*c*) "Old York." Vol. 25, pp. 192—204, 304—317; vol. 26, pp. 181—201 ; vol. 27, pp. 351—367.

(*d*) " The Lives of SS. Callistus and Hippolytus. A Conjectural Chapter of Church History." Vol. 32, pp. 214—226, 321—336.

(*e*) " Dr. Jessop's Henry Walpole." Vol. 34, pp. 323 —326.

(*f*) "English Relics." 1882, vol. 44, pp. 112—126, 272—279, 358—367, 549—556; vol. 45, pp. 82—90, 555—562. 1883, vol. 47, pp. 245—249.

(*g*) "The English Martyrs." 1887, . 59, pp. 1—17, 524—537.

(*h*) "A Layman on the English Martyrs." 1887, vol. 60, pp. 19—28.

(*i*) "The Venerable Adrian Fortescue, Martyr." 1887, vol. 60, pp. 153—170, 340—362. (See No. 20.)

(*j*) "An Incident in the History of the Stuarts." 1887, vol. 60, pp. 476—485.

(*k*) " Blessed Edmund Campion at Douay." 1887, vol. 61, pp. 30—46. (See No. 19.)

(*l*) " Blessed Edmund Campion and Companions, Martyrs." 1887, vol. 61, pp. 457—470.

(*m*) " Dr. Lee and Corporate Reunion." 1887, vol. 62, pp. 14—24.

(*n*) " The Relics of St. Thomas of Canterbury." 1888, vol. 62, pp. 305—324. (See No. 21.)

(*o*) " The Stuart Exhibition." 1889, vol. 65, pp. 341—349.

(*p*) " Blessed Margaret Pole and her Sons." 1889, vol. 65, pp. 514—528.

(*q*) " A Spanish Account of Henry VIII." 1889, vol. 66, pp. 1—13.

(*r*) " Archiepiscopal Jurisdiction." 1889, vol. 66, pp. 153—169. (See No. 25.)

(*s*) " Blessed Edmund Campion and his Ten Reasons." 1889, vol. 66, pp. 373—383.

(*t*) " The Lincoln Case." 1889, vol. 67, pp. 37—49; 1892, vol. 76, pp. 21—34.

(*u*) " Canterbury, our Old Metropolis." 1889, vol. 67, pp. 227—247. (See No. 22.)

(*v*) " The deposed Bishops of England." 1889, vol. 67, pp. 346—365.

(*w*) " A Run into Bavaria." 1889, vol. 67, pp. 493—505; 1890, vol. 68, pp. 57—72.

(*x*) " Italy before the Railways." 1890, vol. 68, pp. 489—504; vol. 69, pp. 27—37, 324—338; pp. 512—523.

(*y*) " The Tombs of the Archbishops of Canterbury." 1890, vol. 69, pp. 210—228. (See No. 23.)

(*z*) " Blessed Juvenal Ancina, of the Oratory." 1890, vol. 70, pp. 24—40. (See No. 28.)

(*aa*) " The Relics of Blessed Thomas More." 1891, vol. 71, pp. 189—200.

(*bb*) "Archbishop Benson's Pastoral." 1891, vol. 71, pp. 323—339.

(*cc*) " Anglo-Roman Papers." 1891, vol. 73, pp. 52—59.

(*dd*) " Memoirs of Cardinal Erskine." 1891, vol. 73, pp. 196—211.

(*ee*) "Catholic England in Modern Times." 1891, vol. 73, pp. 328—343; 489—505; 1892, vol. 74, pp. 41—60, 356—374, 515—527; vol. 75, pp. 27—45. (See No. 29.)

(*ff*) "The Cardinal Archbishop." 1892, vol. 74, pp. 153—172.

This has been reprinted as an Appendix to *Cardinal Manning*, by Dr. J. R. Gasquet. London, 1895.

(*gg*) "Dancing in Churches." 1892, vol. 76, pp. 495—513.

(*hh*) "A Catholic House." 1893, vol. 77, pp. 362—368.

(*ii*) "Audenarde." 1893, vol. 77, pp. 465—475.

(*jj*) "The Roman Breviary." 1893, vol. 78, pp. 349—365.

(*kk*) "A New Witness about Blessed Edmund Campion." 1893, vol. 78, pp. 457—465.

(*ll*) "Faculties for Confession." 1893, vol. 79, pp. 341—359; 1894, vol. 80, pp. 69—92.

To *Letters and Notices.* Roehampton.

(*a*) "College of St. Ignatius, Malta. July 10, 1878." 1878, pp. 165—170.

(*b*) "The English Martyrs and the Society." 1887, 15 pp.

(*c*) "The ex-Jesuits of London." 1891, pp. 104—110.

(*d*) "Coming Beatifications." 1892, pp. 227—229. (Reprinted in the *Tablet* of February 16, 1892.)

To the *Archæologia.*

(*a*) "The Kalendar and Rite used by Catholics since the time of Elizabeth." Vol. 52. (See No. 26.)

(*b*) "On a Wall Painting in St. Anselm's Chapel in Canterbury Cathedral Church." Vol. 52. (See No. 27.)

To *Pastoralia.*

" Reserved Censures." 1892, 8 pp.

Father Morris edited the Historical Series of the publications of the Catholic Truth Society for the first eighteen months of its existence. When he undertook the editorship of the Quarterly Series, he wrote the preface to the first volume he brought out, which was my *Acts of English Martyrs.* He had helped me so much while I was preparing it, that I urged him to let me put his name on the title-page, but he would not allow it.

The Life of Mother Henrietta Kerr, printed at the Manresa Press, Roehampton, 1886—second edition, 1887—also contains a preface and a chapter on Mother Kerr's interior life from the pen of Father Morris.

Other works to which he contributed prefaces are :

The Life of Margaret Clitherow, by Lætitia Selwyn Oliver, 1886.

Faithful unto Death, by J. M. Stone, 1892.

A Manual of Prayers for Youth, Catholic Truth Society, 1893, was edited by Father Morris.

As Postulator for the Beatification of the English Martyrs he wrote many of the Offices and Masses for their feasts, as well as *A Litany of the English Martyrs* (1887, &c.).

To these may be added various leaflets on *Meditation, Examination of Conscience*, and kindred subjects.

English Manuals of Catholic Philosophy.

(STONYHURST SERIES.)

EDITED BY RICHARD F. CLARKE, S.J.

Extract from a Letter of His Holiness the Pope to the Bishop of Salford, on the Philosophical Course at Stonyhurst.

"You will easily understand, Venerable Brother, the pleasure We felt in what you reported to Us about the College of Stonyhurst in your diocese, namely, that by the efforts of the Superiors of this College, an excellent course of the exact sciences has been successfully set on foot, by establishing professorships, and by publishing in the vernacular for their students text-books of Philosophy, following the principles of St. Thomas Aquinas. On this work We earnestly congratulate the Superiors and teachers of the College, and by letter We wish affectionately to express Our good-will towards them."

---

1. **Logic.** By RICHARD F. CLARKE, S.J., formerly Fellow and Tutor of St. John's College, Oxford. Second Edition. Price 5s.

2. **First Principles of Knowledge.** By JOHN RICKABY, S.J., late Professor of Logic and General Metaphysics at St. Mary's Hall, Stonyhurst. Second Edition. Price 5s.

3. **Moral Philosophy (Ethics and Natural Law).** By JOSEPH RICKABY, S.J., M.A. Lond ; late Professor of Ethics at St. Mary's Hall, Stonyhurst. Third Edition. Price 5s.

4. **Natural Theology.** By BERNARD BOEDDER, S.J., Professor of Natural Theology at St. Mary's Hall, Stonyhurst. Second Edition. Price 6s. 6d.

5. **Psychology.** By MICHAEL MAHER, S.J., M.A. Lond.; Professor of Mental Philosophy at Stonyhurst. Third Edition. Price 6s. 6d.

6. **General Metaphysics.** By JOHN RICKABY, S.J. Second Edition. Price 5s.

Supplementary Volume.

Political Economy. By C. S. DEVAS, Esq., M.A., Examiner in Political Economy in the Royal University of Ireland. Price 6s. 6d.

LONDON: LONGMANS, GREEN & CO.

The Subscription price for the above is closed; but the seven Volumes can be had direct from Mr. James Stanley, Manresa Press, Roehampton, London, S.W., for £1 11s. 6d., carriage paid; or without the Supplementary Volume, £1 6s. 6d.

CATALOGUE OF THE

NGLISH MANUALS OF CATHOLIC THEOLOGY,

OF THE QUARTERLY SERIES,

AND OTHER BOOKS

WRITTEN OR EDITED BY

FATHERS OF THE SOCIETY OF JESUS.

MANRESA PRESS,

ROEHAMPTON, LONDON, S.W.

English Manuals of Catholic Theology.

OUTLINES OF DOGMATIC THEOLOGY.

BY

SYLVESTER JOSEPH HUNTER, S.J.

Three Volumes. Price 6s. 6d. each.

London : LONGMANS, GREEN, AND CO.

TREATISES.

In this work an attempt is made to offer to the English reader an outline of the dogmatic theology of the Catholic Church as one connected whole. The language is rich in works of controversy, some of which deal with the Rule of Faith, while others defend particular doctrines, such as Purgatory and the worship of Saints, from the attacks that are made upon them by popular writers ; these works are very valuable, and are useful in showing the worthlessness of the ordinary objections made to the Catholic faith, which most commonly rest upon misrepresentation : but works written to suit particular phases of controversy are necessarily confined to the points which happen to engage attention at the moment, and they fail to exhibit the science of theology as a whole, and to show its essential unity. Courses of theology for the use of students exist in abundance, varying in fulness and excellence, but they are written in Latin, so that they are of less use to a wide circle of readers who would wish to know something on the subject; they are little known beyond the ranks of the clergy. So far as is known, there is no modern work in the English language comparable to those which France owes to Gousset and Germany to Scheeben, who endeavour to deal with the matter in the vernacular, in such a manner as to satisfy the curiosity of all intelligent readers. An attempt is now made to supply this defect.

The work is divided into three volumes, containing twenty-three Treatises, the distribution of which is appended. The treatment may strike the professed theologian as meagre, but it was necessary to compress the vast material, to reduce it to a reasonable compass. No attempt has been made to enforce the rigid exclusion of all matter that is not strictly dogmatic, but portions of history and the like have been admitted as often as they seemed suitable to illustrate the subject. Other Treatises might have been added, as on Hope, on Charity, on Sin, and the like: but it is believed that what are here given hang together sufficiently well, and that these Outlines will admit of being filled up by the readers who go on to study more elaborate Treatises.

The Three Volumes can be had direct from Mr. James Stanley, Manresa Press, Roehampton, S.W., for 15s. 6d., carriage paid.

QUARTERLY SERIES.

25. **The Life of Margaret Mostyn** (Mother Margaret of Jesus), Religious of the Reformed Order of Our Blessed Lady of Mount Carmel (1625-1679). By the Very Rev. Edmund Bedingfield. 6s.

26. **The Life of Henrietta D'Osseville** (in Religion, Mother Ste. Marie), Foundress of the Institute of the Faithful Virgin. Arranged and Edited by the Rev. J. G. MacLeod, S.J. 5s. 6d.

30. **The Life of St. Thomas of Hereford.** By Father L'Estrange, S.J. 6s.

32. **The Life of King Alfred the Great.** By the Rev. A. G. Knight, S.J. 6s.

34, 58, 67. **The Life and Letters of St. Teresa.** Three Vols. By the Rev. H. J. Coleridge, S.J. 7s. 6d. each.

35, 52. **The Life of Mary Ward.** By Mary Catherine Elizabeth Chambers, of the Institute of the Blessed Virgin. Edited by the Rev. H. J. Coleridge, S.J. Two Vols. 15s.

39. **Pious Affections towards God and the Saints.** Meditations for Every Day in the Year, and for the principal Festivals. From the Latin of the Ven. Nicolas Lancicius, S.J. 7s. 6d.

40. **The Life of the Ven. Claude de la Colombiere.** Abridged from the French Life by Eugene Sequin, S.J. 5s.

41, 42. **The Life and Teaching of Jesus Christ** in Meditations for Every Day in the Year. By Father Nicolas Avancino, S.J. Two vols. 10s. 6d.

43. **The Life of Lady Falkland.** By Lady G. Fullerton. 5s.

47. **Gaston de Segur.** A Biography. Condensed from the French Memoir by the Marquis de Segur, by F. J. M. A. Partridge. 3s. 6d.

48. **The Tribunal of Conscience.** By Father Gaspar Druzbicki, S.J. 3s. 6d.

50. **Of Adoration in Spirit and Truth.** By Father J. Eusebius Nieremberg. With a Preface by the Rev. P. Gallwey, S.J. 6s. 6d.
*

56. **During the Persecution.** Autobiography of Father John Gerard, S.J. Translated from the original Latin by the Rev. G. R. Kingdon, S.J. 5s.

59. **The Hours of the Passion.** Taken from the "Life of Christ" by Ludolph the Saxon. 7s. 6d.

62. **The Life of Jane Dormer, Duchess of Feria.** By Henry Clifford. Transcribed from the Ancient Manuscript by the late Canon E. E. Estcourt, and edited by the Rev. Joseph Stevenson, S.J. 5s.

65. **The Life of St. Bridget of Sweden.** By F. J. M. A. Partridge. 6s.

66. **The Teachings and Counsels of St. Francis** Xavier. From his Letters. 5s.

70. **The Life of St. Alonso Rodriguez.** By the Rev. Francis Goldie, S.J. 7s. 6d.

71. **Chapters on the Parables.** By the Rev. H. J. Coleridge, S.J. 7s. 6d.

73. **Letters of St. Augustine.** Selected and Translated by Mary H. Allies. 6s. 6d.

74. **A Martyr from the Quarter-Deck.** Alexis Clerc, S.J. By The Lady Herbert. 5s.

75. **Acts of English Martyrs,** hitherto unpublished. By the Rev. John H. Pollen, S.J. With a Preface by the Rev. John Morris, S.J. 7s. 6d.

77. **The Life of St. Francis di Geronimo,** of the Society of Jesus. By A. M. Clarke. 6s.

79, 80. **Aquinas Ethicus; or, the Moral Teaching** of St. Thomas. By the Rev. Joseph Rickaby, S.J. 2 vols. 12s.

81. **The Spirit of St. Ignatius, Founder of the** Society of Jesus. Translated from the French of the Rev. Father Xavier de Franciosi, of the same Society. 6s.

82. **Jesus, the All-Beautiful.** A Devotional Treatise on the Character and Actions of our Lord. By the Author of *The Voice of the Sacred Heart* and *The Heart of Jesus of Nazareth.* Edited by the Rev. J. G. MacLeod, S.J. Second Edition. 6s. 6d.

83. **Saturday Dedicated to Mary.** From the Italian of Father Cabrini, S.J. With Preface and Introduction by the Rev. R. F. Clarke, S.J. 6s.

84. **The Life of Augustus Henry Law,** Priest of the Society of Jesus. By Ellis Schreiber. 6s.

85. **The Life of the Venerable Joseph Benedict** Cottolengo, Founder of the Little House of Providence in Turin. Compiled from the Italian Life of Don P. Gastaldi, by a Priest of the Society of Jesus. 4s. 6d.

86. **The Lights in Prayer** of the Ven. Louis de la Puente, the Ven. Claude de la Colombière, and the Rev. Father Paul Segneri. 5s.

87. **Two Ancient Treatises on Purgatory. A** Remembrance for the Living to Pray for the Dead, by Father James Mumford, S.J. And Purgatory Surveyed, by Father Richard Thimelby, S.J. With Introduction and an Appendix on the Heroic Act, by Father John Morris, S.J. 5s.

88. **Life of St. Francis Borgia.** By A. M. Clarke, author of the *Life of St. Francis di Geronimo.* The first Life of the Saint written in English. 6s. 6d.

89. **The Life of Blessed Antony Baldinucci.** By Father Francis Goldie, S.J. 6s.

90. **Distinguished Irishmen of the Sixteenth** Century. By the Rev. Edmund Hogan, S.J. 6s.

91. **Journals kept during Times of Retreat** by Father John Morris, S.J. Selected and Edited by Father J. H. Pollen, S.J. 6s.

92. **The Life of the Reverend Mother Mary of** St. Euphrasia Pelletier, First Superior General of the Congregation of Our Lady of Charity of the Good Shepherd of Angers. By A. M. Clarke. With Preface by His Eminence Cardinal Vaughan, Archbishop of Westminster. With Portrait. 6s.

93. **Jesus.** His Life in the very words of the Four Gospels. A Diatessaron. By Henry Beauclerk, S.J. 5s.

94. **First Communion.** A Book of Preparation for First Communion. With many Illustrations. Edited by Father Thurston, S.J. 6s. 6d.

WORKS ON THE LIFE OF OUR LORD.

BY THE REV. H. J. COLERIDGE, S.J.

Published in the Quarterly Series.

INTRODUCTORY VOLUMES.

19, 20. **The Life of our Life.** Introduction and Harmony of the Gospels, new edition, with the Introduction re-written. Two vols. 15s.

36. **The Works and Words of our Saviour,** gathered from the Four Gospels. 7s. 6d.

46. **The Story of the Gospels.** Harmonized for Meditation. 7s. 6d.

THE HOLY INFANCY.

49. **The Preparation of the Incarnation.** New Edition. 7s. 6d.

53. **The Nine Months.** The Life of our Lord in the Womb. 7s. 6d.

54. **The Thirty Years.** Our Lord's Infancy and Early Life. New Edition. 7s. 6d.

THE PUBLIC LIFE OF OUR LORD.

12. **The Ministry of St. John Baptist.** 6s. 6d.

14. **The Preaching of the Beatitudes.** New Edition. 6s. 6d.

17. **The Sermon on the Mount.** To the end of the Lord's Prayer. 6s. 6d.

27. **The Sermon on the Mount.** From the end of the Lord's Prayer. 6s. 6d.

31. The Training of the Apostles. Part I. 6s. 6d.

37. The Training of the Apostles. Part II. 6s. 6d.

45. The Training of the Apostles. Part III. 6s. 6d.

51. The Training of the Apostles. Part IV. 6s. 6d.

57. The Preaching of the Cross. Part I. 6s. 6d.

63. The Preaching of the Cross. Part II. 6s.

64. The Preaching of the Cross. Part III. 6s.

HOLY WEEK.

68. Passiontide. Part I. 6s. 6d.

72. Passiontide. Part II. 6s. 6d.

76. Passiontide. Part III. 6s. 6d.

78. The Passage of our Lord to the Father.
7s. 6d. Conclusion of *The Life of our Life.*

---

38. The Return of the King. Discourses on the Latter Days. By the Rev. H. J. Coleridge, S.J. Second Edition. 7s. 6d.

44. The Baptism of the King. Considerations on the Sacred Passion. By the Rev. H. J. Coleridge, S.J. 7s.6d.

55. The Mother of the King. Mary during the Life of our Lord. By the Rev. H. J. Coleridge, S.J. 7s. 6d.

60. The Mother of the Church. Mary during the first Apostolic Age. By the Rev. H. J. Coleridge, S.J. 6s.

The Prisoners of the King. Thoughts on the Catholic Doctrine of Purgatory. By the Rev. H. J. Coleridge, S.J. New Edition. 4s.

The Seven Words of Mary. By the Rev. H. J. Coleridge, S.J. 2s.

HISTORICAL PAPERS.

EDITED BY THE LATE REV. JOHN MORRIS, S.J.

EDITED BY THE REV. SYDNEY F. SMITH, S.J.

17. **England's Title: Our Lady's Dowry: Its** History and Meaning. By the Rev. T. E. Bridgett, C.SS.R. 1d.

18. **Dr. Littledale's Theory of the Disappearance** of the Papacy. By the Rev. Sydney F. Smith, S.J. 2d.

19. **Dean Farrar on the Observance of Good** Friday. By the Rev. Herbert Thurston, S.J. 1d.

20. **Savonarola and the Reformation.** By the Very Rev. J. Procter, O.P. 3d

21. **Robert Grosseteste, Bishop of Lincoln.** By Mgr. W. Croke Robinson. 2d.

The above numbers in four Volumes, bound in cloth, 1s. each.

22. **The English Coronation Oath.** By the Rev. T. E. Bridgett, C.SS.R. 2d.

BY THE REV. R. F. CLARKE, S.J.

Theosophy. Its Teaching, Marvels, and True Character. Wrapper, 6d.

Spiritualism. Its Character and Results. Wrapper, 2d.

The Existence of God: A Dialogue. New Edition. Wrapper, 6d.

A Pilgrimage to the Holy Coat of Treves. With an Account of its History and Authenticity. With Twelve beautiful Illustrations. Crown 8vo, cloth, 4s.

The Pope and the Bible. Wrapper, 6d.

The Adorable Heart of Jesus. By Father Joseph de Galliffet, S.J. With Preface and Introduction by the Rev. R. F. Clarke, S.J. Fcap. 8vo. 3s.

Theodore Wibaux, Pontifical Zouave and Jesuit. By Father du Coëtlosquet, S.J., with an Introduction by the Rev. R. F. Clarke, S.J. Crown 8vo, handsomely bound in blue and gold. 5s.

Fasti Apostolici. An Annual Record, from our Lord's Ascension to SS. Peter and Paul's Martyrdom. With copious Notes and Appendix. Second Edition. Small 4to, 184 pp. Cloth, 3s. 6d.

Britain's Early Faith. With copious Notes and Appendix. Seventeen chapters, 244 pp. Cloth, 3s.

Afternoons with the Saints. Tenth Edition. 394 pp. Cloth, 3s. 6d. French Edition. Wrapper, 2s.

Evenings with the Saints. Cloth, 3s. 6d.

Bracton : A Tale of 1812. Second Edition. Cloth, 2s.

In the Snow. Ninth Edition. Cloth, 2s.

The Catholic Crusoe. Ninth Edition. With Twelve Illustrations. Cloth, 3s. 6d.

Some Verses of Various Dates. Cloth, 6d. ; wrapper, 4d.

Luther. In Four parts. 172 pp. Cloth, 1s. ; wrapper, 6d.

Is Ritualism Honest? Three Lectures. Third Edition. Including **Begging the Question.** 6d.

Via Crucis: translated from the original of St. Leonard of Port Maurice. Stanzas of the *Stabat*, chiefly by Aubrey de Vere. Seventh Thousand. 3d. and 2d.

The Old Religion of Taunton. 2d.

What is the Bible? Is yours the right book? 1d.

Confession to a Priest. 1d.

Five Minutes' Sermons for the Sundays throughout the Year.

PART THE FIRST. From Trinity Sunday to the Twelfth Sunday after Pentecost. 6d.

PART THE SECOND. From the Thirteenth to the Twenty-fourth Sunday after Pentecost. 6d.

CPSIA information can be obtained
at www.ICGtesting.com
Printed in the USA
BVOW11s0945210316

441129BV00018B/161/P

9 781331 503064